ORDER FROM CHAOS

Social and Aesthetic Harmonies in Boccaccio's Decameron

Marga Cottino-Jones

UNIVERSITY
PRESS OF
AMERICA

Copyright © 1982 by
University Press of America, Inc.
P.O. Box 19101, Washington, D.C. 20036

All rights reserved
Printed in the United States of America

ISBN (Perfect): 0-8191-2841-4
ISBN (Cloth): 0-8191-2840-6

A Luisa, colleghe affezionime, con affetto Maya

To my family, here and in Italy

ACKNOWLEDGEMENTS

To mention individually all the colleagues who have assisted me in the writing of this book would require that I recount here the story of the last ten years of my life. This, obviously, I am not about to do . There are cases, however, where I feel that my debt is so great that a brief acknowledgment is only fair.

Pier Maria Pasinetti watched the book develop and provided encouragement and suggestions. His marvellous sense of humour has often mitigated my innate tendecy to dogmatization. Fredi Chiappelli read the manuscript in its various stages and knew when to be encouraging and when to be critical. He gave the manuscript the kind of searching critique that only a friend dare give and caused me to rethink and rework several parts. Edward F. Tuttle was my adviser on the subtleties of the English language. If my style has not reached the level of refined prose that he had hoped for, the responsibility is all mine.

Among the many colleagues outside of UCLA who have provided encouragement and support, I wish the mention particularly Pamela Stewart and Antonio D'Andrea, Dante Della Terza, Vittore Branca, Giorgio Padoan, Giuseppe Petronio, Gian Paolo Biasin, Laura White, Giuseppe Mazzotta, and Joy Potter.

My research assistants through these many past years, Murtha Baca, Debbie Birns, Posie Di Sesa, Betsy Emerick, Sherrye Mossuto, and Michael Sherberg, have been of the greatest value to me, from the early phase of basic bibliographic research, through the various drafts down to the final product. At every point, I have received valuable assistance from the staff of the Department of Italian at UCLA, particularly from my invaluable Administrative Assistant, Luciana Varlotta. I am also very grateful to the Research Committee of the UCLA Academic Senate for the continuous support that they have provided for my project.

Los Angeles, June 1982

TABLE OF CONTENTS

Acknowledgements .... p. v

Preface .... p. ix

Introduction .... p. 1
   1. Historical Background .... p. 1
   2. Narrative Structures and Interrelations .... p. 4
   3. Narrative Technique .... p. 19
   Notes .... p. 32

Part I: *Individual and Society in Search of Order:*
     Days I-V .... p. 39
     Day I: "Wit in the Midst of Chaos" .... p. 41
     Day II: "The Haphazard Play of Events" .... p. 49
     Day III: "Resourcefulness Within Limits" .... p. 60
     Day IV: "Love in a Hostile World" .... p. 66
     Day V: "Love, Nature, and Society: Towards a
          Harmonious Solution" .... p. 80
     Notes .... p. 97

Part II: *Order Within Reach:*
     Days VI-X .... p. 103
     Day VI: "Wit and Success" .... p. 103
     Day VII: "The Haphazards of Marriage:
          Individual Solutions" .... p. 118
     Day VIII: "Resourcefulness Extended" .... p. 135
     Day IX: "An Exercise in Balance" .... p. 155
     Day X: "Individual in Harmony with Society" .... p. 170
     Concluding Remarks .... p. 191
     Notes .... p. 192

Index .... p. 197

Subject Index to the *Decameron* .... p. 199

PREFACE

As the title suggests, this book is an overall reading of the *Decameron* as an aesthetic model which represents a society in the process of reorganizing itself from a state of chaos into an ordered system of individual and social values. It is a reading which treats the *Decameron's* narrative complexity in close relation to its historical background and shows, in particular, how fiction may develop as a response to an historical crisis by proposing a healthy alternative to a diseased society.

Other critics have approached facets of the *Decameron* with not dissimilar purposes. However, instead of providing episodic illuminations, this book addresses the work's larger architecture, focusing on pervasive structural relationships, e.g., between *cornice* and *novelle*, between narrator and storytellers, as well as between their respective audiences, between clusters of *novelle*, groups of days, which unify the whole. It is my belief that such an approach will heighten our enjoyment of the *Decameron* through an increased understanding of the techniques Boccaccio developed to show, or to imply, connections between the fictional and the historical, the imaginative and the real.

In terms of approach, something useful has been derived from nearly all current critical "strategies." Advances in social history and recent discoveries in biographical and philologic research have helped provide a more accurate, richly detailed context in which to place both author and work. Applying certain methodologic tools popularized by the French "narratologists," I have sought to evaluate Boccaccio's use of the *novella* form. My goal here was not to formulate a general theory of storytelling in the French manner, but rather to penetrate Boccaccio's motives in selecting the *novella* as the major narrative form for the *Decameron*. In line with the Spitzerian faith that in sound literary structures "tout se tient," I examine Boccaccio's use of the *novella*, vis-à-vis the tradition, in the context of the *Decameron* as a whole. But, in the end, my concern lies far less with methodologic experiment than with Boccaccio, the writer of *novelle*, and with his work, as it relates to the society of his time.

I share completely the interest of those modern students of Boccaccio who are fascinated by the complexity of the *Decameron's* narrative structure. Grasping such complexity is at once the greatest challenge to the readers and the greatest gratification the work holds out to them. It arises not merely from the plurality of narrative levels, but from the dynamic interplay among them. Either implicitly or explicitly, this complexity pervades all levels of the work, drawing all its audiences or readerships, through a mirroring or bridging of relationships, into the tension between the fictional world of the *Decameron* and the historical world of its author/narrator.

Much of the present book addresses such interrelations as a significant unifying component of the *Decameron's* message and underlying structure, which throws new light on its multi-tiered movements from misery and chaos towards an ordered, harmonious mode of social life. I found it convenient to divide the book in three parts. The Introduction offers keys to the *Decameron's* sociocultural and historical background and to the literary conventions and narrative techniques that entered into its making. The following two parts closely investigate the relationship between individual and society in the fictional context of the *novelle*, and trace the progression from chaos to order which underlies the narrative. Both Parts I and II aim also at identifying the important connections that exist between the *novelle's* narrative action and the historical world outside the book. Part I focuses on the *novelle* of the first Five Days of storytelling, while Part II concentrates on the ways in which the *novelle* of the last Five Days are a counterpoint to, and elaborate on, the stories in Part I.

INTRODUCTION

1. Historical Background

At the fictional base of the *Decameron's* narrative action lies a historic event — the Black Plague of 1348, which the "onesta brigata" temporarily escapes by moving from the city of Florence to its *"contado."* According to the historians of the period, for at least six months (from March to September, 1348), the plague paralyzed the social, political, and economic life of Florence and its rural surrounds.[1]

Matteo Villani's and Marchionne's chronicles of the plague stress the absence of human compassion and the deterioration of social order in the city and its outskirts. Their historical commentaries correspond to the description of the plague and its consequences in Florence and the *contado* in the "Introduction" to the *Decameron*.[2] Boccaccio's prologue, like the chronicles, concerns itself with dismal social conditions in the Florentine state during the period of the Black Death:

> E in tanta afflizione e miseria della nostra città era la reverenda auttorità delle leggi, così divine come umane, quasi caduta e dissoluta tutta per li ministri e essecutori di quelle, li quali, sì come gli altri uomini, erano tutti o morti o infermi o sì di famiglie rimasi stremi, che uficio alcuno non potean fare; per la qual cosa era a ciascun licito quanto a grado gli era d'adoperare.
>
> ... tra per lo difetto degli oportuni servigi, li quali gl'infermi aver non poteano, e per la forza della pistolenza, era tanta nella città la moltitudine di quegli che di dì e di notte morieno, che uno stupore era a udir dire non che a riguardarlo. Per che, quasi di necessità, cose contrarie a' primi costumi de' cittadini nacquero tra coloro li quali rimanean vivi.
>
> (I Introduction, 23-31)

Historical evidence confirms that the plague was, indeed, "the coup-de-grace in a series of disasters that had caused havoc and undermined the social, economic, and moral foundations laid in previous decades of patient work."[3] No civil laws were maintained, no natural or moral laws were respected: men, in both the city and the *contado*, had no social or personal moral pattern on which to model their lives.[4]

After the Black Plague, the *comune* faced the difficult tasks of reorganizing commercial and industrial activities which had been dormant for months, both in Florence and abroad, and of formulating a policy of social reconstruction. Such activities were particularly difficult at a time when many parts of Europe, Italy especially, were undergoing general economic hardships resulting from a decline in population caused by periodic recurrences of plague and famine, unsettled political conditions, and the plundering of the countryside and cities by marauding bands of discharged soldiers.[5] Radical change seemed the only hope for social rehabilitation.

Matteo Villani, a typical burgher of the time, punctiliously documented the dismal effects of the plague, but was also able to view it apocalyptically as a renewal "of time and the world":

> Non fu universale giudicio di mortalità che tanto comprendesse l'universo, come quella che ne' nostri di avvenne. . . Nella quale mortalità avendo renduta l'anima a Dio l'autore della cronica nominata la Cronica di Giovanni Villani cittadino di Firenze. . . dopo molte gravi fortune, con più conoscimento della calamità del mondo che la prosperità di quello non m'avea dimostrato, propuosi nell'animo mio fare alla nostra varia e calamitosa materia cominciamento a questo tempo, *come a uno rinovellamento di tempo e secolo.*[6]

Such a "renewal," or trend toward recovery, became apparent in various levels of the economy immediately after the Black Death. As G. Brucker observes, there was an increase in the number of shop rentals, guild matriculations, and substantial purchases of real estate, as well as a sharp rise in the value of the gold florin, between 1348 and 1354.[7] Not surprisingly, during these same years Boccaccio composed the *Decameron*, where a similarly optimistic and confident attitude prevails. The high mortality rate among the lower classes had created exceptional opportunities for immigrants from the *contado*: the income of the lower segment of the population soon showed previously unheard-of gains.[8] This phenomenon, coupled with the leveling of wealth and power, seems to have stimulated a more pronounced democratization of society than that before the Black Death. Several factors contributed to this democratization: mercantile difficulties and bankruptcies were more common in the economic sphere, while in the political realm, a larger share of government was assumed by the *Arti minori* after the episode of the Duke of Athens's tyranny. In addition, the *gente nuova*, the social group that consisted of immigrants or descendants of immigrants who had moved to the city from the *contado* throughout the fourteenth century, were rapidly gaining social status. Yet another element which contributed to stronger democratization was the exclusion of the magnates from the higher offices of the *comune*.⁹ According to M. B. Becker, "Arno society during the generation after the thirties was in process of democratization . . . Individuals could identify more easily with the public world."[10] Brucker seems to have an even more subtle and complex conception of the historical circumstances and problems of this generation:

> Two important attributes of this social order were the critical importance of wealth as a determinant of status, and the survival, from the city's medieval past, of a corporate structure and ethos. These qualities, which were blended in the Florentine crucible, were fundamentally irreconcilable. A capitalistic economic order is characterized by risk, uncertainty, flexibility, and sharp fluctuations. It fosters individualism and contributes to social mobility and dislocation through perpetual redistribution of wealth. Conversely, a corporate society order stresses group action; its goals are stability, security, conformity. It gives its members a sense of identity, of belonging; it teaches them to accept the principles of a hierarchic social structure, a sense of social place.[11]

At the same time, the disillusionment of a world half destroyed by the plague seems to have produced a new outlook, not only on the "cause" of all cosmic events and historical occurrences, but on man's chances for survival and success in such a world. According to L. Green's discussion of the different implications of Giovanni and Matteo Villani's views of history, one can see that,

> in the former, providence ensures that right triumphs, in the latter this depends on man's capacity to learn from the past the lessons that God has written into it. Consequently, *the area left to human choice is larger and crucial in a sense that it was not before.* . . *Resourcefulness becomes.* . . *a criterion in its own right,* irrespective of the justification or otherwise of the purpose it is employed for—because *it is a tool in the reduction of the haphazard, accidental play of events to the service of human ends.*[12]

These observations increase our understanding of the Decameronian world, a world which bears striking similarities to the society described by Brucker. Individuals in the *Decameron* often face social "risks" and "fluctuations" of wealth.[13] At the same time, they are constantly concerned with a "sense of social place."[14] "Resourcefulness" becomes the essential aspect of the Decameronian heroes' success; in most *novelle*, a narrative conflict develops when the protagonist uses resourcefulness as the tool with which to find and maintain his social place. And it is this resourcefulness that allows most characters of the *Decameron* to overcome the "haphazard, accidental play of events," and to manipulate the action to the "service of human ends." As for social class, many protagonists of the *novelle*, (as well as the Narrator himself and presumably the ten storytellers), belong to the powerful *gente nuova*[15]. In the historical reality of Boccaccio's times, the link between the *contado* (which provided the raw material for success), and the city (which provided the field of action for success), was a crucial one for this group of "new men" who were responsible for the regeneration of communal morale and economy in the wake of the Black Death. Despite critical claims to the contrary, the *Decameron* portrays neither solely a merchant's world, nor a nostalgic view of patrician society in decline, but offers also a sympathetic view of the *gente nuova's* role in the communal society of the 1350's. In almost every Day of the *Decameron*, these "new men and women" take active roles in society and their contributions are cast in a generally positive light. The link they create between city and *contado* plays an important part in the narrative dynamics of the *Decameron*. Boccaccio, then, proposes a fictional world where individuals of various classes are capable of acting purposefully within their society.

2. *Narrative Structure and Interrelationships*

If we recognize that the *Decameron*, through narrators' descriptions and characters' actions, provides significant documentation of the Florentine plague years, we may then adopt a critical perspective broad enough to advance our understanding of the work's social as well as literary dimensions. This perspective will embrace both the relationship between narrators and their audiences and the treatment of character and action in the *novelle*. It will also focus on the dimensions of space and time which link the fictional realm of the work to the historical world outside the *Decameron*.

There are specific parts of the *Decameron* where the first person Narrator and the ten storytellers individually dominate the narrative space. All these parts make up a specified structural level of the work: the so-called frame or *cornice,*which constitutes a fundamental narrative dimension of the *Decameron*. Through it, Boccaccio conveys the relationships between the storytellers and their audiences. These relationships create a narrative pattern of harmonious and dynamic interactions which constitute a proper backdrop for the fictional world of the *novelle*.

The Narrator's first concern in the "Proemio" is to explain his reasons for writing and to suggest the urgent need for communication. His desire for verbal give-and-take after an unhappy love affair has been fulfilled in the past by the "piacevoli ragionamenti" of his friends.[16] Now, in turn, he feels an obligation to satisfy the need of others in love, especially women. He does this by collecting for them, in written form, tales which a group of ten storytellers (*novellatori*) with whom he is acquainted had previously told to each other. Thus Boccaccio intruduces an important narrative element: the fictive audience of the work.

This fictive audience is composed of two groups. The first is the Narrator's audience, represented by the women in love to whom he refers constantly in the "Proemio," the Introduction to the Fourth Day, and in the Author's Conclusion. They are an ideal public totally sympathetic to the Narrator's pleas and interests. The imagined presence of this ideal audience fulfills his need for communication; the women addressed in the Narrator's mind act as his inspiration, provide him with his reasons for writing, and eventually reassure him of the success of his endeavor.

The second group is composed of the ten storytellers; in the process of storytelling, a fictional situation is created in which each one of them functions as narrator and the others as an audience "inside" the work. These inner audiences act differently from the Narrator's "ideal" audience, since they are not always attuned to each storyteller's intentions. Instead they sometimes disagree, criticize, or question what is narrated, just as a "real" audience would. In the First Day, for instance, we find a dynamic differentiation of the inner audience's reactions, ranging from a generally sympathetic response on the part of the women to Panfilo's story of Ser Ciappelletto ("la novella di Panfilo fu in parte risa e tutta commendata dalle donne. . ." I 2, 2), and on the part of the whole group to Neifile's story of Abraham and Giannotto ('. . . commendata da tutti la novella di Neifile. . ." I 3, 2), to a total lack of comments for Filomena's (I 3), Lauretta's (I 8), Elissa's (I 9), and Pampinea's (I 10) *novelle*. The effect of Dioneo's story (I 4) on the "donne" is, on the other hand, amply described:

> "La novella di Dioneo raccontata prima con un poco di vergogna punse i cuori delle donne ascoltanti e con onesto rossore nel loro viso apparito ne diede segno; e poi quella, l'una l'altra guardando, appena del rider potendosi abstenere, soghignando ascoltarono. Ma venuta di questa la fine, poi che lui con alquante dolci parolette ebber morso, volendo mostrare che simili novelle non fossero tra donne da raccontare. . ."
>
> (I 5, 2-3)

Fiammetta's (I 5), Emilia's (I 6), and Filostrato's (I 7) stories draw pleasant comments, the first from the "donne" ("da tutte commendato il valore e il leggiadro gastigamento dalla marchesana fatto al re di Francia. . ." I 6, 2), the second from the whole group ("Mosse la piacevolezza d'Emilia e la sua novella la reina e ciascuno altro a ridere e a commendare il nuovo avviso del crociato. . ." (I 7, 2), and the third from unidentified listeners ("poscia che udito ebbe lodare la 'ndustria di Bergamino . . . " I 8, 2.). This alternating scheme of audience reactions, repeated each day with appropriate changes, intensifies the dynamic relationship between narrators and their audiences, thus enriching the texture of the work.

Furthermore, this *cornice* level develops its dynamics through the interaction of all the fictional elements. The Narrator interacts with his "ideal" audience and with the storytellers, who in turn function as narrators and audiences. These dynamics are enhanced by the constant superimposition of the Narrator's "ideal" audience on the storytellers' audiences.[17] This brief but recurring interweaving of narrative voices and audiences is evident in the various addresses which open almost all the *novelle*, where Boccaccio's "women in love" momentarily superimpose each storyteller's immediate audience—the *onesta brigata*.[18] The more frequent formulae of addresses are referred to the female audience: among them, "carissime donne" occurs eleven times, "piacevoli donne" nine times, "valorose donne" eight times, and "amorose donne" seven times.[19] Yet the "brigata" counts three men along with its seven women, and therefore should require an ambigeneric form of address. One can only conclude that the Narrator's audience, his "women in love," are the women addressed. And indeed, the Narrator's "dilicate donne innamorate" of the "Proemio" appear again in the "dilicate donne" of the crucial central and last Days (V 2 and X 2). These addresses to an exclusively feminine audience represent ambiguous points of flux between the narrative strata. Through their periodic reappearances, the "amorose donne" open the inner narration of the "brigata" by directly engaging the larger audience of the author-Narrator. Thus, the actual readers of the work become involved with its inner and outer audiences in a complex network of human communication.

This complicated and absorbing play between narrators and audiences subtly draws the readers in and enforces upon them the book's social and personal moral message. Despite the Narrator's contention that his *novelle* are addressed specifically to women in love, they have a broader influence than that directed to the *amorose donne*. One reading public outlined in the Fourth Day's Introduction is, indeed, composed of the many groups of readers whom the Narrator addresses in defending himself from their criticisms. They range from the extreme moralists who state that "onesta cosa non è che io tanto diletto prenda di piacervi (alle donne)" (IV, "Introduzione", 5), to the middle-aged "wise men" who sustain that "alla mia età non sta bene l'andare . . . dietro . . . a ragionar di donne" (IV "Introduzione," 6), to the would-be *litterateurs*, for whom "io farei piu saviamente a starmi con le Muse in Parnaso" (IV "Introduzione," 6), to the materialists, according to whom "io farei più discretamente a pensare donde io dovessi aver del pane" (IV "Introduzione," 7), and finally, to the realists, who believe "in altra guisa essere state le cose da me raccontatevi" (IV, "Introduzione," 7). These reactions to the work reveal the book's influence on many strata of society, and the Narrator's responses, in turn, convey his belief in the literary work's formative influence on its society. Writers, he states, "dietro alle loro favole andando, fecero la loro età fiorire." (IV, "Introduzione," 38). This "fioritura" conveys a positive view of what some men of letters are able to accomplish for their societies, while others, "nel cercar d'aver più pane, che bisogno non era loro, perirono acerbi." (IV "Introduzione," 38).

Even before the *Decameron*, and certainly well after it, Boccaccio infused many of his works with his belief in literature's impact upon society. While in most of his works, the fictional narrators are the ones who voice this belief, in the *Genealogia Deorum Gentilium*, Boccaccio himself defines poetry as "fervor quidem exquisite inveniendi atque dicendi, seu scribendi, quod inveneris", whose essential task is "velamento fabuloso atque decenti veritatem contigere."[20] For the Boccaccio of the *Genealogia*, poets are constantly in search of a suitable isolated location where they can escape the futility and unpleasantness of overcrowded urban life:

> Solitudines incolunt et coluere poete, quia non in foro cupidinario, non in pretoriis, non in theatris, non in capitoliis aut plateis, publicisve locis versantibus, seu turbelis civicis inmixtis, vel mulierculis circumdatis sublimium rerum meditatio prestatur, absque qua fere assidua nec percipi possunt, nec perfici percepta poemata.
>
> (XIV xi)[21]

The annoyances of the urban milieu give way to relaxed contemplation and serenity with a move from city to country:

> simplicia quidem omnia sunt nature opera. Ibi in celum erecte fagi et arbores cetere, opacitate sua recentes porrigentes umbras; ibi solum viridantibus herbis contectum atque mille colorum distinctum floribus, limpidi fontes et argentei rivuli, lepido cum murmure ex ubertate montium declinantes; ibi picte aves cantu frondesque lenis aure motu resonantes bestiole ludentes; ibi greges et armenta, ibi pastoria domus, aut gurgustiolum, nulla domestica re sollicitum; et omnia tranquillitate et silentio plena. Que non solum, satiatis oculis auribusque deliciis suis, animum mulcent, verum mentem in se colligere et ingenium, si forte fessum sit, in vires revocare, atque illud videntur inpingere in desiderium meditationis sublimium et aviditatem etiam componendi; que mira exhortatione suadent libellorum societas et canori circum choreas agentes Musarum chori. Que omnia si rite consideremus, *quis studiosus homo civitatibus solitudines non preponat?*
>
> (XIV xi)[22]

Here Boccaccio recreates an ideal bucolic scene. It offers the poetic mind a suitable model not only for aesthetic enjoyment through the traditional image of nature as a state of perfection, but also for spiritual ease; serenity and contentment foster meditation and the desire for creative expression. As the outcome of such preparation and creation, the written products of the artist's experience, here, his *fabulae*, are not bound for isolation, but are brought back into the social realm where they can affect their audiences:

> Fabulis fessis illustrium virorum circa maxima animis vires persepe restitute sunt; quod non tantum exemplo veteri, sed assiduis demonstratur . . . Fabulis labantium in desidiam mentium in meliorem frugem lapsos revocatos iam novimus . . . Quid multa? Tanti quidem sunt fabule, ut earum primo contextu oblectentur indocti, et circa abscondita doctorum exerceantur ingenia, et sic una et eadem lectione *proficiunt* et *delectant*.
>
> (XIV ix)[23]

According to the *Genealogia*, then, poetic creations, especially *fabulae*, should be conceived in the country. Ultimately, however, they must reach men everywhere and provide them with beneficial and delightful lessons, which in turn may be applied to their personal and social experiences.

The *Decameron* seems to put into practice what the *Genealogia* suggests, in theory, about narrative art. As if in anticipation of the *Genealogia's* poetics, Boccaccio, in the *Decameron's* "Proemio", creates a fictional scaffold on which to build his desired narrative structure. His "novelle o favole" are told by a Narrator and ten narrative voices, and each addresses a different audience with delightful and useful lessons. The storytellers recount these tales orally in a perfected natural environment, removed from the chaos and moral disorder of the city. The Narrator, in turn, transcribes them in written form at a later time in, and for, an urban environment:

> Adunque . . . intendo di raccontare *cento novelle o favole o parabole o istorie* che dire le vogliamo, raccontate in diece giorni da una onesta brigata di sette donne e di tre giovani nel pistelenzioso tempo della passata mortalità fatta . . . Nelle quali novelle piacevoli e aspri casi d'amore e altri fortunati avvenimenti si vederanno così né moderni tempi avvenuti come negli antichi; delle quali le già dette donne . . . *parimente diletto . . . e utile consiglio potranno pigliare, in quanto potranno cognoscere quello che sia da fuggire e che sia similmente*

da seguitare . . .²⁴

(Proemio 13-14; all italics in all quotations
from Boccaccio are mine)

The combined aims of the storytelling, "diletto . . . e utile consiglio", anticipate the *Genealogia's* contention that "fabule . . . una et eadem lectione *proficiunt et delectant.*" The Narrator's belief in the *diletto* and *utilità* of storytelling is later reiterated by the ten storytellers. Dioneo stresses the group's desire for pleasure, "Amorose donne, se io ho bene la 'ntenzione di tutte compresa, noi siamo qui per dovere *a noi medesimi novellando piacere;* e per ciò . . . estimo a ciascuno dovere essere licito . . . *quella novella dire che più crede che possa dilettare*" (I 4, 3). Pampinea emphasizes utility, "Per che, acciò che voi vi sappiate guardare . . . questa ultima novella di quelle d'oggi . . . voglio ve ne renda ammaestrate" (I, 10, 8). Filomena presents both aims, "Al novellare torneremo, nel quale mi par *grandissima parte di piacere e d'utilità similmente consistere*" (I Conclusion, 9).

The storytellers of the *onesta brigata* seem to be the only people who realize the serious problems of their society, which they view in the same catastrophic terms as the Narrator. Verbal exchanges among the seven women reveal certain patterns of social behaviour to which they strongly object. These include the lack of social order, the contempt for family and social traditions, and the corruption of individual and social values. The women's realization of the dangers and evils of the urban world is not, however, merely a passive acknowledgement of its condition but an incentive to remedy its ills. With the outspoken Pampinea as their unofficial leader the women devise a plan to circumvent and overcome the dangers of the plagues. The appearance of the group's three men on this fictional stage enables the members of the "onesta brigata" to abandon the decayed world of the city and to enter another world. This new world, still untouched by social and moral corruption, is, in Pampinea's words, highly reminiscent of the ideal natural setting recommended as a poet's retreat in the previously cited passage of the *Genealogia:*

> . . . s'odono gli uccelletti cantare, veggionvisi verdeggiare i colli e le pianure, e i campi pieni di biade non altramenti ondeggiare che il mare, e d'alberi ben mille maniere, e il cielo più apertamente, il quale, ancora che crucciato ne sia, non per ciò le sue bellezze eterne ne nega, le quali molto più belle sono a riguardare che le mura vote della nostra città; e èvvi, oltre a questo, l'aere assai più fresco, e di quelle cose che alla vita bisognano in questi tempi v'è la copia maggiore e minore il numero delle noie.
>
> (I, Introduction 66-67)

The perfect natural world described in this passage—eventually chosen by the "brigata" as their dwelling place outside the city—suggests, with its regenerative powers, a Christian vision of nature, a type of Earthly Paradise.[25] But it also seems to foreshadow the earthly Renaissance vision of the power of art and the artist to recreate and perfect nature.[26] The ten young people who will be our storytellers actively seek escape from an urban situation plagued not only by disease but by a morbid lack of human contact and social intercourse. Their subsequent retreat becomes an attempt to recreate a socially harmonious life in a restricted country environment. In view of the dramatic action of the whole work, the departure from the city—now a symbol of disease, despair, and social disorder—into the perfected natural world of the secluded country estate—potentially representative of a healthy, happy, and harmonious social order—is in effect the prime mover of the narrative action of the *Decameron*. In fact, it is only after the transfer has been affected that the decision to tell stories can be made. Thus, the fleeing storytellers are more than a narrative device to supply a fictional context for the collected tales; through them Boccaccio presents the socio-historical and ideological bases of his work. Only by fleeing the plague-infested city can the members of the *brigata* find the solitude and serenity needed to create their *favole;* and only through these creations can they benefit the members of their society with "diletto e utilità." Not only the characters in many of the tales, but the storytellers themselves demonstrate the qualities needed for survival in a plague-torn society: resourcefulness, ingenuity, self-control, verbal mastery, and organizational skill. Pampinea is the first among them to show such abilities when she suggests a system of self-government for the "brigata".

> . . . per ciò che le cose che sono senza modo non possono lungamente durare, io, che cominciatrice fui de' ragionamenti da' quali questa così bella compagnia è stata fatta, pensando al continuar della nostra letizia, estimo che di necessità sia convenire esser tra noi alcuno principale, il quale noi e onoriamo e ubidiamo come maggiore, nel quale ogni pensiero stea di doverci a lietamente vivere disporre . . . e questo cotale, secondo il suo arbitrio, del tempo che la sua signoria dee bastare, del luogo e del modo nel quale a vivere abbiamo ordini e disponga.
>
> (I Introduction, 95-96)

If we compare this passage with the initial view of a Florence devoid of law and order, we realize that Pampinea ingeniously outlines a social order which counterbalances all the problems of the city. While in the city "in tanta afflizione e miseria era la riverenda autorità delle leggi . . . quasi caduta e dissoluta tutta . . . per la qual cosa era a ciascun licito quanto a grado gli era d'adoperare," here instead Pampinea stresses the ennobling experience of a well-functioning society based upon the mutual respect and cooperation of its members and their "principle" of governing authority, "nel quale ogni pensiero stea di doverci a lietamente vivere disporre."

As the first queen of the group, Pampinea reasserts the need for order by suggesting that the responsibility for ruling should be divided among all the youths, "E acciò che ciascun pruovi il peso della sollecitudine insieme col piacere della maggioranza e, per conseguente da una parte e d'altra tratti, non possa chi nol pruova invidia avere alcuna, dico che a ciascuno per un giorno s'attribuisca e il peso e l'onore . . ." (I Introduction, 96). These are the first clear indications of the *brigata's* intention to restructure life in the country according to an orderly program of shared participation in government. Such a program guarantees a dynamic interaction among the ten youths in determining their method of self-government, and implies a careful interweaving of personal and communal interests and goals. It is again Pampinea who proposes the method of electing the king or queen of the day "e chi il primo di noi esser debba nella elezion di noi tutti sia: di quegli che seguiranno . . . quegli o quella che a colui o a colei piacerà che quel giorno avrà avuta la signoria . . ." (I Introduction, 96). The proposal allows for one communal decision at the beginning of the first day, and for many different personal decisions on each consecutive day.

Pampinea outlines the daily program on the First Day so that "la nostra compagnia con ordine e con piacere e senza alcuna vergogna viva e duri quanto a grado ne fia . . ." (I Introduction, 98). However, each king or queen will have full responsibility for the day's activities during his or her reign: "e questo cotale, secondo il suo arbitrio, del tempo che la sua signoria dee bastare, del luogo e del modo nel quale a vivere abbiamo ordini e disponga . . ." (I Introduction, 96). This daily routine will include early rising and walking, lunching outside in gardens or meadows, playing games, taking naps, and eventually spending the warmest part of the day "novellando . . . il che può porgere, dicendo uno, a tutta la compagnia che ascolta diletto" (I Introduction, 111). The evenings will then be dedicated to elegant suppers followed by singing and dancing. And yet, even within such a closed, predetermined structure, each youth will be able to exercise his or her personal influence on the day that he or she reigns.

Filomena, the queen of the second day, "formosa e di piacevole aspetto," agrees to reissue Pampinea's "laudevoli e dilettevoli" commands as long as they "o per troppa continuanza o per altra cagione non ci divenisser noiose" (I Conclusion, 7). She thus subscribes to Pampinea's endorsement of periodic change. At the same time, she introduces her own innovation. As opposed to Pampinea's ruling for the First Day, Filomena prescribes set topics for the "novellare," and also frees Dioneo "col consentimento degli altri" from following such restrictions, because he is known to be a "solazzevole uomo e festevole" (I Conclusion, 14). Once the storytelling procedure for the day has been set,

Filomena takes the *brigata* for a walk towards an enchanting new location, where the ladies find an original pastime that they will pursue again in the conclusion of the Sixth Day:

> E da seder levatasi, verso un rivo d'acqua chiarissima, il quale d'una montagnetta discendeva in una valle ombrosa da molti albori fra vive pietre e verdi erbette, con lento passo se n'andarono. Quivi, scalze e con le braccia nude per l'acqua andando, cominciarono a prendere varii diletti fra se medesime.
>
> (I Conclusion, 15)

During her reign Filomena thus fulfills her duties by maintaining a balance between accepting her predecessor's decisions and introducing original measures which include participation by other members of the *brigata*.

These balanced rapports between current and past governing authorities, and between these authorities and their subjects, are maintained in each of the subsequent days. In the Third Day, Neifile is crowned queen and with her bold decisions she soon overcomes the shyness she seems to show at the moment of her coronation, "del ricevuto onore un poco arrossò, e tal nel viso divenne qual fresca rosa d'aprile o di maggio in su lo schiarir del giorno si mostra, con gli occhi vaghi e sintillanti non altramenti che matutina stella, un poco bassi" (II Conclusion, 3). Neifile's intention, readily accepted by her subjects, is to suspend the storytelling for the next two days, Friday and Saturday, for religious and hygienic reasons:

> . . . il venerdì, avendo riguardo che in esso Colui che per la nostra vita morì sostenne passione, è degno di reverenza; per che giusta cosa e molto onesta reputerei che, a onor di Dio, più tosto a orazioni che a novelle vacassimo. E il sabato appresso usanza è delle donne di lavarsi la testa, di tor via ogni polvere, ogni sucidume che per la fatica di tutta la passata settimana sopravvenuta fosse; e soglion similmente assai, a reverenza della Vergine madre del Figliuolo di Dio, digiunare . . .
>
> (II Conclusion, 5-6)

Furthermore, Neifile is the organizer of a move to new lodgings, "perciò che noi qui quatro dì dimorate saremo, se noi vogliam tor via che gente nuova ci sopravenga, reputo oportuno di mutarci di qui e andarne altrove; e il dove io ho già pensato e proveduto" (II Conclusion, 7). The "bellissimo e ricco palagio" that Neifile chooses is the new setting in which the *brigata* will spend all the remaining days of their sojourn in the idyllic Tuscan countryside.[27] Neifile's innovative actions, then, balanced by her acceptance of a set topic of the *novellare* as well *novellare* as well as of the scheduled daily routine, open new possibilities for dynamic relationships between the ruling authority and its subjects. Moreover, Neifile's two-day suspension of narration will be repeated by Lauretta one week later as queen of the Eighth Day:

> . . . volendo il buono essemplo datone da Neifile seguitare, estimo che onesta cosa sia che domane e l'altro dì, come i passati giorni facemmo, dal nostro dilettevole novellare ci astegnamo, quello a memoria riducendoci che in così fatti giorni per la salute delle nostre anime adivenne.
>
> (VII Conclusion, 17)

Lauretta does not linger on the hygienic reasons given by Neifile, thus exercising a certain independence in ruling her own day. When Filostrato, the first elected king, assumes the privileges of the crown in the Fourth Day, his actions and manner of supervising the *brigata's* life do not differ much from his predecessors'. In one way, however, he does introduce an innovation that will produce a balancing effect in the next day. He asks the storytellers to narrate tales about "coloro li cui amori ebbero infelice fine . . ." (III Conclusion, 6), a theme which stands in marked contrast to the *brigata's* established aim of seeking happiness. This decision is not readily accepted by the *brigata*. Fiammetta sees such a choice to be in conflict with the expectations of the whole group: "dove per rallegrarci venuti siamo, ci convenga raccontar l'altrui lagrime . . ." (IV Conclusion, 2).

Still, one can find in Fiammetta's words the implication of a well-composed balance of opposites when she assumes that Filostrato "Forse per temperare alquanto la letizia avuta li giorni passati l'ha fatto . . ." (IV 1, 2). The implied need for balance becomes even more convincingly demonstrated in the second *novella* of that day where Pampinea, "più disposta a dovere alquanto recrear loro (le compagne) che a dovere, fuori che del comandamento solo, il re contentare . . ." (IV 2, 4), decides "alquanto gli animi vostri pieni di *compassione* per la morte di Ghismunda forse con *risa* e *con piacer* rilevare" (IV 2, 7). Eventually Dioneo decides at the end of the day to change the sorrowful mood into a happy one. With this change, he sets the stage for Fiammetta, who, as the next queen, will follow his advice whereby "senza andar più dietro a così dolorosa materia, da alquanto più lieta e migliore incomincerò, forse buono indizio dando a ciò che nella seguente giornata si dee raccontare" (IV 10, 3). Filostrato himself, in crowning Fiammetta queen of the Fifth day, stresses the same need for change, "Io pongo a te questa corona sì come a colei la quale meglio dell' aspra giornata d'oggi, che alcuna altra, con quella di domane queste nostre compagne *racconsolar* saprai . . ." (IV Conclusion, 3). In fact, Fiammetta's choice for her day's storytelling will be "ciò che a alcuno amante, dopo alcuni fieri o sventurati accidenti, felicemente avvenisse . . ." (IV Conclusion, 5), where the adverb "felicemente" stands in opposition to the wording of Filostrato's command to narrate love stories of "infelice fine." Emilia, in the introduction to her story, (V 2), exemplifies each storyteller's involvement in the creation of dramatic oppositions in narrative choice and tone within the *novelle:* ". . . e per ciò che amare merita più tosto diletto che afflizione a lungo andare, con molto mio maggior piacere della presente materia parlando ubidirò la reina, che della precedente non feci il re" (V 2, 3). Filostrato, in the opening lines of his *novella* of the Fifth Day (V 4), recognizes the need to say "alcuna cosa per la quale io alquanto vi faccia ridere" (V 4, 3). He thus counterbalances his previous choice of a sad topic for the Fourth Day and brings harmony between himself and the women. The queen, at the end of Filostrato's *novella,* praises the success of his effort to balance the effect of the preceding day: "Sicuramente, se tu ieri ci affligesti, tu ci hai oggi tanto dileticate, che niuna meritamente di te si dee ramaricare" (V 5, 2). In addition, Fiammetta introduces another slight innovation at the end of the Fourth Day by asking Filostrato to sing the final *canzone:*

> Filostrato, io non intendo deviare da' miei passati; ma sì come essi hanno fatto così intendo che per lo mio comandamento si canti una canzone; e per ciò che io son certa che tali sono le tue canzoni chenti sono le tue novelle, acciò che più giorni che questo non sien turbati de' tuoi infortunii, vogliamo che *una ne dichi qual più ti piace* . . .
> (IV Conclusion, 9)

This slight deviation from the normal procedure is repeated in the Sixth Day, where Dioneo, elected king of the Seventh Day, asks Elissa, queen of the Sixth, to sing the final canzone: "Bella giovane, tu mi facesti oggi onore della corona, e io il voglio questa sera a te fare della canzone; e per ciò *una fa che ne dichi qual più ti piace*" (VI Conclusion, 40). Dioneo's wording is almost identical to Fiammetta's. This verbal similarity does not recur in the request for *canzone* singing at the end of any of the other days.[28] Yet the intentions of both speakers in requesting the king and queen of that particular day to sing the last *canzone* are markedly different. Fiammetta attempts to contain the effects of Filostrato's unhappiness on the *brigata* to a single day, thus acknowledging the disharmony created by his selection of love tales with "infelice fine." Dioneo, on the other hand, seeks to create a feeling of harmony by reciprocating Elissa's kindness to him with a kind action towards her. By addressing her as "Bella giovane," he touches on the unifying principle of beauty—a quality that is common to all the "belle donne" of the *brigata*—and to the "tanto bella . . . valle delle Donne" which has been the setting for both the women's and the men's late afternoon outing.

This balancing of similarities and differences in the verbal structure finds a parallel in the group's communal interests and goals as well. At the beginning of her rule of the Sixth Day, Elissa proposes a new topic of *novellare* that will stress, instead of emotions, the power of the mind and the beauty of appropriate verbal expression: "chi, con alcun leggiadro motto tentato, si riscotesse, o con pronta risposta o avvedimento fuggì perdita o pericolo o scorno" (V Conclusion, 3). The narrative order in which matters relating to the *brigata*'s life are usually presented is disrupted twice under Elissa's reign: first at the end of the Fifth Day by Dioneo, who insists, to the women's great amusement and the queen's eventual irritation, on suggesting ribald titles for his final *canzone* ("Monna Aldruda, levate la coda, Chè buone novelle vi reco . . . Alzatevi i panni, monna Lapa . . . Monna Simona imbotta imbotta, E' non è del mese d'ottobre"); and then at the beginning of the Sixth Day by the servant's quarrel about women's sexual habits. "Madonna," says Licisca of Tindaro, "costui mi vuol far conoscere la moglie di Sicofante . . . mi vuol dare a vedere che la notte prima che Sicofante giacque con lei messer Mazza entrasse in Monte Nero per forza e con ispargimento di sangue . . ." (VI Introduction, 8). These erotic references recall Dioneo's teasing exploits of the night before while foreshadowing the thematic variations of the following day's *novelle* when Dioneo will rule. The balancing dynamics of narration are particularly clear in the Sixth Day, where there is an opposition between the opening scene dominated by the servants' view of sexual matters in equivocal, bawdy terms, and the Conclusion, with its idealized presentation of the perfect *locus amoenus*, the "Valle delle Donne . . . tanto bella e tanto dilettevole" (VI Conclusion, 19).

The "Valle delle Donne" is described in traditional terms; its "chiarissimo fiumicello" forms "un piccolo laghetto" surrounded by "sei montagnette di non troppa altezza . . . Le piagge delle quali . . . erano . . . tutte di vigne, d'ulivi, di mandorli, di ciriegi, di fichi . . . piene . . . (e) di boschetti di quercioli, di frassini e d'altri arberi verdissimi e ritti . . ." and is embellished by "tutto un prato d'erba minutissima e piena di fiori porporini e d'altri . . ." (VI Conclusion, 20-24). This wholly positive natural scene is preceded by a contrasting negative account of city life described by Dioneo:

> Or non sapete voi che, per la perversità di questa stagione, li giudici hanno lasciati i tribunali? le leggi, così le divine come le umane, tacciono? e ampia licenzia per conservar la vita è conceduta a ciascuno?
>
> (VI Conclusion, 9)

In this passage an opposition is again suggested between a negative city world devoid of justice and moral order, and a delightful natural environment, "una delle belle cose del mondo," where beauty, joy, peace, and comfort prevail with inner order and harmony. Dioneo, then, manifests his individuality in choosing this setting as the backdrop for the aesthetic experience of storytelling during the day of his rule, as if such an ideal location might counterbalance the audacious and often rather immoral narrative situations in the *novelle* of this day. First the women and later the men undergo a symbolic purification in the *valle* by bathing in the clear waters of the "piccol laghetto." This purification offsets the ambiguous atmosphere created by Dioneo's choice of subject-matter, "le beffe le quali o per amore o per salvamento di loro le donne hanno già fatte a' lor mariti . . ." (VI Conclusion, 6). Besides performing a socially therapeutic function for the *novellatori* themselves, the *locus amoenus* of the "Valle delle Donne" also counteracts the potentially negative social and moral impact of the *beffa novelle*. The natural environment functions as a dramatic counterpart both to the social world of the storytellers and to the aesthetic world of the *novelle*. Through the ritual of bathing, and through moving the *brigata* to the "Valle delle Donne," a balanced rhythm which harmoniously merges the physical and the ideal, the course and the refined, the sexual and the spiritual, is successfully created.

At the end of the Seventh Day, Dioneo crowns Lauretta queen, and she, as previously mentioned, follows Neifile's example by setting aside the next Friday and Saturday to abstain "dal . . . dilettevole novellare . . ." (VII Conclusion, 17). Lauretta, however, introduces a slight change—instead of announcing this decision as soon as she is made queen, as Neifile did, she postpones doing so until after supper, when the *brigata* is ready to retire for the night. At the end of her rule Lauretta crowns Emilia queen, stressing her beauty as her major virtue, "Madonna, io non so come piacevole reina noi avrem di voi, ma bella la pure avrem noi: fate adunque che alle vostre bellezze l'opere sien rispondenti . . ." (VIII Conclusion, 1). Emilia's immediate reaction to such flattery is one of modesty, "un pochetto si vergognò e tal nel viso divenne quali in su l'aurora son le novelle rose . . ." (VIII Conclusion, 2). Soon enough, however, she reveals her other gifts, among them a clear insight into the *brigata's* need for healthy changes in daily routine. Indeed, Emilia becomes the first ruler to allow her subjects a free choice of topic without being compelled to do so by time restrictions, as was Pampinea during her first day as queen. The reasons Emilia gives for her choice are clearly inspired by a desire to ensure a balanced and wholesome rhythm in the *brigata's* affairs:

> . . . Avendo riguardo quanti giorni sotto certa legge ristretti ragionato abbiamo, che, sì come a bisognosi, di vagare alquanto e vagando riprender forze a rientrar sotto il giogo non solamente sia utile ma opportuno. E per ciò quello che domane, seguendo il vostro dilettevole ragionar, sia da dire non intendo di ristrignervi sotto alcuna spezialità, ma voglio che ciascuno secondo che gli piace ragioni, fermamente tenendo che la varietà delle cose che si diranno non meno graziosa ne fia che l'avere pur d'una parlato; e così avendo fatto, chi appresso di me nel reame verrà, sì come più forti, con maggior sicurtà ne potrà nell'usate leggi ristrignere.
>
> (VIII Conclusion, 4-5)

Panfilo, elected king of the last day by Emilia, will accordingly fulfill her wish and request the company to return to the fixed topic rule:

> Innamorate donne, la discrezion d'Emilia, nostra reina stata questo giorno, per dare alcun riposo alle vostre forze arbitrio vi diè di ragionare ciò che più vi piacesse; per che, già riposati essendo, giudico che sia bene il ritornare alla legge usata, e per ciò voglio che domane ciascuna di voi pensi di ragionare sopra questo, cioè: di chi liberalmente o vero magnificamente alcuna cosa operasse intorno a' fatti d'amore o d'altra cosa.
> (IX Conclusion, 4)

Panfilo eventually asserts individuality as king by convincing the *brigata* to return to the city after their fortnight sojourn in the country. His resolution is motivated by a concern for the *brigata*'s communal wellbeing: ". . . acciò che per troppa lunga consuetudine alcuna cosa che in fastidio si convertisse nascer non potesse . . ." (X Conclusione, 6), as well as for their social position and reputation, "e perché alcuno la nostra troppo lunga dimoranza gavillar non potesse . . ." (X Conclusion, 6). At the same time, Pamfilo does not hesitate to indicate the importance of the contribution that each member of the brigata has made to the group's welfare, "avendo ciascun di noi la sua giornata avuta la sua parte dell'onore che in me ancora dimora . . ." (X Conclusion, 6). With this last statement, Pamfilo seems to suggest that the experience of ruling has sharpened their sense of social and moral responsibility to their troubled society. Each member of the *brigata* may thus be able to face the complex and dangerous world of the city with the resourcefulness and moral integrity that he or she will need when they all return.

In the "Author's Conclusion," the Narrator himself states that the work's readers as well as the storytellers have moral responsibility. He reiterates his desire to use the *novelle* as didactic tools suited to specific "tempi" and "persone":

> "Ciascuna cosa in se medesima è buona a alcuna cosa, e male adoperata può essere nociva di molte; e così dico delle mie novelle. Chi vorrà da quelle malvagio consiglio e malvagia operazion trarre, elle nol vieteranno a alcuno . . . e chi *utilità* e *frutto* ne vorrà, elle nol negheranno, né sarà mai che altro che utile e oneste sien dette o tenute, se a que' tempi o a quelle persone si leggeranno per cui e pe' quali state son raccontate."
> (Author's Conclusion, 13-14)

The "tempi" fall into two periods: first, the late spring of the plague year, 1348—the time of the storytellers' oral narration[29]—and second, the years immediately following the plague—the time of the Narrator's transcription of the tales. The Narrator specifies in the "Proemio" that he is recording *novelle* that had been "raccontate . . . da una onesta brigata di sette donne e di tre giovani nel pistelenzioso tempo della *passata* mortalità" (Proemio 13). In the Introduction he again stresses this difference in time between the oral recounting of the *novelle* and their publication. This differentiation is sharpened when he explains his decision not to mention the real names of the storytellers, especially those of the ladies, because:

> . . . io non voglio che per le raccontate cose da loro, che seguono, e per l'ascoltate *nel tempo avvenire* alcuna di loro possa prender vergogna, essendo *oggi* alquanto ristrette le leggi al piacere che *allora* . . . erano non che alla loro età ma a troppo più matura larghissime . . .
> (I Introduzione, 50)[30]

The three adverbial forms in this passage indicate the two-phase process of *novelle*-narration; "allora" suggests an earlier moment—that of the oral narration—and "oggi" a later date—that of the written version. The projected "tempo avvenire" suggests the Narrator's desired communication with future audiences outside the work. This treatment of the time of narration creates a close connection between the narrators—the first person Narrator and the ten storytellers, especially the women among them—and their audiences, and consequently suggests a constant reciprocal influence of narrative matters on readers and of readers on narrators. We have here, *in nuce*, an insight into the multi-level relationship between the narrator, the work of literature, and its audience.

This same passage illustrates the process of human communication which a work of literature can initiate in a social environment. The Narrator personally knows the storytellers and feels a respectful empathy for them—at least for the ladies—which he implies by his decision to spare them future embarrassment by withholding their real names. This kindness and respect, and the presence of an actual relationship between the Narrator and the storytellers, echoes the feeling expressed by the Narrator in the "Proemio". There he was at once reacting with gratitude and love to those friends who had helped him in the past with consoling words, and was, at the same time, offering his own understanding to the women in love whom he expected to help in the future. The work's fundamental purpose thus becomes the act of concerned communication among individuals of all times in oral as well as in written form.

Through the device of the independent Narrator's point of view, Boccaccio establishes, at an early stage of the work, a harmonious tone of communication that works on both aesthetic and social levels. The narrative "word" becomes thus an active and useful means of urging individual and social change. The *novellatori* themselves, as well as the Narrator, may offer their respective audiences fruitful lessons to succor them in times of hardship. Given the harsh reality of the period in which the members of the "onesta brigata" gather to relate their tales, these lessons must attempt to deal with the most pressing needs of the ailing Florentine commune; the need for more vital integration of individual and communal interests, the need for more effective interaction between the "gente nuova" and established class groups, and the need for a concerned reevaluation of men's and women's rights in a changing society.

3. Narrative Technique

Boccaccio started writing the *Decameron* after he had mastered other prose forms. Through the romances in verse *Filostrato* and *Teseida*, the *Filocolo*, a romance in prose, and the *Comedia delle Ninfe*, he had worked his way to *Fiammetta*, an elegy. These works all present similarities in characterization, structural organization, and ideology; the characters belong almost exclusively to the aristocracy and are developed in ample descriptive sequences around the themes of love and adventure (the latter extensively in *Filocolo* and *Teseida* and less so in *Filostrato, Comedia delle Ninfe* and *Fiammetta*). Their organizational patterns, for the most part, are dominated by temporal and logical sequences describing the actions and counteractions of the main characters. Narrative voices speak almost exclusively in prefaces, where fictionalized background passages provide insights into the works' composition and ideology. Each plot, because it treats the themes of love and adventure, is directed toward an aristocratic audience which shares the characters' concern for courtly virtues and behavior.

From the point of view of narrative technique, there is a steady improvement in the use of language and characterization; it ranges from the longwinded, often abusively monotonous *Filocolo*, to the well-proportioned *Comedia delle Ninfe* and *Fiammetta*, works which show a good mastery of characters' psychology and a complex development of narrative sequences. These later writings also reveal other innovations. Where in previous works the narrative voice is confined to the preface and/or conclusion, in the *Comedia delle Ninfe* a prose fiction with interspersed *canzoni*, the narrator enters the fictional world itself. He becomes a sort of voyeur in the work's last scene where he parallels, although less happily, the main character's situation. In the same work seven nymphs recount their life stories to each other and Ameto, the main male character, with a resulting multiplication of narrative voices. The message, then, is slightly different; rather than encouraging courtly virtues and behavior, as in previous works, the author now stresses Ameto's intellectual and spiritual enlightment which has come about through the process of storytelling.

In the *Fiammetta* a new narrative technique is introduced with the insertion of the narrator directly into the fictional world and in fact, the narrator is the main character of the story, madonna Fiammetta . The *Fiammetta's* purpose is twofold: it at once reaches out to an unfaithful lover to win him back — and thus reaffirms the values of courtly love—at the same time, it attempts to warn women against love and the suffering it brings—and thus rejects courtly love to exalt communication as life's essential component. These last works thus show an increasing complexity of narrative technique, especially in the treatment of the narrator's role, in the multiplication of narrative voices, in the use of storytelling and in ideology.

In the *Decameron* Boccaccio pushes his innovations further with an even more complex use of narrator and narrative voices. At the same time he concentrates on the possibilities of a shorter narrative form, the *novella* or *novellina*. This was a most popular form in thirteenth-century narrative, as evidenced by the collections of *exempla* or *novelline* common to the literary traditions of Spain, France, and Italy.[31] The collections included, among many others, various adaptions and translations of the *Story of Barlam and Josafat*,[32] *Galila and Dimna*,[33] and the *Book of Sinbad*.[34] All of these collections and their many translations and adaptations are based on the *exemplum*[35] or *novellina* form. A short tale centered around one special theme or event, the *novellina* presents a moral or social lesson with the help of examples or proofs chosen from historical, religious, or popular traditions of the past. Works such as the *Exempla* of Jacques de Vitry and the *Factorum ac dictorum memorabilium* of Valerius Maximus owe their popularity to their use of historical tradition for practical purposes and anecdotal learning. The choice of a particular example or set of examples reveals the need for a proof or witness on which to base a certain definition of life or social behavior. From the abundant examples of this kind of narrative we may deduce that at the end of the thirteenth century the cultural needs of the times were satisfied by an "exemplary" form of literature which, through its direct involvement with daily life, contributed to shaping the moral, social, and political views of its readers. Similar collections of *exempla* or *novelline* also appear in Italian: *Fiore dei Filosafi*,[36] *Conti di antichi cavalieri*,[37] *Fiori di Virtù*,[37] and *Novellino*,[38] among them. All share a common goal, to instruct their readers and to spur them on to improved behavior:

> Ed acciò che li nobili e gentili sono, nel parlare e nell'opere, quasi com'uno specchio, appo i minori . . . facciamo qui memoria d'alquanti fiori di parlare, di belle cortesie e di belli amori, secondo che, per lo tempo passato, hanno fatto già molti. E chi avrà cuore nobile ed intelligenzia sottile, sì li potrà somigliare . . . ed argomentare, e dire, e raccontare . . . *a prode ed a piacere di coloro che non sanno e disiderano di sapere.*
> (Novellino, p.p. 8-9)

From this and similar prefaces, we may conclude that the *novellina* is a literary form that urges its readers to learn for the purpose of personal enjoyment and moral and social improvement. Boccaccio recounts the "novelle" in his

Decameron with the purpose of offering "diletto e utile consiglio" to his readers, so that they may "cognoscere quello che sia da fuggire e che sia similmente da seguitare" (Proemio, 13, 14). His choice of the *novella* is thus made intentionally and is based on a clear understanding of this narrative genre's traditional function. Yet, in comparison with its antecedents, the *novella* form used in the *Decameron* shows innovations in narrative structure, narrator's intention, and ideology. It also provides a human prototype and social model strikingly similar to the reality of fourteenth-century Italy.

A comparative analysis of *Decameron* I 3 and its source, *Novellino* LXXIII, will highlight the essential components of each and will isolate those elements of the *Decameron* which are unique to Boccaccio. In the *Novellino* tale, "Come il Soldano avendo bisogno di moneta volle coglier cagione a un giudeo,"[40] concision is the guiding narrative principle. There is no *exordium*, and the tale opens in *medias res* without any preparatory statements or lengthy descriptions of the main characters, "Il Soldano avendo bisogno di moneta, fo consigliato che cogliesse cagione a un ricco giudeo, ch'era in sua terra, e poi li togliesse il mobole suo ch'era grande oltre numero." The characters are introduced as "Il Soldano" and "un ricco guideo," the former as the subject of the first two sentences of the story, and the latter of the third. The first sentence opens with "Il Soldano" followed immediately by a gerundive clause revealing Saladin's exclusively monetary motivation, "avendo bisogno di moneta." This phrase is followed by a passive construction, "fo consigliato," where Saladin, while grammatically still functioning as the subject, semantically becomes the object of the advice from undefined counselors. This anonymous advice triggers Saladin's intent to act against the "ricco giudeo," an intention rendered with the subjunctive verbal forms "*cogliesse* cagione" and "li *togliesse* il mobole suo." These dependent clauses, suggesting the possible actions of a (thus far) passive subject, are followed by relative clauses in the indicative mood which define the "ricco giudeo," "ch'era in sua terra," and his wealth, "ch'era grande oltra numero." In this way, the only connection between the two characters is reduced to what the "ricco giudeo" possesses. The following sentence presents the "Soldano" in action, "mandò per questo giudeo e domandolli." No transition is provided between the anonymous advice and Saladin's decision to act upon it. The indirect question after "domandolli" reintroduces a subjunctive construction, "qual *fosse* la miglior fede." This is followed by another gerundive, "pensando," related to Saladin, which balances the previous "avendo bisogno." These two gerundive forms function as the only qualifiers for the character of the "Soldano," the first one specifying an external condition (his socio-economic situation), and the second an inner one, neither of which is apparently too sound or dependable. Contrary to the previous anonymous advice conveyed in indirect speech, passive forms, and subjunctive mood, Saladin's thoughts are now expressed in direct speech and in present and future indicative tenses, "'S'elli dirà la giudea, io li dirò ch'elli pecca contro la mia; e se dirà la saracina, ed io dirò: 'Dunque, perchè tieni la giudea?'" The speech is evenly balanced in two main sequences, each is built upon an "if" clause followed by a main clause, connected in the first sequence to a declarative clause, and in the second to an unanswered interrogative.

The similarity in the syntactical structure is strengthened by the repetition of the same verbal forms "dirà," "dirò," which produces a monotonous rhythm. The whole speech, in its simplified, repetitive form, is Saladin's one-sided wishful projection of his future dealing with the Jew.

The following sentence introduces the Jew who "udendo la domanda del signore, rispose così," and promptly initiates his counteraction. In this case no transition is provided to prepare for the apparently impromptu "parable inside the tale" improvised by the Jew as a reply to Saladin's question:

> Messere, elli fu un padre, ch'avea tre figliuoli, ed avea un suo anello, con una pietra preziosa, la miglior del mondo. Ciascuno di costoro pregava il padre, ch'alla sua fine li lasciasse questo anello. Il padre, vedendo che catuno il volea, mandò per un fine orafo e disse: 'Maestro, fammi due anella, così appunto come questo, e metti in ciascuno una pietra, che somigli questa.' Lo maestro fece l'anella così appunto, che nessuno conoscea il fine, altro che 'l padre. Mandò per li figliuoli, ad uno ad uno, ed a catuno diede il suo, in sacreto: e catuno si credea aver il fine, e niuno ne sapea il vero, altri che 'l padre loro. E così ti dico delle fedi, che sono tre. Il Padre di sopra sa la migliore, e li figliuoli, ciò siamo noi, ciascuno si crede avere la buona. (pp. 143-144)

The parable offers a three-way comparison between (1) the father of the parable and the heavenly father, (2) the three sons and mankind divided into religious sect, and (3) the three rings and the three major religions. The parable correctly conveys the traditional triadic series of religions, while, curiously enough, Saladin in his own two-cola monologue, had only mentioned two, "la giudea" and "la saracina." This detail, present in the parable and insisted upon by the Jew "(E così dico delle fedi, che sono tre)", seems to imply an intellectual superiority on the Jew's part, when compared to the incompleteness of Saladin's questioning—a superiority which may well warrant his eventual outwitting of Saladin. The Jew's linguistic skills vis-à-vis the shortcoming of Saladin's character seem to sanction such an interpretation.

While the main themes suggested by Saladin's question and by the parable's message deal with spiritual realities, the parable's linguistic and semantic context convey exclusively economic realities. The motives of the relations between father and sons are purely possession-oriented; the father's possessions include on a level of equal syntactical weight, his sons and an object, his precious ring. The latter is dealt with much more at length than the former, so that it occupies a dominant place in the narrative, *"avea tre figliuoli,* ed *avea un suo anello,* con una pietra preziosa, la miglior del mondo." The sons relate to their father through an exclusively possession-oriented urge for the ring, "Ciascuno . . . pregava il padre, ch'alla sua fine li lasciasse questo anello . . . catuno *il volea."* The father responds to their desire by having the object reproduced twice, thus satisfying their needs in an equally materialistic way. The parable closes with the Jew's interpretation of its paradigmatic meaning.

Saladin's reaction to the Jew's parable takes place through syntactical forms similar to the ones used in the opening sentences of the *novellina* and again through a two-cola format, which hints once more at an unresolvable conflict, "Allora il Soldano, *udendo* costui cosi riscuotersi, *non seppe* che si dire di coglierli cagione: *sì lo lasciò andare."* The gerund form introduces another qualifier for Saladin, this time connected with a sensorial as well as an intellectual perception, *"udendo* costui cosi riscuotersi". The main verb in its negative form, "non seppe," clearly expresses the passivity and irresolution of Saladin's character, already intimated in the earlier passive construction "fo consigliato" and in his two-cola monologue. His final action "lo lasciò andare" again underlines Saladin's weakness through its semantically non-active construction.

On the whole, this *novellina* shows a simple syntactical structure made up of short sentences which are either paratactically coordinated or are expressed in simplified hypotactical sequences, "Il Soldano *mandò . . . e domandolli";* or "elli fu un padre ch'*avea* tre figliuoli, *e avea* un suo anello . . ."; or *"fammi* due anella così . . . *e metti* . . ." The lexical options are limited; nouns and verbs are of the simplest and most obvious choice, and only a handful of the most common adjectives are present, such as *ricco, grande, migliore, preziosa, buona, fine,* and *vero.* There is repetition of the same word — *giudeo, anello, pietra* — or of the same expression: *"s'elli dirà . . . io dirò . . . e se dirà . . . e io dirò"; "fammi due anella così appunto . . . fece l'anella così appunto . . ."* or *"cogliesse cagione . . . coglierli cagione."* This lexical limitation is accentuated by the presence of the same words, i.e.*fine,* used more than once with a different meaning each time, creating a false aura of complexity where in reality no such effect exists: "alla sua *fine,"* meaning "end, death", "un *fine orafo,"* meaning "refined, excellent," "nessuno conoscea il *fine,"* meaning in a pronominal form, "the real one," and repeated in the same way later in "catuno si credea aver il *fine."*

The brevity and concision of the story are thus heightened by the simplicity of the syntax, the economy — even monotony — of the lexicon, and the abruptness of narrative transitions. This is seen specifically in the progression from Saladin's question to the Jew's answer, where the parable is introduced suddenly without any narrative preparation. The same happens at the end of the parable, when Saladin's reaction to it comes equally abruptly.

The characters themselves are represented mostly in sketchy outlines and from a purely external perspective. Their motivations are limited and no change occurs to them either physically or intellectually as a result of their encounter. The moral significance of the story is spelled out at the end of the Jew's parable, while the social significance is implicit in the weakness of Saladin's character. The difficulty which these two characters have in communicating is pointedly stressed not only by the abruptness of narrative transition, but also by Saladin's one-sided monologue. When the Jew contradicts Saladin with his parable the potentate becomes incapable of forcing him into an uncomfortable situation. Lack of thoughtful communication is also obvious among the characters of the parable whose only rapport is based on their possessive urge for the ring.

The human prototype created in this *novellina*, especially through the character of the "Soldano," is, therefore, a very limited one; it is primarily money-oriented, and is incapable of communication, it unsuccessfully projects spiritual needs as pretexts for possessive urges and lacks intellectual and social power. This is less the case of the Jew, whose inventiveness and intellectual promptness in the time of need in part balance Saladin's weaknesses. His parable, however, conveys the same view of a world ridden by materialistic instincts and incapable of communication on any but a money-oriented level.

Novellino LXXIII is a direct source of *Decameron* I 3, where it is adopted by the technique of amplification. The *novella* opens with an eloquent two-part *exordium*, the first part of which provides a narrative connection both with the previous *novella* and with themes presented in earlier *novelle* of the day. It aims also, as most of Day I tales do, at stressing the didactic value that narrative matter has on its audience:

> La novella da Neifile detta mi ritorna a memoria il dubbioso caso già avvenuto a un giudeo. Per ciò che già e di Dio e della verità della nostra fede è assai bene stato detto, il discendere oggimai agli avvenimenti e agli atti degli uomini non si dovrà disdire: a narrarvi quella verrò, la quale udita, forse più caute diverrete nelle risposte alle quistioni che fatte vi fossero.
> (I 3, 3-4)

The second part of the *exordium* introduces the novella's main theme:

> Voi dovete, amorose compagne, sapere che, sì come la sciocchezza spesse volte trae altrui di felice stato e mette in grandissimi miseria, così il senno di grandissimi pericoli trae il savio e ponlo in grande e sicuro riposo.
> (I 3, 4-5)

After the address to the "amorose compagne," the passage is equally balanced in two corresponding rhythmical parts—two hendecasyllables plus a seven-syllable verse—which are semantically antithetical, "come la sciocchezza . . . trae altrui di felice stato e mette in grandissima miseria" versus "così il senno di grandissimi pericoli trae il savio e ponlo in grande e sicuro riposo." The basic opposition of the *novella* is introduced by the antithetical pair *sciocchezza-senno* and *miseria-fortuna*, which suggests the main conflict between Saladin's need and Melchisedec's riches. From this antithesis springs the test through which Melchisedec's *senno*—and Saladin's as well—will eventually be proven. This opposition is strengthened by other antitheses, such as, in the first part the actions of *trae* versus *mette*, and the conditions of *felice stato* versus *grandissima miseria*. These correspond word by word to the antitheses in the second part of the passage; *trae* versus *ponlo*, and *grandissimi pericoli* versus *grande e sicuro riposo*. These contrasts are further emphasized by the antithetical relationship between *altrui* of the first part—impersonal, anonymous, and with a negative connotation—and *il savio* of the second part, which refers to the positive character of the *savio giudeo*. This whole *exordium* amplifies and modifies its source, the *Novellino* tale. In its two parts, it has the specific narrative functions of creating meaningful connections between this story, the preceding *novelle*, and the audience, and of anticipating the main theme and mood of the *novella* to come through rhythmic, lexical, and syntactical parallelisms and antitheses.

The characters presented also modify the source material. The protagonists, Saladin and Melchisedec, are introduced with brief but precise descriptions which are relevant to the development of the story. Saladin's background is provided with particular emphasis on his exceptional *valore*. This quality is an ambiguous motivation inasmuch as it is at once the admitted cause of his success as a world conqueror, and the implied source of his state's disastrous financial condition:

> Il Saladino, il valore del quale fu tanto, che non solamente di piccolo uomo il fé di Babilonia soldano ma ancora molte vittorie sopra li re saracini e cristiani gli fece avere, avendo in diverse guerre e in grandissime sue magnificenze speso tutto il suo tesoro e per alcuno accidente sopravenutogli bisognandogli una buona quantità di denari, né veggendo donde così prestamente come gli bisognavano avergli potesse, gli venne a memoria un ricco giudeo, il cui nome era Melchisedech, il quale prestava a usura in Alessandria.
> (I 3, 6-7)

"Il Saladino" is here syntactically isolated at the opening of the passage, where it stands alone before a long series of dependent clauses. Only in the next to the last line of the period is the main verb "venne alla memoria" introduced. Several of the dependent clauses that follow "Il Saladino" introduce different subjects, frequently personified abstractions, which act upon the initial subject, "Il Saladino." Such is the case of personified "valore," which is used as an agent to transform Saladin's existence -"di piccolo uomo *il fé* di Babilonia sovrano," and to establish his military superiority, "molte vittorie sopra li re saracini e cristiani *gli fece* avere." Two infinitive sentences made up of impersonal forms and abstract nouns present Saladin's extreme need for financial help, "per alcuno *accidente sopravenutogli bisognandoli* una buona *quantità* di denari." These clauses seem to underplay Saladin's active role in the crisis of his financial disaster. Two other gerundial forms depend directly on Saladin. One conveys essential information about his military and social behavior, "*avendo* in diverse guerre e in grandissime sue magnificenze *speso* tutto il suo tesoro," and the other introduces his intellectual activity, "né *veggendo* donde così prestamente come gli bisognavano avergli potesse." These last two clauses, depending on "veggendo," convey Saladin's involuted thoughts by inserting one of the clauses ("come gli bisognavano") in the center of the other. Anastrophic inversion of the verbs "avergli potesse" at the end of both clauses accentuates the breach in regular syntax. Up to this point both syntax and lexicon give us information about the main events of Saladin's life and the salient traits of his character. They build up to a particularly critical personal and social situation. All logical connections are provided for a thorough understanding of his character and his future actions. The critical moment introduced by "né veggendo . . ." is viewed from inside the character of Saladin himself. Syntactical disorder and confused word arrangement convey Saladin's disordered thoughts, and linguistically reflect his mental embarrassment and confusion.

At this moment, the main verb is introduced with "gli venne a memoria"; but "un ricco giudeo" immediately follows and becomes the regular subject of the clause. This creates a strong syntactical break, or anacoluthon inasmuch as "Il Saladino," who seemed to be the main clause's subject up to that point, is suddenly demoted to a secondary position and is only incidentally identifiable with the indirect object, "gli." In his stead, "un ricco giudeo" becomes the center of the grammatical and semantic interest, and is qualified by the two dependent relative clauses that follow: "il cui nome era Melchisedec, il quale prestava a usura ad Alessandria." Two important details are thus introduced here that were not present in *Novellino* LXXIII: (1) the Jew's name—which addition focuses more narrative attention on Melchisedec, and (2) the Jew's profession as a money-lender which provides a logical reason for Saladin's choice. With the introduction of the principal verb and clause, the syntax brings the antithetical tone of the passage to a harmonious close by pulling the two characters together in identical roles; one as the apparent and the other as the real subject of the same verb. In this way, regardless of the differences in characters and situations, this careful syntactical arrangement lays the foundations for potential understanding and communication between Saladin and Melchisedec in the conflicting actions to come.

The last part of this paragraph resumes Saladin's train of thought. As his plot develops, his thoughts acquire a less orderly syntactical pattern than we saw previously:

> E pensossi costui avere da poterlo servire quando volesse, ma sì era avaro che di sua volontà non l'avrebbe mai fatto, e forza non gli voleva fare; per che, strignendolo il bisogno, rivoltosi tutto a dover trovar modo come il giudeo il servisse, s'avisò di fargli una forza da alcuna ragion colorata.
>
> (I 3, 7)

The syntactical construction in the first part of this passage hinges on a main verb, "pensossi." All subsequent clauses depend on that verb; the infinitive "costui avere . . ." and its hypothetical qualifier "quando volesse," clearly so. The oppositive consecutive, "ma sì era avaro," with its consequential clause, "che di sua volontà non l'avrebbe mai fatto" and its coordinate "e forza non gli voleva fare," are more ambiguosly so. The mood and tenses of the verbs "era" and "voleva" suggest, in fact, that these clauses are coordinate to the principal "pensossi." However, if this were so they would describe the character of the Jew from the narrator's point of view and thus create a contradiction between this description and the essence of the character which emerges later. This flaw is, however, easily dismissed if these two clauses are seen as representing not the narrator's but the character's point of view. They thus indicate a sudden change in Saladin's thoughts from the indirect speech of the previous infinitive and subjunctive clauses to an *impromptu* and unmarked direct speech, possibly prompted by the *Novellino* source. This sudden shift reveals an intellectual ambivalence in Saladin's approach to the Jew. It also suggests (through the ambivalence of the syntactical construction) Saladin's anxious misinterpretation of reality. His misinterpretation will explain the apparent contradiction in the character of the Jew, whose behavior is very different from what Saladin projects it to be. The sultan's view of Melchisedec as "sì avaro che di sua volontà non l' avrebbe mai fatto," is untenable when compared with Melchisedec's actions; as soon as Saladin openly requests his help, the Jew "liberamente d'ogni quantità che il Saladino il richiese, il servì." (I 3, 18). The expression "e forza non gli voleva fare" should be seen as an indirect utterance of Saladin's tortuous thinking. Indeed, the statement is contradicted in the following paragraph, where Saladin's determination to make the Jew serve him is heavily underscored, "rivoltosi *tutto* a *dover* trovar modo come il giudeo il *servisse*," and "*fargli una forza da alcuna ragion colorata.*" Contradiction also emerges in Saladin's direct question to Melchisedec about the faiths where, while on one hand he praises the Jew for his superior wisdom—"tu se'savissimo e nelle cose di Dio senti molto avanti" (I 3, 8)—on the other he challenges this wisdom by posing a question which obviously camouflages a ruse, "per ciò io saprei volentier da te quale delle tre leggi tu reputi la verace, o la giudaica o la saracina o la cristiana." Another noticeable change from the source occurs here in Saladin's correct use of the traditional three faiths rather than two. The rivals appear to be equally intelligent and thus a harmonious resolution of their conflict is possible.

Melchisedec's reply is then carefully anticipated with a lengthy description of the Jew's character:

> Il giudeo, il quale veramente era savio uomo, s'avisò troppo bene che il Saladino guardava di pigliarlo nelle parole per dovergli muovere alcuna quistione, e pensò non potere alcuna di queste tre più l'una che l'altre lodare, che il Saladino non avesse la sua intenzione; per che, come colui il qual pareva d'aver bisogno di riposta per la quale preso non potesse essere, aguzzato lo 'ngegno, gli venne prestamente avanti quello che dir dovesse; e disse . . .
> (I 3, 9-10)

The qualifiers for "il giudeo," often conveyed by adverbial forms, stress his intellectual lucidity and penetration, *"veramente* era *savio* . . . *S'avisò troppo bene* . . . *pensò* . . . *aguzzato l'ingegno* . . . gli venne *prestamente* avanti . . ." In contrast to the complex syntactical arrangements of Saladin's contorted thought-processes, the syntactical order is respected here. Syntactical organization and lexicon again carefully establish the primary traits of a narrative character, which in this case are wisdom, clarity of perception, and human insight. In view of these characteristics, a basic conflict takes shape between the two characters of Melchisedec and Saladin.

This conflict produces the narrative action of the story; which, as in all *novelle* of the *Decameron*, corresponds to a process of transformation undergone by the main character or characters at the hands of others.[41] Generally, this tranformation unfolds in three steps. The novella of the King of Cyprus (I 9) for instance, one of the simplest *novella* structures in the whole *Decameron*, is indicative of this narrative technique. The initial situation is created by the king's cowardice, which, in a second moment, is bitterly denounced by the "donna di Guascogna," with the result of transforming the king from a coward to a just and courageous man. The narrative action of the story, then, centers on the transformation undergone by the king upon the "donna di Guascogna's subtle reproach. Another—and this time more elaborate—example is provided by the *novella* of "lo scolare e la vedova" (VIII 7), where the basic narrative action develops in three steps with a repetitive pattern. At first, it is the *vedova* who, through ridicule, indifference, and ruthlessness, changes an infatuated and unwise lover into a hateful and shrewd antagonist. In a second moment, it is the *scolare* who acts as the agent of the counteraction that transforms the *vedova* from a beautiful and naively credulous lover into a physically ravaged creature cured of love and its cruelly playful inspirations. While in the *novella* of the King of Cyprus only one course of transformational actions was performed by the "donna di Guascogna" (as the agent) upon the king (as the object), in the *novella* of "lo scolare e la vedova," the transformational process takes place through a repetitive pattern that alternates agent and object. The three steps are (1) an initial conflict, (2) a transformational process, and (3) a final changed situation.

In the story of Melchisedec and Saladin, the transformational process occurs as well and assumes a subtly complicated pattern. In a first moment, it is Saladin who, under a false pretense, creates a situation whereby Melchisedec should be obliged to change from a miser into a financial provider. In a second moment, however, Melchisedec, with the device of a "novellina within a novella", counteracts Saladin through a clear-minded overview of the whole situation and transforms the latter into the object of his own counter-attact. Instead of a self-centered and anxiety-ridden tyrant in need, Saladin changes into a generous, friendly, and financially solvent sovereign. The final situation shows the outcome of this complex interaction. Melchisedec, whom Saladin had wrongly imagined to be a miser, corrects Saladin's opinion and offers him all his *fortuna*, thus eliminating the latter's initial *miseria*. Saladin, in turn, as the object of the transformation performed by the "savio giudeo," sincerely opens his mind to Melchisedec and eventually offers him everlasting friendship and protection. The final moment of the *novella* shows a vision of balance and order that neatly contrasts with the initial moment when a conflict was afoot and society disunited.[42].

The narrative device that brings about the transformation of Saladin is of course the "novellina within the novella." As in *Novellino* LXXIII, it functions as a paradigmatic rendering of the narrative situation projected by Saladin in his question to the Jew. If compared to the *Novellino* parable, however, the *novellina* presents a linguistic pattern which corresponds to the intellectual thoroughness and refinement of its narrator. Melchisedec's narration avoids illogical abruptness, needless repetitiveness, or rhythmic monotony. He recognizes the relevance of Saladin's question and introduces the *novellina* as the best means to arrive at a suitable reply, "Signor mio, la questione la qual voi mi fate è bella, e a volervene dire ciò che io ne sento, mi vi convien dire una novelletta, qual voi udirete." (I 4, 10-11). The *novellina* is then amplified in two ways. The ring-giving ceremony becomes (1) a family tradition passed down from generation to generation as a ritual gesture, and (2) it assumes a symbolic value which overshadows the purely monetary urge of the *Novellino* characters:

> un grande uomo e ricco fu già, il quale intra l'altre gioe
> più care che nel suo tesoro avesse . . . era uno anello
> bellissimo e prezioso . . . ordinò che colui dé suoi
> figliuoli appo il quale . . . fosse questo anello trovato,

> che colui s'intendesse essere il suo erede e dovesse da tutti gli altri esser come maggiore onorato e reverito. E colui al quale da costui fu lasciato tenne simigliante ordine ne' suoi discendenti . . . e in brieve andò questo anello di mano in mano a molti successori, e ultimamente pervenne alle mani a uno il quale avea tre figliuoli belli e virtuosi e molto al padre loro obedienti, per la qual cosa tutti e tre parimenti gli amava.
> (I 3, 11-13)

A neat syntactical distinction is made between the materialistic possession of the jewels, and the relationship between father and sons—a distinction which was missing in the *Novellino*. The jewels are introduced at the opening of the paragraph as the direct object of the family founder's possessions. The ring is the most precious of all and it also becomes the symbol of family tradition and power. The sentimental bond between the latest owner of the ring and his sons is, instead, described at the end of the paragraph. It is based exclusively on human values; that is, the three sons long for the ring because it represents honor and the father's recognition, "vaghi ciascun d'essere *il più onorato tra i suoi*" (I 3, 13) The father arrives at his decision to have two additional rings made which are identical to the original, because of his desire "di volergli tutti e tre soddisfare" (I 3, 14).

The end of the *novellina* is clearly an *amplificatio* of the corresponding passage in the *Novellino*:

NOVELLINO	DECAMERON (I 3, 16)
"E così vi dico delle fedi che sono tre. Il Padre di sopra sa la migliore, e li figliuoli, ciò siamo noi, ciascuno si crede avere la buona."	E così vi dico, signor mio, delle tre leggi alli tre popoli date da Dio padre, delle quali la quistion proponeste: ciascuno la sua eredità, la sua vera legge e i suoi comandamenti dirittamente si crede avere e fare, ma chi se l'abbia, come degli anelli, ancora ne pende la quistione.

The *Decameron's amplificatio* of the first sentence from this *Novellino* passage moves in two directions: (1) towards the addressee and (2) towards its topic, the "fedi." The addressee is introduced in two instances; "signor mio," whereby Melchisedec acknowledges Saladin's social status in the same way he did at the opening of his speech, and "delle quali la quistion proponeste," which acknowledges Saladin as the originator of the question debated in the *novellina*. This kind of amplification stresses the social dimension of respect and refinement which defines the relationship between the two characters. The "fedi" of the *Novellino* become the "tre leggi alli tre popoli date da Dio padre." "Tre leggi" is a repetition of the same "tre leggi" in Saladin's question; the repetitive use of "tre" connects the *leggi* with the *popoli* and, by inference, with the *anelli* and *figli* of the *novellina*. This careful *amplificatio* thus provides a clear, logical link between the story and Saladin's question.

The second sentence from the *Novellino* also undergoes *amplificatio*. Once again the elaborations are determined by a need for syntactical clarity and logical sequences. Semantically, the social horizons are opened to new energies and interests. The pronominal form "ciascuno" connects with the previous "tre popoli," each of which is presented in terms of its fervid dedication to its own traditions and social structure. "la sua eredità, la sua vera legge e i suoi comandamenti dirittamente si crede avere e fare." Such dedication is nonexistent in the *Novellino* statement "e li figliuoli, ciò siamo noi, ciascuno si crede avere la buona." A decidedly human rather than superhuman outlook is stressed in the *novella's* final phrase "ma chi se l'abbia, come degli anelli, ancora ne pende la quistione." In the *Novellino*, God is seen as obviously omniscient, "Il Padre di sopra sa la migliore." In the *Decameron*, instead, the situation, viewed in exclusively human terms, remains unsolved, "ancora ne pende la quistione." Saladin's reaction brings about the story's denouement in such a way that both characters accept a harmonious solution of the original conflict, with sympathetic rapport and intelligent understanding.

Boccaccio's *novella*, then, when compared with its *Novellino* source, is innovative on several levels. Syntax and lexicon show a degree of linguistic refinement and intellectual discrimination on the narrator's part that was absent in the earlier tale. They provide a rich and elaborate pattern of meaning and unveil a logical semantic development that stresses the realism of the genre. The main characters, aptly modulated by such linguistic subtlety, are in charge of their actions and appropriately confront each other on intellectual as well as social grounds.

The human prototype which emerges in the *Decameron* is basically different than that in the *Novellino*, which we have seen to be materialistically oriented, lacking in intellectual refinement or social power, and incapable of communication. Neither Saladin nor Melchisedec is limited to exclusively materialistic concerns. Their confrontation in the *novella* has a moral as well as a social dimension, which is absent from the *Novellino* story. An intelligent Saladin accepts defeat and his honesty and sincerity are rewarded by Melchisedec's generosity. Man is seen as capable of change and improvement, and the human world is able to recognize and reward virtue. The social status of the two main characters is also carefully limned: Saladin, as "dì Babilonia sultano," occupies a position of power never undermined by his needy situation; Melchisedec, with all his riches, belongs to a lower class because of his profession as moneylender. The linguistic conventions used by Melchisedec in his addresses to Saladin leave no doubt about this social differentiation, nor does Saladin's eventual gratitude, which conveys a feudal lord's reward to his trusty subject, "*gli donò grandissimi doni* e sempre per suo amico l'ebbe e in grande e onorevole stato *appresso di sè il mantenne*" (I 3, 18). These social differences are not, however, rigid. They seem rather to be overshadowed by the importance attributed to intellectual awareness, whatever social class an individual may belong to. Melchisedec's wisdom, intelligence, and resourcefulness earn him not only Saladin's gratitude, but his friendship as well, "sempre per suo amico l'ebbe."

Boccaccio's use of the *novella* genre thus demonstrates his understanding of its function as the proper "poetic" instrument to captivate fourteenth century audiences and through "pleasant" topics convey to them a whole set of instructional material on how to live meaningfully in—and eventually improve upon—a changing and disorderly society.

At the same time, Boccaccio innovates upon the traditional tale not only in terms of linguistic refinement, but also in terms of more complex characters facing social and moral questions unknown in the former tales. Built as it is upon a central narrative nucleus in which main characters undergo a transformation, the *Decameronian novella* substantiates Green's point that "the area left to human choice is larger and (more) crucial."

Boccaccio's expert manipulation of narrative relationships and his refinements of the *novella* technique foster an interpretation of the *Decameron* as a fictional world intentionally reworking the historical reality for his readers' enjoyment and learning. As such, the *Decameron* was a precious model for its contemporary readers in search of social and personal moral patterns with which to face the dismal situation in fourteenth-century Florence.

What follows is a detailed reading of the *Decameron* in terms of its overall structure. Through the discussion of its narrative action, characters' interrelations, and space and time dimensions, this reading will trace the development from Day I through Day X of the relationship between individual and society, in the narrative context of the one hundred *novelle*.

NOTES

1. Gene Brucker, *Florentine Politics and Society, 1343-1378* (Princeton: Princeton University Press, 1962), p.9.

2. For similarities on the specific topics of
   1) the beginning of the plague
   2) its symptons
   3) the ways the sick were treated
   4) the lawlessness and disorder caused by the plague, see the following points of contact to be found for each topic in Boccac-

cio's *Decameron*, Marchionne's *Cronaca fiorentina*, and Matteo Villani's *Cronica:*

1) *Decameron*, "Introduction," 8
Marchionne, I, viii, 136, Rubrica 634a, p. 230
Villani, Cap. II, 8-9

2) *Decameron*, "Introduction," 19
Marchionne, I, viii, 136, Rubrica 634a, p. 230
Villani, Cap. II, p. 8

3) *Decameron*, "Introduction," 19
Marchionne, I, viii, 136-137, Rubrica 634a, p. 230
Villani, Cap, II, p. 9

4) *Decameron*, "Introduction," 23, 27
Villani, Cap. IV, p. 9.

3. Anthony Molho, ed., *Social and Economic Foundations of the Italian Renaissance* (New York: John Wiley & Sons, 1969), p. 3.

4. Armando Sapori, *Le crisi delle compagnie mercantili dei Bardi e dei Peruzzi* (Firenze: Olschki, 1932), 131-32; 140.

5. Brucker, p. 14.

6. "Cronica di Matteo Villani dall'anno MCCCXVIII al MCCCLXIII," in *Croniche di Giovanni, Matteo, e Filippo Villani*, Biblioteca Classica Italiana, sec. XIV, No. 21, (Trieste, 1857); vol. 2, 6-387; p. 8.

7. Brucker, pp. 11-12.

8. Meillard Meiss, *Painting in Florence and Siena After the Black Death* (Princeton: Princeton University Press, 1951), p. 69.

9. Marvin B. Becker, *Florence in Transition* (Baltimore: Johns Hopkins University Press, 1968), vol. I, 178-179; vol. II, 94-95.

10. Becker, vol. II, p. 66.

11. Gene Brucker, *Renaissance Florence* (New York: John Wiley & Sons, 1969), p. 90; Lauro Martines discusses the corporate state in communal Italy in "The Communes around 1200", in his book *Power and Imagination: City-States in Renaissance Italy*, (New York: Alfred A. Knopf, 1979), 34-44. Aldo Scaglione discusses Medieval Mercantile Ethic in "Boccaccio, Chaucer, and the Mercantile Ethic", in *Literature and Western Civilization*, Vol. II, "The Medieval World", eds. David Daiches & A. Thorby (London: Aldas Press, 1973), 579-600.

12. Louis Green, *Chronicle into History: An Essay on the Interpretation of History in Florentine Fourteenth Century Chronicles* (Cambridge: Cambridge University Press, 1972), 70-72.

13. Typical examples of social "risks" can be found in the characters of Masetto (III,1), the "Pallafreniere" (III,2), Giletta di Narbona (III,9), Guiscardo (IV,1), Lorenzo (IV,5), Salvestra (IV,8), Pietro Boccamazza (V,3), Ricciardo Manardi (V,4), Teodoro (V,7), Madonna Filippa (VI,7), etc. "Fluctuations of wealth" occur in the adventures of merchants such as Rinaldo d'Este (II,2), Alessandro degli Agolanti and his uncles (II,3), Landolfo Rufolo (II,4), Madonna Beritola and her sons (II, 6), the Count of Antwerp (III,8), Federigo degli Alberighi (V,9), Cecco Angiolieri and Cecco di Fortarrigo (IX, 4), etc.

14. This concept of a search can be sensed especially in many characters of the Third and Seventh Day, and particularly on the part of the husbands in III, 3 and 5, and VII 4,5, and 8.

15. Brucker, *Florentine Politics*, p. 27; see also E. Repetti, *Dizionario geografico, fisico, e storico della Toscana*, (Firenze, 1833-43); p. 41.

16. "Piacevoli ragionamenti "eventually comes to refer to *novelle* collections in the Renaissance, as in Agnolo Firenzuola's *Ragionamenti*.

17. I have treated this topic in my essay on "Comic Modalities in the *Decameron*" in *Versions of Medieval Comedy*, ed. Paul Ruggiers (Norman: University of Oklahoma Press, 1977), 429-49. Significant insights in the narrators-works-readers relationships are offered by W. Iser's "Indeterminacy and the Reader's Response in Prose Fiction" in *Aspects of Narrative*, ed. J. Hillis Miller (New York: Columbia University Press, 1971) 1-45; by L. Nelson, Jr. "The Fictive Reader: Aesthetic and Social Aspects of Literary Performance," *Comparative Literature Studies*, XV, 2 (June 1978), 203-210; and by J. H. Potter, "Boccaccio as Illusionist: The Play of Frames in the *Decameron*," *The Humanities Association Review*, XXVI, 4 (Fall 1975), 327-345

18. The only exceptions are II 5 and 8; III 4, 7 and 9; IV 1; V 5; and VII 1 and 6.

19. In the whole work "belle donne" (II 2, 10; VI 2; VII 8; VIII 2), "giovani donne" (I 9; IV 3; VI 1, 6; X 4) and "graziose donne" (I 2; III 10; IV 5; VIII 6,10) each occur five times, "bellissime donne" (III 1; V 7; IX 3), "vezzose donne" (V 3; VI 10; IX 1) three times: "amabili donne" (V 8; IX 9), "care compagne" (I 8; IV 7), "dilettose donne" (V 1; VIII 5), "dilicate donne" (V 2; X 2), "leggiadre donne" (VI 9; IX 10), twice; and "amorose compagne" (I 3), "bellissime giovani" (IV 10), "care giovani" (I 6), "carissime donne mie" (VII 2), "donne mie belle" (I 5), "gentilissime donne" (IX 5), "graziosissime donne" (II 4), "innamorate giovani" (V 10), "laudevoli donne" (IX 6), "magnifiche donne" (X 8), "mansuete mie donne" (X 10), "morbide donne" (X 5), "nobili donne" (X 3), "nobilissime donne" (VII 5), "onorabili donne" (X 1),

"reverende donne" (VII 9), "savissime donne" (IX 8), "pietose donne" (IV 9), "ragguardevoli donne" (X 7), "splendide donne" (X 6), "vaghe giovani" (VI 8), and "valorose giovani" (I 10), once only.

20. G. Boccaccio, *Genealogia Deorum Gentilium, Liber XIV*, in *Opere in versi — Corbaccio — Trattatello in laude di Dante — Prose latine — Epistole*, Pier Giorgio Ricci, ed. (Milano & Napoli: Ricciardi, 1965); XIV, vii, pp. 940-42. English translation from: Charles S. Osgood, *Boccaccio on Poetry* (New York: Liberal Arts Press, 1956) 39. "A sort of fervid and exquisite invention, with fervid expression, in speech or writing, of that which the mind has invented"; ". . . it veils truth in a fair fitting garment of fiction."

21. Osgood, p. 55: "Poets have sought and still seek their habitation in solitudes because contemplation of things divine is utterly impossible in places like the greedy and mercenary market, in courts, theatres, offices, or public squares, amid crowds of jostling citizens and women of the town. Yet unless such contemplation is practically uninterrupted, the poet can neither conceive his works, nor complete them."

22. Osgood, pp. 56-57: "All nature's works are simple. There the beeches stretch themselves, with other trees, toward heaven; there they spread a thick shade with their fresh green foliage; there the earth is covered with grass and dotted with flowers of a thousand colors; there, too, are clear fountains and argent brooks that fall with a gentle murmur from the mountain's breast. There are gay song-birds, and the boughs stirred to a soft sound by the wind, and playful little animals; and there the flocks and herds, the shepherd's cottage, or the little hut untroubled with domestic cares; and all is filled with peace and quiet. Then, as these pleasures possess both eye and ear, they soothe the soul; then they collect the scattered energies of the mind, and renew the power of the poet's genius, if it be weary, prompting it, as it were, to long for contemplation of high themes, and yearn for expression — impulses wonderfully reinforced by the gentle society of books, and the melodius bands of the Muses moving in stately dance. In the light of all this what studious man would not prefer remote places to the city?"

23. Osgood, pp. 50-51: "By fiction, too, the strength and spirits of great men worn out in the strain of serious crises, have been restored. This appears, not by ancient instance alone, but constantly . . . Through fiction, it is well known, the mind that is slipping into inactivity is recalled to a state of better and more vigorous fruition . . . Such then is the power of fiction that it pleases the unlearned by its external appearance, and exercises the minds of the learned with its hidden

truth; and thus both are edified and delighted with one and the same perusal."

24. Giovanni Boccccio, *Decameron:* edizione critica secondo l'autografo Hamiltoniano, a cura di Vittore Branca (Firenze: Accademia della Crusca, 1976).

25. See A. Bartlett Giamatti, *Earthly Paradise and the Renaissance Epic* (Princeton: Princeton University Press, 1966) especially Chapter I, "Gardens and Paradises," pp. 11-93. Lucia Marino aptly discusses the *Cornice's* moral allegory in her book. *The Decameron cornice: Allusion, Allegory, and Ideology* (Ravenna: Longo, 1979).

26. See E. William Tayler, *Nature and Art in Renaissance Literature*, (New York, 1964), especially Chapter III, "The Medieval Contribution," pp. 72-101.

27. In the part of his *Cronica* dedicated to "Stato e Finanza della Repubblica Fiorentina," in the first half of the '300 before the plague of 1348 (of which he himself was a victim), Giovanni Villani underscores the wealth of the Florentines by mentioning their properties in the country:

> non v'era cittadino popolano o grande che non avesse edificato o che non edificasse in contado grande e ricca possessione, e abitura molto ricca, e con begli edificii e molto meglio che in città; e in questo ciascuno ci peccava e per le disordinate spese erano tenuti matti. E sì magnifica cosa era a vedere, che i forestieri non usati a Firenze, venendo di fuore, i più credevano per li ricchi edificii e belli palagi ch'erano di fuori alla città d'intorno a tre miglia, che tutti fossero della città . . . che in altre contrade sarebbono chiamate castella. Insomma si stimava che intorno alla città a sei miglia aveva tanti ricchi e nobili abituri che due Firenze non avrebbono tanti . . .

Cronica di Giovanni Villani, Libro XI, Capitolo XCIV, in *Croniche di Giovanni, Matteo e Filippo Villani* (Trieste: Biblioteca Classica Italiana, 1857). The first dwelling place of the *brigata* in the *Decameron* is just about "due piccole miglia" (I 38) from Florence; the second "bellissimo e ricco palagio" where they move four days later is about "dumila passi" from the former. (I 313). These indications coincide with Villani's description and demonstrate Boccaccio's penchant for realistic details even in the *cornice* passages, as if to further stress the connection between poetry and life.

28. I, Conclusion, 16: "comandò la reina che una danza fosse presa e, quella menando la Lauretta, Emilia cantasse una canzone da' leuto di Dioneo aiutata . . ."
   II, Conclusion 11: "menando Emilia la carola, la seguente canzone da Pampinea, rispondendo l'altre, fu cantata . . ."
   III, Conclusion, 9-10: "Filostrato, per non uscir del cammin tenuto da quelle che reine avanti a lui erano state . . . comandò che la Lauretta una danza prendesse e dicesse una canzone . . ." to which Lauretta replies that she does not know too many songs, and Filostrato in direct speech continues, "Niuna tua cosa potrebbe essere altro che bella e piacevole; e per ciò tale quale tu l'hai, cotale la dì'" (III, Conclusion, 10).
   V, Conclusion, 7: "E avendo già con volere della reina Emilia una danza presa, a Dioneo fu comandato che cantasse una canzone . . ." Dioneo replies in rather "scabrosì" terms, and the queen, "allora un poco turbata . . . disse: 'Dioneo, lascia stare il motteggiare e dinne una bella; e se no, tu potresti provare come io mi so adirare'" (V, Conclusion, 14).
   VII, Conclusion, 9: "Ma alla fine la reina comandò a Filomena che dicesse una canzone . . ."
   VIII, Conclusion, 8: "Alla fine la reina, per seguire de' suoi predecessori lo stilo . . . comandò a Panfilo che una ne dovesse cantare . . ."
   IX, Conclusion, 7: "comandò il re a Neifile che una ne cantasse a suo nome . . ."
   X, Conclusion, 9: "e menando la Lauretta una danza, comandò il re alla Fiammetta che dicesse una canzone . . ."

29. The time of the *onesta brigata*'s meeting in Santa Maria Novella in Florence should be some time after July, 1348. The Narrator, after indicating that the plague appeared in the city in the spring, "quasi nel principio della primavera dell'anno predetto orribilmente cominciò i suoi dolorosi effetti, e in miracolosa maniera, a dimostrare" (Introduction, 9), comes to specify that it reached its peak between March and July of that same year: "infra 'l marzo e il prossimo luglio vegnente . . . oltre a centomilia creature umane si crede per certo dentro alle mura della città di Firenze essere stati di vita tolti" (I, Introduction, 47). It is just about this time that the *brigata* appears;" . . . stando in questi termini la nostra città, d'abitatori quasi vota, addivenne, si come io poi da persona degna di fede sentii, che nella venerabile chiesa di Santa Maria Novella, un martedì mattina . . . si ritrovarono sette giovani donne . . ." (I, Introduction, 49).

30. See Vittore Branca's comments in his "Prefazione" to the *Decameron*, a cura di Vittore Branca, (Firenze: Le Monnier, 1965), p.xiv.

31. Antonio D'Andrea studies another interesting element of the *Decameron's* narrative structure in his "Le Rubriche del *Decameron*" *Yearbook of Italian Studies* (1973-75), 41-67.

32. See S. Battaglia's "Dall'esempio alla novella" in *Filologia Romanza* VII (1960), 21-84, and Pamela Stewart's "Boccaccio e la tradizione retorica: la definizione della novella come genere letterario", in *Stanford Italian Review* I (1979), 67-74.

33. Translated into Latin in the twelfth century by Pedro Alonso with the title *Disciplina clericalis*, and also found in the *Legenda aurea* of Jacopo da Varazze (1230-98).

34. Taken from the *Panchatranta*, translated into Persian and Arabic and later into Latin c. 1275 by Ihoannes da Capua under the title *Directorium vitae humanae*.

35. A Spanish version of the *Book of Sinbad* was made in 1238 under the title *Libro de los enganos y asayamentos de las mujeres*, and two Italian twelfth-century adaptions probably derived from French or Franco-Venetian texts entitled *Libro dei sette savi*.

36. A translation into Italian of the *Speculum Historiale* of Vincent de Beauvais, made around 1264-80.

37. A collection of approximately twenty stories probably written between 1280 and 1300.

38. A collection of parables from approximately the same time as the *Conti*.

39. A charming collection of anecdotic tales composed between 1280 and the end of the century.

40. See *Novellino*, a cura di L. Di Francia, (Torino: UTET, 1948), *novella* LXXII, 142-144.

41. I have dealt with this particular problem in "Observations on the Structure of the *Decameron* novelle" in *Romance Notes*, XV (1974), 1-10.

42. See my "Saggio di lettura della Prima Giornata del *Decameron*" in *Teoria e Critica*, 1(1972), 111-138.

PART I

Individual and Society in Search of Order: Days I-V

1. The fictional world of the Decameronian *novelle* is the most complex level in the structure of the work. The one hundred *novelle* seem to be organized in two sequences, the first including Days I-V and the second, Days VI-X.[1] Several critics share this view of the *Decameron* as a two-part structure with clear correspondences between the parts. Recently Pamela Stewart reconsidered this approach and offered supplementary supporting evidence for it, precisely pinpointing the many structural correspondences which link the first and second sequences of the *Decameron:*

> La prima parte tratta, nelle giornate II, III e V, di imprese o avventure (d'amore o d'altro) a lieto fine, e nella IV di amori infelici. La seconda parte tratta, nelle giornate VII e VIII, di beffe e, nella Giornata X, del contrario, e cioè della generosità nei "fatti d'amore o d'altra cosa". Ciascuna delle due parti ha così un tema dominante e in ciascuna di esse una giornata è dedicata al rovesciamento di esso. Inoltre, la Terza Giornata, come abbiamo già ricordato, riprende e continua il tema della Seconda, ma ristringendolo ("sarà ancora più bello che un poco si restringa del novellare la licenzia", II. concl.8). Un rapporto simile, ma rovesciato, si riscontra fra la Settima Giornata, dedicata alle beffe "le quali, o per amore o per salvamento di loro, le donne hanno già fatte a' loro mariti", e l'Ottava, in cui il tema delle beffe viene volutamente generalizzato ed esteso ad una più larga varietà di rapporti umani: in essa, infatti, si ragiona "di quelle beffe che tutto il giorno o donna ad uomo o uomo a donna o l'uno uomo all'altro si fanno" (VIII. concl. 4). Ancora: allo spostamento di luogo, deciso alla fine della Seconda Giornata (II. concl.7) ed effettuato al principio della Terza, col trasferirsi al *bellissimo e ricco palagio* (III. Introd.2-3), corrisponde nella seconda parte il trasferimento della brigata nella Valle delle donne, deciso alla fine della Sesta Giornata (VI. concl. 38) e effettuato al principio della Settima (VII.Introd.2-4). Come si è già discusso, tanto la prima quanto la seconda parte hanno inizio, con una giornata introduttiva, dedicata all'abilità verbale: rispet-

> tivamente la Prima e la Sesta. Questo rapporto fra la Prima e la Sesta Giornata non esclude però un ulteriore rapporto fra la Prima, il cui tema non è preliminarmente annunciato, e la Nona, che è senza tema. Cosicchè tanto la prima quanto la seconda parte vengono ad avere ciascuna una giornata senza tema prestabilito.[2]

These structural correspondences reinforce parallel contextual correspondences between characters, actions, space, and time in the *novelle* of the two parts.

As a whole, the *novelle* repeat the *cornice's* pattern of transformation from a disharmonious to a stable social structure. As we previously noted, the storytellers' environment shifts dramatically at the beginning of Day I from urban chaos to controlled and harmonious life in the country. From then on, through the enlightened guidance of each member of the *onesta brigata*, their condition gradually improves and finally becomes perfected. Similarly, in the world of the *novelle*, a parallel, though slower, transformation takes place, notably in the first five days of narration. By the beginning of the Sixth Day, the world of the storytellers and that of the *novelle* characters seem to converge and to level off at a peak. A second sequence then begins in which situations similar to those in the first five days are explored in greater depth through the perspective of now self-confident and socially responsible *novelle* characters.

The *novelle* commence with a negative view of both individual and society which continues through Day IV. The First Day, opening with the *novella* of Ser Ciappelletto, abounds with examples of vice and corruption, while in the *novelle* of the Second Day, the characters lack self-motivation and fail to understand their environments. In the Third Day, individual characters begin to show glimmers of understanding, although the Fourth Day's tales challenge that awareness and present a deadly conflict between individual and society. Day V then introduces individuals who are able to recognize the problems created in their environments by their love affairs. They cleverly succeed in manipulating their worlds so as to overcome all obstacles, eventually reassert their rights to love, and become successfully integrated in their societies.

In the second moment, Days VI through X, individual and society are usually in harmony with each other. The characters interact vigorously with their society and gain an increasing potential for learning and improving. Through urban encounters (Day VI), marital affairs (Day VII), professional relationships (Day VIII), and finally through a broad spectrum of human relationships in Day IX, they gain insight into the human condition. In Day X, which closely parallels Day V, individual and society are at their best, and the natural world often provides a basis for a perfect form of existence. The theme of nature's meliorative powers throughout this second moment of storytelling, and especially in the Day X *novelle*, recalls the similar motif in the *cornice* sequences: there the idyllic setting has a regenerative effect on the storytellers themselves.

I will analyze the first five days of the *Decameron* in different sub-chapters, examining the treatment of characters, action, point of view, and the dimensions of space and time in the *novelle*. This analysis will also call attention to the narrative tone that informs each day and will note the transformations that occur in the individual-society relationships among the *novelle* characters.

2. Day 1: Wit in the Midst of Chaos

The First Day, according to Branca, deals largely with human shortcomings.[3] It begins with the "piggior uom forse che mai nascesse" (I 1) and closes with an invective against female presumptuousness (I 10). It progresses from a wholly negative view of society to portraits of individuals capable of counterbalancing with intelligence and wit sinful attitudes in themselves (I 4 and 10) and in others (I 5,6,7,8,9, and 10). All vices are embodied in Ser Ciappelletto (I 1) and in the Roman "clerici" of I 2, while each following *novella* concentrates on a particular human defect. The more viciously antisocial sins, hypocrisy (I 3 and 6), avarice (I 7 and 8), and lust (I 4 and 5), recur more frequently than do such lesser vices as prodigality (I 3), cowardice (I 9), and feminine hauteur (I 10).

The dimensions of time and space vary extensively among the Day I *novelle*, ranging from the present (I 1,2,4,6,8, and 10) to the past (I 3,5,7, and 9) and occurring in foreign locales (I 1,2,3, and 9), Tuscany (I 4,6, and 10), and northern Italy (I 5,7, and 8).

The individuals treated in this day's *novelle* span a broad social spectrum. We see the self-seeking, money-hungry mercantile class in the commercial world of Ser Ciappelletto in I 1, in the Paris of Giannotto in I 2, and in the Florence of the naive "valentuomo" in I 6. The aristocracy is represented both in Italy, by the Marchesana of Monferrato in I 5 and Cane della Scala in I 7, and in foreign lands by Saladin in I 3, the King of France in I 1 and 5, and the King of Cyprus in I 9. Representing the many levels of religious authority we find the Pope, mentioned in I 1 and 2, the cardinals of I 2, the abbot and the monk of I 4, the hypocritical inquisitor of I 6, and the Abbott of Cluny in I 7.

The professional class is represented by Melchisedec, the Jewish merchant and money-lender of I 3, Bergamino, the professional courtier of I 7, and the wise scholar of I 10. Female characters, a class in their own right, span a wide variety of types, from the honest and intelligent Marchesana of Monferrato in I 5, to the enterprising and outspoken "donna di Guascogna" in I 9, to the presumptuous but ultimately contrite monna Malgherida in I 10.

Although no specific topic is set for this day's storytelling, verbal wit and storytelling skills recur everywhere as motifs and cause the basic transformation of narrative situations and characters in each *novella* of the day. Witty *motti* underscore or produce changes in I 2,4,5,6, and 9; they cause crucial improvements of characters in I 8,9, and 10. Storytelling skills are mastered by the protagonists of I 1,3, and 7 in order to improve their difficult personal situations. The importance of verbal wit and storytelling skills in these *novelle* of the First Day clearly suggests, even at this early stage — and to an even greater degree in Day VI — Boccaccio's undeniable belief in the power of the word. It also suggests his desire to explore all possible variations of the storyteller-audience relationship through the fictional world of his *novelle*.

From an overall view, the First Day's *novelle* present antithetical relationships spatially, temporally, and thematically.[4] Their conflictive tone not only parallels the chaotic backdrop of urban disaster in the *cornice* sequences, but creates a narrative tension in organization as well as in content of the *novelle*. In each *novella* of this day, in fact, the narrative drama derives from the interaction of a main character and an opponent, and their conflict produces a transformation either in the initially uncooperative character or in the narrative situation. This interaction is clear especially in *novelle* I 8 and 9, both of which are based on one transformational pattern: I 8 concerns Guglielmo Borsieri's intention to counter and eliminate Erminio's avarice; I 9 the woman from Guascogna's intention to reproach the King of Cyprus' cowardice. In the former *novella* Erminio is viewed at the outset as uncooperative and wholly avaricious; at the end, he is shamed by Guglielmo's remark that he should improve his beautiful new home by having the figure "Cortesia" painted there: "Fateci dipingere la Cortesia" (I 8,16). He is thus transformed into a liberal and generous man. In the latter, the King of Cyprus is completely passive at the beginning; at the end he becomes active in upholding honor and justice. The woman from Guascogna brings about his transformation through her ironic understatement: " . . . che tu m'insegni come tu sofferi quelle (ingiurie) le quali io intendo che ti son fatte . . ." (I 9,6). In both cases the transformed character unwittingly faces a cognizant opponent who teaches him a lesson in civic virtue through a witty verbal exchange. The outcome is an improved personal as well as social relationship. Erminio, presented initially as one who "d'avarizia e di miseria *ogni altro* misero e avaro che *al mondo* fosse soperchiava oltre misura" (I 8,5), is relocated at the end within the spatial borders of his native Genoa and the temporal limitations of his times, and becomes a civic example of liberality and kindness: *"il più liberale e 'l più grazioso gentile uomo* e quello che *più e' forestieri e i cittadini onorò che altro che in Genova fosse a' tempi suoi"* (I 8,18).

The same is true of the King of Cyprus, who, at the beginning of the story is unaware of the responsibility of his royal post — "di . . . rimessa vita e da . . . poco bene . . . con vituperevole viltà" (I 9,5) — while at the end he becomes the epitome of royal virtue for his age: "rigidissimo persecutore divenne di ciascuno che *contro allo onore della sua corona alcuna* cosa commettesse *da indi innanzi"* (I 9, 7).

In more complex *novelle* the intentions of an initially active character are frustrated and redirected by the actions of a supposedly inferior or passive opponent. Such is the case in most *novelle* of this day (I 3,4,5,6,7,and 10), where the same plot pattern is repeated with a careful diversification of basic details and especially of the verbal means used to bring about the transformation. In the *novella* of Saladin and Melchisedec (I 3) hypocritical Saladin intends to trick the socially inferior Melchisedec into giving him the money he needs. Melchisedec's intelligence provides him with the means—the parable within the *novella*—to escape Saladin's trap and to prove himself superior to Saladin. The parable by which Melchisedec makes a clever substitution of three rings for the three faiths of Saladin's question, is a verbal device which allows the "inferior" character to chastise and indirectly admonish his superior without disrupting the social hierarchy.[5] The authoritative character (in this case Saladin) ultimately regains the upper hand by perceiving the hidden moral of the parable. His final action thus eliminates the hypocrisy and bad faith of his initial behavior and allows the two main characters to be reconciled within a social situation that offers the best to both: "Il giudeo liberamente d'ogni quantità che il Saladino il richiese il servì, e il Saladino poi interamente il sodisfece; e oltre a ciò gli donò grandissimi doni e sempre per suo amico l'ebbe e in grande e onorevole stato appresso di sè il mantenne" (I 3,18).

The device of telling a story within the *novella* is used in another tale of the same Day, the story of Cane della Scala's atypical inhospitality towards Bergamino (I 7).[6] Bergamino uses his short tale about Primasso and the Abbot of Cluny to the same end as Melchisedec; that is, to chastise and admonish Cane without breaking the social code that forbids an inferior to criticize his superior. Again the inferior succeeds in redeeming his opponent and the final situation is satisfactory for both of them:

> Messer Cane, il quale intendente signore era, senza altra dimostrazione alcuna ottimamente intese ciò che dir volea Bergamino . . . E fatto pagare l'oste di Bergamino e lui nobilissimamente d'una sua roba vestito, datigli denari e un pallafreno, nel suo piacere per quella volta rimise l'andare e lo stare.
> (I 7, 27-28)

This same superior/inferior conflict is also present in I 4, where an oversexed young monk is in serious danger when his abbot intends to punish his lustful activities.[7] The abbot's intention, however, is never realized because the young monk successfully traps his superior in a similarly compromising situation, thus reducing the older monk to his own level and consequently, through his witty remarks, frustrating his plans for harsh punishment:

> . . . voi ancora non m'avavate mostrato che 'monaci si debban tar dalle femine premiere, come da' digiuni e dalle vigilie; ma ora che mostrato me l'avete, vi prometto, se questa mi perdonate, di mai più in ciò non pec-

care, anzi farò sempre come io a voi ho veduto fare.
(I 4,21)

The eventual equality of the two main characters in I 4 is suggested through a linguistic device; groups of adverbs which serve initially to define one character are finally used for the other. In their first appearance, the adverbs "fieramente," "men cautamente," "prestamente," and "dirittamente" characterize the impulsive and audacious young monk: "egli *fieramente* assalito fu dalla concupiscenza carnale" (I 4,6); *"men cautamente* con lei scherzava" (I 4,7); *"prestamente*seco molte cose risolse" (I 4,9); "al fine imaginato da lui *dirittamente* pervenne" (I 4,6). Adverbs such as "pianamente" and "chetamente" instead describe the behavior of the more mature abbot: *"pianamente* passando" (I 4,7); *"chetamente* s'accostò" (I 4,7); *chetamente* andatose." (I 4,14); *"pianamente* la cominciò a confortare" (I 4,7). At the *novella's* climax, these same adverbs are applied to the opposite character to mark the moment of transformation: i.e., when the young monk realizes that the abbot is near his cell, his first words to the girl are "statti *pianamente*'" (I 4,10), an adverbial qualification that had been connected with the abbot up to that moment. And later, when the abbot is with the girl, the young monk, who *"chetamente"* n'andò ad un pertugio" (I 4,19), adopts the behavior of the abbot. The abbot, in his turn, seems to undergo a similar transformation. The change in his attitude toward sex becomes apparent through the use of the same group of adverbial phrases previously reserved for the young monk:" . . . sentì *subitamente* non meno cocenti gli stimoli della carne" (I 4,15); and when confronted with the young monk's retort, he *"prestamente"* realizes the need for an alliance without compromise. Not only is the transformation of each character underlined, but their motivations are reduced to the same level. Thus the two characters are equated through their respective behavioral transformations revealed primarily by adverbial forms.

These transformations seem to indicate, as much in I 4 as in the previously discussed *novelle* 3 and 7, an intentional stress on what Green has called "resourcefulness" as "criterion in its own right . . . a tool in the reduction of the haphazard, accidental play of events to the service of human ends."[8] In all the cases we have considered, the "haphazard" and "accidental" quality of the human situation in which the "inferior" characters find themselves is indeed eliminated by their resourcefulness, most commonly revealed in witty verbal exchanges. Their resourcefulness comprises intellectual awareness, wittiness of utterance, promptness to act, and belief in the triumph of the individual, coupled with a recognition of the need for social stability. As Brucker has pointed out, such recognition allows an individual to strive for his "social plane" in a "hieratic social structure."[9]

This belief in the intellectual and verbal abilities of the individual appears in even more forceful terms in I 5,6, and 10. These *novelle* teach not only a social lesson, but a moral one as well. In I 5 the King of France's intention to seduce the

Marchesana of Monferrato during her husband's absence is frustrated by the Marchesana's ingenuity.[10] She prepares a dinner of hens and in her speech to the King she offers a clever explanation by equating them to women: "'le femine, quantunque in vestimenti e in onori alquanto dall'altre variino, tutte per ciò son fatte qui come altrove'" (I 5,15). As in the previous *novelle*, the social status and intellect of the character who initiates the action — in this case, the King — is proven by his quick comprehension of the Marchesana's innuendo:

> Il re, udite queste parole, raccolse bene la cagione del convito delle galline e la vertù nascosa nelle parole, e accorsesi che invano con così fatta donna parole si gitterebbono e che forza non v'avea luogo . . .
> (I 5,16)

The outcome in this case is a radical dissociation between the opposing characters; no further interaction is possible after the Marchesana conveys her social and moral lesson to the king, who

> senza più motteggiarla, temendo delle sue risposte, fuori d'ogni speranza desinò; e, finito il desinare, acciò che il presto partirsi ricoprisse la sua disonesta venuta, ringraziatala dell'onor ricevuto da lei, accomandandolo ella a Dio, a Genova se n'andò.
> (I 5,17)

The same narrative pattern appears in *novelle* 6 and 10, where two opposing characters are set against each other and one eventually publicly exposes and reproaches the other. In these two *novelle*, which are set in more contempory times than is I 5, the narrative tone is influenced by the narrator's diatribes which occur in each tale. These two tirades, one delivered by Emilia against priests (I 6), the other by Pampinea against women (I 10), take off on the two most common topics of medieval satire. They reflect widespread resentment at these two major social groups' respective vices of hypocrisy and presumptuousness.[11] In both cases the outcome is similar to that of the previous *novella*; the character who initiates the action must later reconsider his or her initial intentions. The development of the narrative, however, is different in the two stories.

In I 6 the "'nquisitore sentendo trafiggere la lor (the other clerics') brodaiuola ipocrisia, tutto si turbò" (I 6,20). After he is shown up by the *valentuomo*, the inquisitor wants to submit his opponent to another painful penance, thus demonstrating unwillingness to recognize his own faults. Although the *buon uomo's motto* affects no change in the inquisitor, at least the good man's resourcefulness is recognized and accepted congenially by the lay society.[12]

In the tenth *novella*, the initial diatribe against women reaches violent proportions in Pampinea's severe criticism of contemporary vanity:

45

> ... colei la quale si vede indosso li panni più screziati e più vergati e con più fregi si crede dovere essere da molto più tenuta e più che l'altre onorata, non pensando che, se fosse chi adosso o indosso gliele ponesse, uno asino ne porterebbe troppo più che alcuna di loro: né per ciò più da onorar sarebbe che uno asino ...
> (I 10, 5-6)

The wise maestro Alberto of Pampinea's *novella* cleverly criticizes the woman's presumptuousness and her lack of intellectual skill with his leek metaphor:

> come che nel porro niuna cosa sia buona, pur men reo e più piacevole alla bocca è il capo di quello, il quale voi generalmente, da torto appetito tirate, il capo vi tenete in mano e manicate le frondi ... E che so io, madonna, se nello elegger degli amanti voi vi faceste il simigliante? E se voi il faceste, io sarei colui che eletto sarei da voi, e gli altri cacciati via.
> (I 10,17-18)

The outcome, however, is much more balanced here than in the two previously discussed *novelle:* madonna Malgherida, contrary to Maestro Alberto's negative attitude toward feminine intellect, understands his parable quite well and amiably accepts his criticism: "'Maestro, assai bene e cortesemente gastigate n'avete della nostra presuntuosa impresa ...'" (I 10,19). The *novella* presents a final view of congeniality and social ease where all are in harmony, "ridendo e con festa" (I 10,20). Its social lesson is directed not only at the fictional characters of the *novella*, but also — and more importantly — at the inner female audience who are reminded twice to profit from the exemplary behavior of the characters in the story: first, at the beginning of the tale, with "acciò che voi vi sappiate guardare ... questa ultima novella ... voglio ve ne renda ammaestrate, acciò che, come per nobiltà d'animo dall'altre divise siete, così ancora per eccellenzia di costumi separate dall'altre vi dimostriate" (I 10,8); and finally at the end, with "così la donna, non guardando cui motteggiasse, credendo vincer fu vinta: di che voi, se savie sarete ottimamente vi guarderete" (I 10,20).[13] These carefully handled links between individuals belonging to two different fictional levels of the work — the *novella* characters and the *cornice* audience — foreshadow the Day's Conclusion where the "onesta brigata" once again assumes the entire fictional space of the work. At the same time, they foreshadow the Sixth Day, where the same interconnections between *novelle* and *cornice* characters are made and even greater emphasis is placed upon witty utterances.

We have left for last the discussion of the *novella* of Ser Ciappelletto (I 1),[14] which seems to encompass most, if not all, of the main points touched upon in this First Day of the *Decameron:* the close relationship between storytellers and their audiences; the value of "resourcefulness," especially as it is manifested in verbal exploits; the Florentine citizen's need for a "sense of identity" or "belonging" to a particular society or group, especially when confronted by hostility and unpopularity in a foreign land; and the wholly human, rather than heavenly oriented perspective of the story.

In the *exordium* Pamfilo, the narrator of the *novella*, says he will prepare his audience for the story he is about to narrate. He stresses the precariousness and misery of the human condition, and assigns to God the sole possibility for relief of suffering:

> Manifesta cosa è che, sì come le cose temporali tutte sono transitorie e mortali, così in sè e fuor di sè esser piene di noia, d'angoscia e di fatica e a infiniti pericoli sogiacere; alle quali senza niuno fallo né potremmo noi, che viviamo mescolati in esse e che siamo parte d'esse, durare né ripararci, se spezial grazia di Dio forza e avvedimento non ci prestasse.
>
> (I 1,3)

In the closing paragraphs, Pamfilo once again stresses man's total dependence on God, now addressing himself directly to the members of the "onesta brigata":

> E per ciò, acciò che noi per la sua grazia nelle presenti avversità e in questa compagnia così lieta siamo sani e salvi servati, lodando il suo nome nel quale cominciata l'abbiamo, Lui in reverenza avendo, ne' nostri bisogni gli ci raccomanderemo, sicurissimi d'essere uditi.
>
> (I 1,91)

What differentiates this *novella* from all the others of this day is the complexity of levels on which it functions and the ironic conflict between Pamfilo's statements and the *novella's* narrative matter. On the one hand the storyteller's introduction and conclusion emphasize man's limited role in the universe; on the other, his tale presents the theme of man's verbal omnipotence and ingeniousness. Such a conflict in the first *novella* of the *Decameron* foreshadows a parallel moment in the last, where Dioneo's introductory and concluding comments also conflict ironically with his tale. Reversing Pamfilo's narrative technique in I 1, Dioneo, in the introduction and conclusion to X 10, irreverently ridicules his characters' lack of humanity, while in the *novella* itself, he presents them as superior examples of untainted humanity.

In I 1, the theme of man's complete reliance upon God's beneficence is challenged as soon as the main character of the *novella* appears; at that moment, we become aware only of man's omniscience and self-reliance, not of his reliance upon God. The importance and complexity of the human world in I 1 is established not only through the historical setting but through the diverse social strata of the characters. We are first introduced to messer Musciatto Franzesi, "di ricchissimo e gran mercatante in Francia cavalier divenuto" (I 1,7), who lives at the Parisian court of the King of France. When messer Musciatto first appears, he is setting out for Tuscany with the King's brother, messer Carlo Senzaterra, at Pope Boniface VIII's bidding. Musciatto's move from Paris to Tuscany initiates other such moves on the part of his many clients, among them Ser Ciappelletto. As Ciappelletto travels from Paris to Burgundy on messer Musciatto's request, the narrative shifts accordingly through various social levels from royalty, to aristocracy, to high bourgeoisie, and eventually to low bourgeoisie — the status of Ciappelletto, a notary, and his Florentine hosts, the usurers living in Burgundy. From this moment on Ser Ciappelletto becomes the initiator of all action in the tale.

Ser Ciappelletto is the prototype of the man of superior mind whose abundant verbal talents help him manipulate every facet of life that concerns him. As a notary in Paris, he had handled many situations to his own and his clients' benefit and had pursued evil with the greatest pleasure.[15] During his final confession, while still a stranger among the "borgognoni, uomini riottosi e di mala condizione e misleali" (I 1,8), he manipulates the situation with equal finesse, and through his confession carefully plans an outcome that will benefit his hosts and himself. He is consequently granted sainthood and offered large sums in alms by those same evil *borgognoni* whose money — ironically enough — he had been sent to regain for his master.

Ciappelletto's confession proves his keen perception of the ways of men on earth — *not of their rapport with God*. He reveals his insight when explaining to his hosts his desire to confess:

"Io ho, vivendo, tante ingiurie fatte a Domenedio, che, per farnegli io una ora in su la mia morte, né più né meno ne farà . . . lasciate fare a me, ché fermamente io acconceró i fatti vostri e' miei in maniera che starà bene e che dovrete esser contenti."

(I 1,28-29)

Man has little to do with God's realm, Ser Ciappelletto suggests; man can act and produce change only in the human realm. Ser Ciappelletto's designs are carried out to perfection: through his persuasive eloquence he not only succeeds in integrating himself (albeit *post mortem*) and his hosts into the hostile Burgundian society, but appeases the Burgundians by creating — in himself — a new saint for them to worship. (Their dedication and zeal reveal that sainthood is not commonplace among Burgundians.) Furthermore, Ser Ciappelletto placates the religious community of his confessor, whose church gains power and prestige as center of the new cult of "Saint Ciappelletto."

The social contexts of greed and violence which are the settings for Ser Ciappelletto's depravity are ironically balanced at the end of the *novella* by the "pious" society of church-goers and relic seekers who rip Ciappelletto's garments to shreds under the benevolent eyes of a clergy eager for alms. No more fitting comment could have been made about the basic selfishness of human beings. Pope, king, upper-and lower-class businessmen, Burgundian citizens and their clergy are all implicated as self-seekers. And it is fitting that the scoundrel *par excellence*, Ser Ciappelletto, sees through them all and manipulates them to his own advantage.

We recognize in this *novella* what Brucker calls the "irreconcilable properties that create the dynamics of the Florentine crucible" in the *Trecento*. On one side, we see the predominance of "individualism" typical of the "capitalistic economic order." "Socialy mobility and dislocation" existed both in the high and middle levels of the bourgeois society of the time. Messer Musciatto, the Florentine usurers, and Ser Ciappelletto himself are characteristic of such an order. On the other side, we can still recognize the qualities of a "corporate social order" with its goals of "stability, security, conformity" and its need for the individual "sense of identity" and of "belonging." These qualities are visible in both the Italian characters and in the Burgundians. The common interests of these conflicting groups provide a background for the eventual resolution of the narrative which is engineered by Ser Ciappelletto.

As the opening story of the *Decameron*, this *novella* presents in Ser Ciappelletto all of the qualities needed for success in human endeavors: keen foresight, an awareness of human needs and foibles, an ability to conform to any environment, and prudence to handle difficult situations. At the same time, this story also reveals all the potential dangers of which human beings should beware, suggesting that "the haphazard, accidentaly play of events "might hinder the success of the ways of man on earth.

3. Day II: The Haphazard Play of Events

This "haphazard, accidental play of events"[16] is the theme of the Second Day's *novelle*, which Queen Filomena decrees should deal with "chi da diverse cose infestato, sia oltre alla speranza riuscito a lieto fine" (I Conclusione, 11). The main characters of this day lack control over their environments and personal situations. Their passivity is reflected through the special handling of the spatial dimension; each character becomes the victim of chance by leaving his or her native surroundings. Such is the case for Martellino and his Florentine actor friends (II I), who find themselves in the northern town of Trevigi; for Rinaldo d'Este (II 2), who is in transit between Ferrara and Verona; for the Florentine Alessandro degli Agolanti (II 3), who practices usury in England; for the Amalfi-born Landolfo Rufolo (II 4), a pirate who plunders the shores of Cyprus; for Andreuccio da Perugia (II 5), who attempts to buy a horse in Naples: for madonna Beritola and her sons (II 6), who escape from Sicily and find harsher life on the peninsula; for Alatiel (II 7), who wanders from Babylon to the southern coast of Europe; for the Count of Antwerp and his children (II 8), who are exiled from France to England; for Ginevra (II 9), who must flee her own country and move from Genoa to Alexandria; and finally for Ricciardo da Chinzica (II 10), who follows his wife from Pisa to Monaco and is unable to successfully accomplish his marital mission there.

The spatial dimension seems, therefore, to be a primary obstacle for the main characters as they attempt to cope with new surroundings (with the possible exceptions of Ginevra in II 9 and Bartolomea in II 10). Shift in location is used to warn against the dangers that a foreign environment may create for an individual regardless of his social position.

The characters of this day represent all social strata: western aristocracy (II 3,6, and 8), eastern potentates (II 7 and 9), merchants (II 2,3,4,5, and 9), professional men (II 1 and 10), and the lower classes (II 2,4,5). The clergy enters only in II 3, where the Pope becomes the "deus ex machina" who provides a solution for the dilemmas of Alessandro and the King of England's daughter. Female characters assume the main roles in many *novelle* of this day, as they will in Day VII: madonna Beritola in II 6; Alatiel in II 7; Ginevra in II 9; and Bartolomea in II 10. They also function in other *novelle* either as opponents to the main characters (II 5 and 8) or as their allies (II 2). In this Second Day, the theme of love is not of major concern in and of itself, but it does provide the means for social change in the last four *novelle*. In II 8 and 9 love causes the main characters a catastrophic loss of social status, while in II 10 social diminishment is accompanied by a compensating gain in freedom and richness of life.

The First Day's narrative pattern of conflict between pairs of individuals becomes much more intricate in Day II, where we find increasing numbers of characters, activities, locations, and time schemes. The Day II *novelle* span not only essential moments in the lives of their characters (as in II 1,2, and 5), but extend over whole life sequences (as in II 3,4,6,7,8,9, and 10). Particularly effective in this day is the use of the image of the sea, present in II 4,6,7,9, and 10. With its undulating to-and-fro-movement, it comes to represent the fluctuating uncertainty of fortune and the "haphazard" course of human life.[17]

Often in these *novelle*, we find a harshly critical description of urban society, notable in the misadventures of Martellino in Trevigi (II 1), of Alessandro in London (II 3), of Andreuccio in Naples (II 5), and of the Count of Antwerp in Paris (II 8). At the same time, the natural environment is often the background for violent and destructive deeds, as in the tale of Rinaldo d'Este and his encounter with the *masnadieri* (II 2), or in the case of Landolfo Rufolo and his disastrous sea adventures (II 4). The natural world often forces the central character to endure inhumane hardships. Such is the case of madonna Beritola, who is shipwrecked on the island of Ponza (II 6), of Alatiel, who is subjected to physical violence and humiliation (II 7), and of Ricciardo da Chinzica, whose wife is kidnapped at sea (II 10).

While the environment is often hostile, many of the adventures in the *novelle* describe a pattern which alternates from misfortune to good fortune. In II 2, for instance, Rinaldo suffers from cold weather in the countryside and is reduced to the level of an animal: "il pianto e 'l triemito che Rinaldo faceva, il quale pareva diventato una cicogna" (II 2,22). His fortunes improve—thanks to his unshakeable faith in St. Julian[18] —when a "donna vedova del corpo bellissima" provides him with a warm bath, clothing, a good dinner, and a night of love. In II 3 we find a similar but more complex alternation in the narrative. In the first phase of the *novella*, three Florentine brothers suffer a loss of money and prestige and later reverse their circumstances by moving to London. There they regain their riches and make possible their return to Florence. The second phase of the tale commences with the introduction of Alessandro, their nephew. His adventures, in turn, develop on two levels, one related to his affairs in London and the other concerning the three brothers in Florence. This second level repeats the movement towards misfortune, again causing the brothers to lose their money and social position. The first level, however, evolves in an alternating pattern: 1) circumstances in London change from positive to negative; 2) a decision is made to abandon London and return to Florence; 3) a fortuitous meeting takes place enroute with the "falso abate"; 4) a positive outcome results from the meeting with the tryst of Alessandro and the "falso abate" "in villa"; 5) a positive resolution is achieved through the couple's travels from the "villa" to Rome, Florence, Paris, and finally back to London where they are completely and happily integrated into a rich and satisfactory social life. The love episode "in villa' in this *novella* catalyzes reversals of the unfortunate circumstances previously created in the city. The country episode therefore has a positive connotation whereas in the preceding *novella* of Rinaldo (II 2), it had a markedly negative one.

After the country episode in II 3, city conditions improve, both for Alessandro and for his three uncles. A similar narrative rhythm which varies in treatment of the city/country relationship takes place in II 8. In the *novella* the Count of Antwerp loses his high standing at the French court and is compelled to flee, penniless and with his children, to London, Wales, and then Ireland. After having lost everything, he retraces his steps, returning from Ireland to Wales, where he finds that his son has been made a martial of the king; thence to London, where he acknowledges his daughter's marriage to the son of another martial; and finally back to France again, where he is restored to former honor and wealth. Here, in contrast to the stories of Alessandro and Rinaldo, no special presentation of natural elements spurs a turning point in the Count's fortunes. Instead, the condition of the natural environment fluctuates, as do the changing fortunes of the Count and the other characters connected with him.

This fluctuation of fortune is often symbolized by the sea, which provides the background for several of the *novelle*. In II 4, for example, the vicissitudes of Landolfo's fortunes are closely connected with his sea voyages: 1) from Ravello to Cyprus, he loses all his riches; 2) from Cyprus to the open sea, he turns to piracy and gains even more than he lost; 3) from the sea to an island, he loses all again; 4) from the island back out to sea, he encounters a terrifying storm and grabs onto a floating chest for dear life; 5) from the sea to Corfu, he discovers that the chest is full of jewels; and finally 6) from Corfu to Ravello, he reaches home richer than when he departed.

The action of II 7 is also projected through a series of ocean voyages which emphasize the currents in Alatiel's fortunes.[19] In her first mishap, a storm at sea destroys the ship on which her father has sent her to her fiancé. Washed ashore on an island, she is rescued by a man who is struck by her beauty and becomes her lover. The pattern is repeated throughout the *novella* as Alatiel, seemingly losing her individuality, is admired, possessed, and then stolen away from a previous lover and possessed by yet another and another. An interesting variation in this general pattern is introduced when Costanzio kidnaps Alatiel from the Duke of Athens. While in the previous kidnaping episodes, two lovers had been brutally murdered — one in bed, and the other at his bedroom window — and others had either been thrown into the sea or killed in a duel, in this sequence there is no bloodshed at all, and a new setting is introduced: the *giardino*. The garden is not only the backdrop for Costanzio's first view of Alatiel ("fatto in un bellissimo giardino, che nel luogo dove la donna dimorava era, apparecchiare un magnifico desinare, loro la seguente mattina . . . a mangiar con lei menò" II 7, 66), but it is also the place from which he later kidnaps her as they stroll toward the seashore. The garden is thus linked at once with beauty and with sexually motivated violence.

Similar use is made of the *locus amoenus* in II 6, a *novella* which shares the narrative pattern of the other tales of this day. Like II 3, the action in this story is divided into two parts: the first concerns madonna Beritola's adventures; the second, the adventures of other characters, especially those of her elder son Giusfredi. As in the previous tales, the sea plays a dominant role in the separation and ultimate reunion of madonna Beritola and the other characters in the story. As the tale begins, Beritola, her children, and their nursemaid flee from Sicily and are shipwrecked on the uninhabited island of Ponza. Thus Beritola is, from the outset, an outcast from civilized society. Her isolation is exacerbated when a pirate raid deprives her even of her children and their nurse. Beritola seeks consolation with the *cavriuoli* as her life slowly descends to an animal-like state:

> parendo alla gentil donna avere nel diserto luogo alcuna
> compagnia trovata, l'erbe pascendo e bevendo l'acqua .
> . . quivi e a vivere e a morire s'era disposta, non meno
> dimestica della cavriuola divenuta che de' figliuoli. E

> così dimorando *la gentil donna divenuta fiera* . . .
> (II 6, 16-17)

With the introduction of Currado Malaspina and his entourage — here again, the sea affects their sudden appearance — Beritola's isolation draws to an end. The Malaspinas take her to their castle and she is reintegrated into human society. We thus have the following pattern emerging in the first part of the novella:

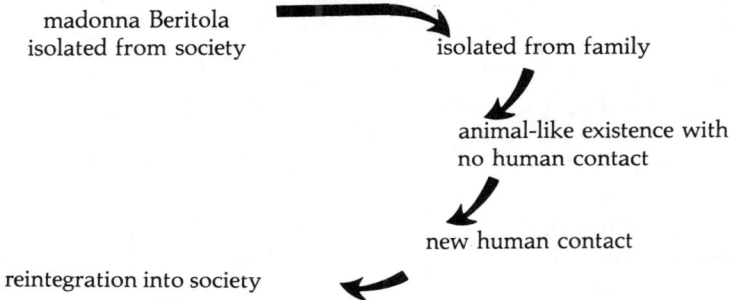

At this juncture, one would expect that the reintegration into her family would be completed in the near narrative future. It is, however, at this first stage of reintegration that chronology is suspended and a flashback focuses on the adventures of madonna Beritola's sons, simultaneous with her isolation on Ponza. Her elder son, Giusfredi, arrives at the court of the same Currado Malaspina and, as a servant, he falls in love with Currado's daughter. Here the narrative device of the *locus amoenus* comes into play with its suggestions of love and beauty and at the same time of potential violence and sorrow:

> in un luogo dilettevole e pien d'erba e di fiori e d'alberi chiuso (i due giovani) ripostisi, a prendere amoroso piacere l'un dell'altro incominciarono. E. . . in ciò dalla madre della giovane prima e appresso da Currado soprapresi furono.
> (II 6,37-38)

The *locus amoenus*, a hidden, natural setting, becomes the backdrop for a clandestine love affair between individuals of different classes, an affair repugnant to those who would rigidly maintain the existing social hierarchy. Such treatment of the *locus amoenus* motif is unique among the *novelle* of the Second Day and foreshadows the extensive role it will play in the stories of "infelice fine" in the Fourth Day.[20]

Currado, after having imprisoned his daughter and Giusfredi for over a year, learns of Giusfredi's aristocratic origin and consequently accepts him as a son-in-law. Giusfredi's love experiences are clearly the focal point of the second narrative moment II 6. They precede Beritola's recognition of and reunion with both Giusfredi and her younger son, "lo Scacciato," and their eventual reunion with Arrighetto in Sicily. The narrative pattern could be graphically represented as a full circle beginning and ending in Sicily:

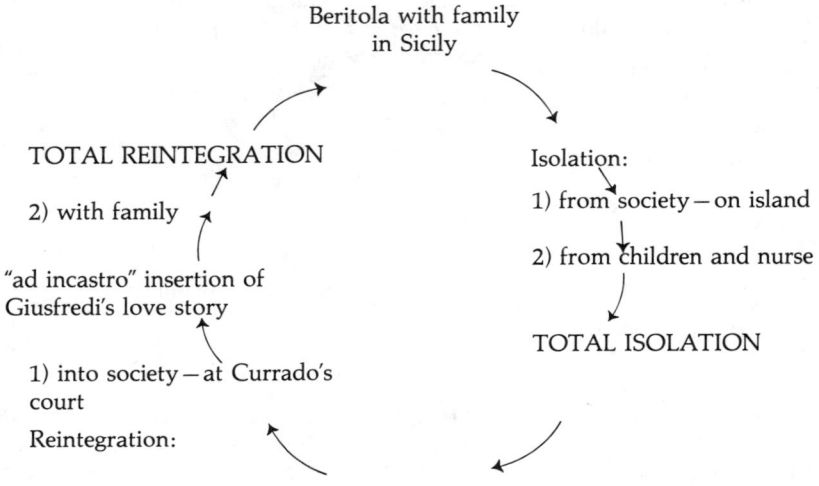

The same circular pattern is repeated in many of the other *novelle* of this day. Martellino and his friends travel from Florence to Trevigi, where they undergo a series of misadventures and eventually are sent back to Florence (II 1). Rinaldo d'Este, en route home from Bologna, is attacked by brigands and suffers a series of first negative, then positive adventures before he returns whence he set out (II 2). Landolfo Rufolo sets forth from Ravello and, after a long succession of misadventures at sea, returns safely to Ravello (II 4). Andreuccio naively faces the Neapolitan underworld and miraculously survives it to return safely to his native Perugia (II 5). Alexandria is Alatiel's point of departure and, after her innumerable love adventures, her point of return (II 7). Paris is both starting and ending point of the Count of Antwerp's misfortunes (II 8). Bernabò and Ginevra reside in Genoa and, after many unhappy adventures, they return there together (II 9). For messer Ricciardo, the aged judge of II 10, Pisa is the place where his married life begins happily and ends tragically after a trip to Monaco.

This circular pattern of narrative action is enhanced by the frantic and fragmented activities of diverse characters in diverse locations. Many narrative sequences, in fact, either involve a single protagonist in a series of different situations (II 1,2,4,5,7, and 8), or introduce different characters who temporarily assume the role of protagonist (II 3,6,9, and 10). In all cases, this fragmentation of narrative action accentuates the conception of a world in which precariousness, instabilility, and chance predominate. A character may undergo an entire sequence of experiences, positive and/or negative, without ever knowingly initiating or terminating them. Each of the sequences into which the narrative is fragmented consists, in turn, of a series of fluctuations in fortune which further accentuates the broken rhythm of the narrative.

The *novella* of Andreuccio da Perugia (II 5),[21] recounted by Fiammetta as a contrast to the preceding *novella* of Landolfo Rudolfo because of its compressed time span, is a classic example of this pattern. Once the story's time frame is established, references are made to its various settings. Andreuccio is from Perugia, a northern city; "non essendo mai più fuori di casa stato" (II 5,3), he decides to go to Naples to buy horses. After spending one day and one night in Naples, he returns to Perugia the following morning on his friends' advice: "parve per lo consiglio dell'oste loro che costui incontanente si dovesse di Napoli partire; la qual cosa fece prestamente e a Perugia tornossi . . ." (II 5,85). The circumscription of the *novella* by the day long Perugia-Naples-Perugia pattern functions as a commentary on the naive and circumscribed life of its protagonist, who eventually learns not to trust the unsavory characters he meets in Naples. The movement from north to south and back reflects the recurring up and down rhythm found in many sequences of the *novella*.[22]

The first sequence, concerning Andreuccio's arrival in Naples and his maladept dealings with the horse-traders, reveals initial elements that are essential to the development of the action: the audience learns of Andreuccio's naiveté through the storyteller's comments: "per mostrare che per comperar fosse, *sì come rozzo e poco cauto* più volte in presenza di chi andava e di chi veniva trasse fuori questa sua borsa de' fiorini che aveva" (II 5,3). The purse of florins is the catalyst for the unwinding of the whole plot because it lures "una giovane ciciliana bellissima, ma disposta per piccol pregio a compiacere a qualunque uomo," who *"senza vederla egli,* passò appresso di lui e la sua borsa *vide* e subito seco disse: 'Chi starebbe meglio di me se quegli denari fosser miei?'" (II 5,4). The conflict between Andreuccio and the *ciciliana* is foreshadowed by their respective degrees of awareness, linguistically conveyed through the verb *vedere*. Andreuccio does not see the *ciciliana* and will not see through her deception until too late; the *ciciliana* immediately sees his purse and his naiveté and she will manipulate Andreuccio until she has stolen his florins. In a second sequence involving the *ciciliana's* ruse, Andreuccio again changes his lodgings, this time moving from his hotel to the *ciciliana's* home in the Malpertugio district. Fiammetta aptly comments: "quanto sia onesta contrada il nome medesimo il dimostra" (II 5,14). Once in the house, Andreuccio climbs the stairs, "salendo su per le scale . . . la vide in capo della scala farsi a aspettarlo" (II, 5,14). The ruse ends with Andreuccio's fall from the upper floor into a narrow alley below, where he lands in the local latrine: "tutto della bruttura, della quale il luogo era pieno, s'imbrattò" (II 5,38). The up and down rhythm of the story is thus in harmony with the diverse adventures of its protagonist, who, by the end of the sequence, finds himself at the lowest possible state of affairs: alone, covered with filth, deprived of his florins, and unable to find his way back to his hotel. Although Andreuccio is able, consequently, to counteract all his misfortunes, he does so as a mere pawn of circumstance, as much a victim of good fortune as he was of ill luck and foolishness.

It is again physical detail detached from personal motivations which initiates the succeeding narrative sequence. In the first part of the *novella*, the purse of florins attracted the *ciciliana's* attention; as Andreuccio's fortunes reach bottom and begin to mount again, it is his stench that attracts the two thieves who become his allies:

> E mentre parlavano, disse l'uno: "Che vuol dir questo? Io sento il maggior puzzo che mai mi paresse sentire;" e questo detto, alquanto alzata la lanterna, ebber veduto il cattivel d'Andreuccio . . .
>
> Andreuccio taceva, ma essi avvicinatiglisi con lume il domandarono che quivi così brutto facesse . . .
>
> (II 5,58-59)

Once again Andreuccio is presented in a passive light, as object rather than agent of the narrative action. The narrator, Fiammetta, interjects her own commentary, and again stresses Andreuccio's naiveté and complete lack of awareness: "Andreuccio, *sì come disperato*, rispuose ch'era presto" (II 5,62), and later, "Andreuccio, *più cupido che consigliato* . . . " (II, 5,64).

As Andreuccio accompanies the thieves, his location shifts again, from their lair to the cathedral where they plan to rob an archbishop's tomb. But the trip is interrupted by a stop at the public well, where the thieves dip Andreuccio so that he may wash himself. His descent into and emergence from the well not only emphasizes the continual up and down pattern of the *novella*, but foreshadows Andreuccio's last such movement of the night: his descent into the tomb of the archbishop and his reemergence with the precious ruby in hand. Andreuccio's ascent from the well is his first self-motivated action of the night's adventures. He instinctively clutches the edge of the well at the moment his would-be helpers release him, and miraculously saves his own life. Instinct for self-preservation spurs him into action in his most horrifying adventure of the night, and prevents him from being entombed alive with the corpse of the archbishop. Here again chance befriends him, providing him with a new ally to unwittingly abet his escape. Finally, in the early light of dawn, Andreuccio returns to his hotel and finds safe passage back to Perugia. The cycle of events is complete.

In Andreuccio's *novella* all major narrative elements—character, action, space, and time—underscore certain dangers that only chance (or, as we shall see in the next day, an astute and enterprising individual) is able to neutralize. Naiveté and passivity are especially vulnerable to greed; gullibility and ignorance of ethnic differences place characters in equally precarious situations. Andreuccio personifies these weaknesses and the shady types he encounters are only too eager to capitalize on his deficiencies. The progression of exaggerated up and down movements and the geographic circularity of Andreuccio's adventures underscore the precariousness of his world. The unfolding of the *novella* in black night provides a metaphorical equivalent for its haphazard action and underworld characters. Narrative tone, however, is not dark: the storyteller views Andreuccio benevolently throughout the tale—as we see by her asides—and coaxes a similar indulgence from her audience. Andreuccio's ability to plunge into disastrous situations and to rebound from them again and again makes him an especially lively and sympathetic character. His tremendous vital energy and his instinct for self-preservation unite him with other memorable characters in the *Decameron* and reveal the narrator's belief in the power of human resourcefulness.

As in previous *novelle* of the Second Day, the action in the ninth and tenth tales is fragmented into many narrative sequences. In these last two *novelle*, however, the role of the main character shifts from sequence to sequence and women predominate. In the ninth *novella* geographic divisions are closely related to the differentiation of roles.[23] The first sequence, which takes place in Paris, presents Ambrogiuolo and Bernabò discussing women. Bernabò praises his wife Ginevra's chastity and virtue; Ambrogiuolo denigrates all women. A wager of 5,000 florins on Ginevra's incorruptibility ensues.

A second narrative sequence begins in Genoa, where Ambrogiuolo discovers that Bernabò's boasts about his wife's virtue are well-founded. He nevertheless succeeds, through deception, in seeing her naked, and steals some trinkets from her boudoir. He returns to Paris and unjustly claims his reward. At this point the chagrined Bernabò returns to Genoa and orders a servant to murder Ginevra. She, as far as the tale has progressed, has performed only a passive role, as topic of conversation and wager or as unwitting victim of deceit and revenge.

In the following sequence we first see Ginevra in action: she dutifully follows the servant to the place where she is told she will meet Bernabò. Ginevra's would-be murder is staged in "un vallone molto profondo e solitario e chiuso d'alte grotte e d'alberi" (II 9,39) which metaphorically suggests the ensuing isolation of her "social death" when she flees from Genoa. Through her eloquence Ginevra convinces the servant not to kill her and persuades him to exchange his garments—"il tuo farsetto e un cappuccio" (II 9,40)—for her own clothes, which he will bring back to Bernabò as proof of her death. He secures her promise that she will never again be seen in Genoa: "e io ti giuro . . . che io mi dileguerò e andronne in parte che mai né a lui né a te né in queste contrade di me perverrà alcuna novella" (II, 9,40).

The last, long sequence of the story presents Ginevra-Sicuran, disguised as a man, now actively involved in creating her own destiny. As a servant in the sultan's court in Alexandria, she not only convinces him that she is a man, but proves her superior wisdom and exceptional abilities. It is in Alexandria that she brings about her reunion with Bernabò and Ambrogiuolo and sees that justice is done. Her honesty is proven, Bernabò's distrust reproached, and Ambrogiuolo's deceit punished:

> Ambruogiuolo il dì medesimo che legato fu al palo e unto di mele, con sua grandissima angoscia dalle mosche e dalle vespe e da' tafani, de' quali quel paese è copioso molto, fu non solamente ucciso ma infino all'ossa divorato: le quali bianche rimase e a' nervi appiccate, poi lungo tempo, senza esser mosse, della sua malvagità fecero a chiunque le vide testimonianza. E così rimase lo 'ngannatore a piè dello 'ngannato.
>
> (II 9,75)

In this *novella* geographical locations provide an interesting contrast between the so-called civilized Western World and the exotic Orient. Paris and Genoa, major representatives of Western European culture and civilization, are the settings for callousness, deceit and vengeance. And although we would expect all manner of corruption in the luxuriant East, it is in Alexandria that virtue is recognized and rewarded and that the evil perpetrated in the "civilized" world is finally punished. Ginevra's transformation into Sicuran da Finale after her "social death" in the "vallone . . . profondo e solitario" is strong commentary on the vulnerability of women in a world dominated by men who are obsessed with their own honor and prowess. A question remains at the story's end: Would the sultan have consented to the "captain's" plan, had he known that Sicuran was actually a woman? His surprise at the end leaves us in doubt:

> Il soldano, il quale sempre per uomo avuta l'avea, questo vedendo e udendo venne in tanta maraviglia, che più volte quello che egli vedeva e udiva credette più tosto esser sogno che vero. Ma pur . . . la verità conoscendo, con somma laude la vita e la constanzia e i costumi e la virtù della Ginevra, infino allora stata Sicuran chiamata, commendò.
>
> (II 9,70)

Ginevra seems to be quite sure that no one would have helped her, had she not decided to disguise herself as a man. By eliminating — at least temporarily — her feminine vulnerability, she demonstrates her superiority of character and intellect to a world of men who had ignored them. Her awareness of the feminine dilemma is made clear in her words to the sultan:

> "'Signor mio, assai chiaramente potete conoscere quanto quella buona donna gloriar si possa d'amante e di marito: ché l'amante a un'ora lei priva d'onor con bugie guastando la fama sua e diserta il marito di lei: e il marito, più credulo alle altrui falsità che alla verità da lui per lunga esperienza potuta conoscere, la fa uccidere e mangiare a' lupi . . .'"
>
> (II 9,64)

Ginevra's resourcefulness and intelligence not only foreshadow the enterprising characters of the Third Day and the resourceful women of the Seventh, but suggest the theme of feminine rights which is treated extensively in II 10. In this *novella*, the sea once again plays a significant role in the unfolding of the tale, for it is through a sea voyage that madonna Bartolomea finds her ideal mate in the pirate Paganino da Monaco. The city of Pisa, her home, stands in direct opposition to the open sea: while the sea brings her freedom and fulfillment of love, Pisa represents deceit, parental tiranny, and unnatural marriage to an old man. When her husband, Ricciardo da Chinzica, finds her in Monaco after Paganino has kidnapped her, she is transformed from the wife he had known in Pisa. She triumphantly proclaims the right to choose her own mate and defends the superiority of natural laws over unnatural constraints:

> "'Del mio onore non intendo io che persona, ora che non si può, sia più di me tenera: fosserne stati i parenti miei quando mi diedero a voi! Li quali se non furono allora del mio, io non intendo d'essere al presente del loro . . . E dicovi così, che qui mi pare esser moglie di Paganino e a Pisa mi pareva esser vostra bagascia, pensando che per punti di luna e per isquadri di geometria si convenieno tra voi e me congiugnere i pianeti, dove qui Paganino tutta la notte mi tiene in braccio e strignemi e mordemi, e come egli mi conci Dio vel dica per me.'"
>
> (II 10,37-38)

While madonna Bartolomea liberates herself from an unhappy situation and takes command of her own destiny, she simultaneously destroys Ricciardo and causes his madness and death: "in tanta mattezza per dolor cadde, che andando per Pisa, a chiunque il salutava o d'alcuna cosa il domandava, niuna altra cosa rispondeva, se non: 'Il mal furo non vuol festa'; E dopo non molto tempo si morì" (II 10,42). This novella thus emphasizes the freedom sought by youth in confrontation with the oppressive rules of an older, more stable urban society, and hints at what will be one of the main topics of social satire in Day VIII, that is, professional misfits.

These last two *novelle* seem to differ from all the previous tales of the Second Day, for both Ginevra and madonna Bartolomea succeed, like the individuals in Day III, in controlling their own lives—but only when removed from their native enviroments. Such a change, it seems, is necessary for the women to prove their worth and gain their freedom. Human resourcefulness thus reemerges in these last two *novelle* of the Second Day to allow Bartolomea and Ginevra to prevail over those deficient individuals who threaten them. We shall see these themes again in the Fifth Day where awareness and enterprise coupled with a change in environment are important narrative concerns.

4. Day III: Resourcefulness Within Limits

With the Third Day of *novellare* some essential changes emerge in the *cornice* that aid in understanding the unique elements of this day. Neifile becomes queen, and decides to move the *onesta brigata* to another retreat. The storytellers' new abode is situated in a perfect *locus amoenus* where all sensual and intellectual pleasures are provided. The artistic and intelligent arrangement of natural elements supplies a profusion of delights: the hues of flowers and grass, the beautiful fountain and roving animals in the *loco naturale,* the perfume of flowers and vines, and the music of water and birds create an array to delight each sense. Such emphasis within the Introduction to the Third Day on nature and the senses suggests their significance within this day's *novelle* as well.

Neifile's impulse for individuality is shared by several other storytellers as they attack the hypocrisy and injustice of many contemporary attitudes. Filostrato begins by calling into question the belief that nuns lack sexual drive:

> assai sono di quegli uomini e di quelle femine che sì sono stolti, che credono troppo bene che, come a una giovane è sopra il capo posta la benda bianca e indosso messole la nera cocolla, che ella più non sia femina né più senta de' feminili appetiti se non come se di pietra l'avesse fatta divenire il farla monaca . . .
> (III I,2)

He criticizes the hypocrisy of those who, "se . . . alcuna cosa contra questa lor credenza n'odono, così si turbano come se contra natura un grandissimo e scelerato male fosse stato comesso . . ." (III I,3), while underscoring the naturalness of sexual desires—even among nuns. He highlights Masetto's shrewdness in fulfilling his "concupiscibili appetiti," which disproves the misconception that "la zappa e la vanga e le grosse vivande e i disagi tolgano del tutto a' lavoratori della terra i concupiscibili appetiti e rendon loro d'intelletto e d'avedimento grossissimi" (III I,4). Filomena, in turn, attacks clergymen and their presumptuousness, describing them as "il più stoltissimi e uomini di nuove maniere e costumi," who "si credono più che gli altri in ogni cosa valere e sapere" (III 3,3). She praises the "bella donna" who brilliantly tricks "uno solenne religioso" into unwittingly arranging amorous trysts in the third *novella* of this day. Emilia, who has already attacked religious hypocrisy in I 6, continues her criticism in the seventh *novella*. There Tedaldo, her tale's protagonist, delivers a lengthy and venomous diatribe (III 7,33-54) against the "frati . . . d'oggi" who are interested only in "femine e . . . richezze; e tutto il loro studio hanno posto e pongono in ispaventare con romori e con dipinture le menti degli sciocchi . . ." (III 7,36).

Neifile's individual initiative not only elicits social criticism, but draws into focus the resourcefulness of those characters in the *novelle* of this day, who, as the announced theme states, "alcuna cosa molto disiderata con industria acquistasse o la perduta recuperasse" (II Conclusion,9).

In this day, sexual love is the chief concern of each *novella*. The main characters are all motivated by sex and call their resourcefulness into play in fulfilling their desires. With one exception (Giletta in III 9), all *novelle* concern extra-marital affairs. Satisfactory fulfillment is generally achieved only at the end of the *novelle* (with the exception of III 2 and 10) and conveys an improvement in each lover's personal life. As in the other days, the characters represent all social strata: the aristocracy appears in III, 2,3,5,6,7,and 9; the wealthy bourgeoisie—urban merchants as well as landed gentry—in III 3,4,8,and 10; the professional class in III 9; lower class rustics and citydwellers in III 1 and 2; and the religious orders in III 1,3,4,8,and 10. Female characters are particularly important in several *novelle* where they either initiate the action (III 3,9, and 10) or play major supporting roles (III 6 and 8). In all cases women are a force for social change and individual freedom, as seen previously in II 8 and 9.

Contrary to Days I and II, change in geographic status does not play an essential role in the Third Day, where neither precariousness nor chance predominates. Many characters dwell in one place throughout their lives (III 3,6 and 8). When seen in transit, characters are described as returning to their place of origin after a brief interval abroad (III 4,5,7 and 10), and in other tales (III 1 and 2) they relocate at the beginning of the *novella* and remain in their new abodes permanently. Again, only the *novella* of Giletta is an exception to the general pattern of the day; the treatment of geographic locations in her story more nearly parallels that of the Second Day.

From the point of view of narrative structure, each *novella* of the Third Day works on two levels: a conscious one, representing the active character in the story, and an unconscious one, representing the character(s) who is (are) the "object" of the former's action. These two levels in turn correspond to two semantic levels of meaning, described in Todorovian terms as "essence," or reality, and "appearance."[24] This interaction of fictional levels which is found again in Days VII and VIII, produces a narrative pattern that dramatically conveys a complex world where the characters struggle to achieve a delicate balance between personal relationships and social traditions.

Interaction between characters, especially where gulls are exploited by their more astute antagonists, creates the atmosphere of a "comedy of errors." In the *novella* of Masetto and the nuns (III 1) for example, an equivocal situation develops from Masetto's cunning manipulations of reality and appearance. In the first narrative moment, he decides to present himself to the nuns as a passive deaf-mute and is sure that he will be welcomed without suspicion:

> A Masetto . . . venne nell'animo un disidero sì grande d'esser con queste monache, che tutto se ne struggeva . . . e . . . cominciò . . . a pensare che via dovesse tenere a dovere potere esser con loro . . . Per che, molte cose divisate seco, imaginò: 'Il luogo è assai lontano di qui e niuno mi vi conosce; se io so far vista d'esser mutolo, per certo io vi sarò ricevuto.'
>
> (III 1,11-12)

It is Masetto's deaf-mute demeanor that induces the nun's steward to hire him "a lavorar l'orto delle monache," and it is again his silent, inviting presence that induces the nuns and their abbess to put him to his sexual labors. In this first sequence, then, the silent character, a supposed dupe, is actually the initiator of all action, while the speaking characters unwittingly bring Masetto's plans to fruition.

In a second narrative moment, Masetto becomes the loquacious agent[25] of his fortunes as he "miraculously" addresses the abbess: "'sono io, per quello che infino a qui ho fatto, a tal venuto che io non posso fare né poco né molto; e per ciò o voi mi lasciate andar con Dio o voi a questa cosa trovate modo'" (III 1,37). Masetto's fortune is secure because the nuns both enjoy his presence and cannot risk his departure. Unable to send him away, they make him steward of the convent. Masetto has cleverly manipulated reality and appearance by projecting the myth of his own simplicity in order to exploit the simplicity of others. The comic dimension of the *novella* consists in the transposition of roles between gull and gulled. Such is the case not only for Masetto and the nuns, but also for the *bella donna* and her gullible confessor in III 3, for Zima and the overconfident husband in III 5, for Ricciardo and Catella in III 6, and for the *santo abate* and Ferondo in III 8.

Like Masetto's, the *santo abate's* comedic manipulation of reality in III 8 functions by pitting conscious and unwitting actions against each other.[26] Motivated by his desire for Ferondo's wife, the abbot plans and executes jealous Ferondo's round trip to Purgatory with the aid of a "magic" potion and a willing accomplice. Ferondo, for his part, is thoroughly duped and believes that he had died and gone to Purgatory in just punishment for his overweaning jealousy. The two levels of action, real and apparent, proceed simultaneously to stress the equivocal nature of the narrative. Ferondo's gullibility both allows and encourages the confusion of reality and appearance, as we see in his willing acceptance of all explanations given to him. When Ferondo asks a question, he accepts the response as reality, and proceeds to ask another question based on the dubious answer he has just received. A repetitive equivocal pattern of questions and responses is thus produced, to create an effective comic rhythm:

> Ferondo, piangendo e gridando, non faceva altro che domandare: 'Dove sono io?'
> A cui il monaco rispose: 'Tu si' in Purgatoro.'
> 'Come?' disse Ferondo 'Dunque son io morto?'
> Disse il monaco: 'Mai sì . . .
> Al quale il monaco portò alquanto da mangiare e da bere; il che veggendo Ferondo disse: 'O mangiano i morti?'
> Disse il monaco: 'Sì, e questo che io ti reco è ciò che la donna che fu tua mandò stamane alla chiesa a far dir messe per l'anima tua' . . .
> Disse allora Ferondo: 'Domine, dalle il buono anno! Io le voleva ben gran bene anzi che io morissi . . .'
> (III 8, 39-45)[27]

A similar juxtaposition of reality and appearance occurs in the *novelle beffe* of the Seventh and Eighth Days, where natural settings often provide freedom from social restrictions and facilitate interpersonal relationships. In the *novella* of Masetto, the natural world described within and without the convent walls seemed to represent the overwhelming predominance of natural needs over moral restrictions. The same could have been said for the country monastery of I 4 and for the sea environment of II 10. Moral intentions and physical instincts are in sharp contrast in the natural world of Rustico the hermit and Alibech (III 10). This contrast is comically encapsulated in the expression "rimettere il diavolo in inferno," which with its linguistic sign suggests the moral intention of the hermit and Alibech, while metaphorically it symbolizes the fulfillment of their sexual desires.

The *novella* of Giletta and Beltramo (III 9) deals with the dichotomy between natural and urban environments in a still different way. Alternating locations correlate with the actions of the main characters: If we trace the locations, our scheme would be:

1) COUNTRY-Rossiglione: Giletta and Beltramo (united as children)
2) CITY-Paris: Giletta and Beltramo (unwilling)

3) COUNTRY-Rossiglione: Giletta alone
4) CITY-Florence: Giletta (incognito) and Beltramo
5) COUNTRY-Rossiglione: Giletta and Beltramo reunited

The country seems to provide what Barthes would call the "parametrical dimension"[28] of the protagonist, Giletta, and it prepares her for the central action of the *novella*. The countryside is, in fact, not only the setting in which Giletta falls in love with Beltramo, but it is the place in which she is allowed to express her managerial skill and wisdom in government. Through her experience in the country she is prepared for her later roles as *chatellaine* and wife. The city, on the other hand, functions as a backdrop for the "cardinal functions" or "nuclei" of the narrative,[29] for it is in Paris that Giletta cleverly induces the king, in exchange for her competent medical advice, to give her Beltramo in marriage despite Beltramo's strong objections. Giletta must then initiate a series of actions to counter Beltramo's opposition and effect their physical and emotional union. After her marriage in Paris, Giletta returns to the country as a wise *chatellaine* and reveals further fundamental details of her noble character. In the decisive sequence in Florence, Giletta shows her resourcefulness and initiative by causing an unwitting Beltramo to consummate their marriage. He unknowingly grants her the seemingly impossible preconditions he had established for their legitimate union: his precious ring and an offspring. A happy ending unfolds at last in the country with a jubilant society surrounding Giletta and her family. In this concluding scene the Boccaccian vision of perfected human society, later presented in the grandiose conclusion to the last *novella* of the *Decameron*, is first anticipated.

We find again that an equivocal two-level pattern operates in Giletta's tale: on one level, Giletta is a conscious and far-sighted agent motivated by love; on the other, her fellow characters become her unwitting pawns. It is the constant presence of conscious/unconscious oppositions set against alternating backgrounds of city and country that creates the equivocal pattern of this *novella*.

The same pattern of conscious/unconscious oppositions appears in III 3,4,5,6,and 7, and its treatment varies in each case. In III 3, for example, a third character — that of the gulled confessor — is introduced to aid the *bella donna* in arranging meetings with the *valente uomo* she admires. Her conscious manipulation of the unknowing friar allows her to instruct her lover in his behavior towards her. Again we have two levels of perception functioning simultaneously: one conscious, through which the *donna* treats future actions as if they had occurred in the past; and one unconscious, through which the confessor acts on the woman's fabricated complaints and unwittingly converts them to instructions — rather than reproofs — for her lover. The confessor thus ironically turns the woman's falsehoods into truths by instructing her lover to perform the same brazen acts of which she had previously "complained."[30]

Nature appears in this *novella* only briefly, but at a crucial point: the union of the lovers can be achieved only if the *valente uomo* enters the woman's garden and climbs a tree to reach her window. The garden, then, is the narrative trigger for sexual love. While in this *novella*, as in II 6 and 7, the garden suggests fulfillment of love, here the continuity and pleasure of love are stressed rather than the often violent consequences of the Second Day. The *giardino* functions similarly in the *novella* of Zima (III 5), who wishes to arrange a meeting with a woman who is forbidden to address him. Not one to accept defeat without a struggle, Zima speaks in her stead. According to the words he puts into her mouth, he will be allowed to come to her through her garden:

> 'quel giorno il quale tu vedrai due asciugatoi tesi alla finestra della camera mia, la quale è sopra *il nostro giardino*, quella sera di notte, guardando ben che veduto non sii, fa che per *l'uscio del giardino* a me te ne venghi: tu mi troverai ivi che t'aspetterò, e insieme avren tutta la notta festa e piacere l'un dell'altro . . .'
>
> (III 5,22)

Here the narrative technique used in III 3 is reversed, for it is through the woman's silence rather than through her speech that the lover fulfills his desires. Pretending to speak the woman's thoughts, he projects actions that each of them will perform in the future. The presence of the woman's husband, who acts as foil for Zima, enables the lovers to meet with his unwilling aid. His participation in affecting a consummation of the love is reduced, however, to a passive role, unlike the confessor in III 3. Unaware that Zima is speaking both for himself and for the woman, her husband stands silently by — out of earshot — gloating over his triumph.[31] The same pattern is thus at work again, with its comic interplay of conscious and unconscious action, and with the added dimension of speech versus silence to play off III 3. Speech versus silence, also the basis for Masetto's adventures in III 1, recurs in the *novella* of King Agilulf's groom (III 2), who silently impersonates the king in order to visit the queen's bed-chamber. The king himself, once aware of the silent substitution made in his wife's bed, responds in kind with a furtive plot of his own. Only at the end of the *novella* is the silence between the antagonists broken with the king's terse "'Chi 'l fece nol faccia mai più, e andatevi con Dio'" (III 2,30).

The Third Day's repeated pattern of conscious and unconscious action reappears in III 6 with Ricciardo's ruse to possess an unwilling Catella. Playing upon Catella's jealousy of her husband, Filippello, Ricciardo fabricates a tale of illicit love between her husband and his own wife, and persuades Catella to impersonate her rival at a tryst with Filippello. She is taken in by Ricciardo's guile and unknowingly becomes his lover, believing that he is Filippello. Ricciardo, alone aware of his complex machinations, enjoys Catella's embraces through his power to distort reality. Once again reality and appearance are interchanged:

what seems to be, is not (i.e., Catella is not making love to Filippello, but to Ricciardo), and what seems not to be, is (i.e., Catella, the "faithful wife," is making love to another man).

Tedaldo's relationship with the other characters in III 7 is similarly based upon the play of appearance and reality. Tedaldo, in fact, is believed to have been murdered by the husband of the woman he has always loved. All of his actions must, therefore, be directed toward reestablishing the reality of his own existence, first to his beloved, then to the authorities, and finally to his family and the Florentine society. The *novella* ends with a crescendo of reconciliations and reunions from the individual to the social level.[32]

This Third Day, then, reveals new and intriguing aspects of the Decameronian world. We see characters drawn largely from Boccaccio's contemporary society who operate in a limited and controlled environment which they manipulate to suit their own ends. Intelligence and awareness predominate as weaker characters are gulled by their intellectual superiors. Individual resourcefulness, especially when sexually motivated, and restricted environments, where no forces hostile to the lovers may enter, emerge as central concerns of the day.

5. Day IV: Love in a Hostile World

In the Fourth Day, under the rule of Filostrato—the unhappy lover—antagonistic forces confront lovers and eventually disrupt their union. In place of the previous day's dramatic alternations of fortune, the "infelici" lovers of the Fourth Day meet universally miserable fates, often suffering death or isolation in environments where no real communication or sympathy is possible among conflicting characters.

The Introduction to the Fourth Day prepares readers and audiences for tales of conflict between lovers and forces antagonistic to them. The Narrator, who has not addressed his readers since the Introduction to the First Day, appears again in this day's Introduction. He appeals to his ideal audience, his "carissime, discrete, valorose, giovani, gentilissime, belle done," in a defense against his "reprensori" who have attacked him on moralistic and practical grounds for his writings on behalf of women:

> hanno detto che voi mi piacete troppo e che onesta cosa
> non è che io tanto diletto prenda di piacervi . . . E . . .
> hanno detto che io farei più discretamente a pensare
> donde io dovessi aver del pane . . .
> (IV Introduction, 5-7)

The defense extols, on the one hand, the "natural power" of love: "gli altri e io, che v'amiamo, naturalmente operiamo; alle cui leggi, cioè della natura, voler contrastare troppo gran forze bisognano, e spesse volte non solamente invano ma con grandissimo danno del faticante s'adoperano" (IV Introduction, 41-42). On the other hand, as Filostrato did in III 1, it criticizes those who oppose love: "chi non v'ama," he tells his female audience, "e da voi non disidera d'essere amato, sì come persona che i piaceri né la vertù della naturale affezione né sente né conosce, così mi ripiglia . . ." (IV Introduction, 32). The lack of understanding between the Narrator and his misinformed critics on the subject of love and its natural power presents a controversial atmosphere and foreshadows the conflictive situations in the *novelle* of this day.

The stories, widely dispersed in geographic terms, seem to suggest that such conflictive situations are ubiquitous in human society: both foreign and Italian locations are represented (France in IV 3 and 9, Africa in IV 4), and among the latter, northern (IV 2 and 6), central (IV 7 and 8), and southern (IV 1,4,5,and 10) locations are backdrops for the narratives. Furthermore, in some *novelle*, a change in space is functionally essential for the development of the action (IV 2,3,and 5) or for its conclusion (IV, 3,5,and 9). Frate Alberto in IV 2 must move from Imola to Venice, where no one knows him, in order to find the proper environment to continue his life of imposture. The three couples in IV 3 must abandon Marseille to avoid the social and legal repercussions of the women's unauthorized seizure of their family's riches. By selecting an island foreign to all the main characters, a place free from all social pressure, they suit their needs ideally. Social pressure, however, is not replaced by any kind of inner moral law, and thus, after a short while, the primitive instincts of revenge and self-gratification resurface. A tragic outcome of dispersion and death results. In the *novella* of Lisabetta (IV 5) the geographical shift from San Gimignano in Tuscany, to Messina in Sicily, plays an important role in the development of action and characters. Lisabetta's morose passion for Lorenzo and the absence of human compassion or communication around her are readily traceable to her "foreign" origin and her subsequent inability to adapt herself to an unfamiliar environment. Her brothers move from Messina to Naples because they fear that if Lorenzo's brutal murder is discovered, their integration into the community will be threatened. A similar action is undertaken by Guiglielmo Rossiglione for the same reasons in IV 9, after he murders his friend and neighbor Guardastagno and his wife commits suicide: "Messer Guiglielmo, vedendo questo, stordì forte e parvegli aver mal fatto; e temendo egli de' paesani e del conte di Proenza, fatti sellare i cavalli, andò via" (IV 9,24).

Time as well as space is manipulated in this day's *novelle* to enrich the complexity of the tragedies confronting some of the more able characters. Ghismonda's exceptional intelligence and foresight would immediately set her among the most successful characters of a Tuscan commune. But placed in a stifling southern feudal environment, as she is in IV 1, she is destined for destruction.[33] Ghismonda's conflict with her father suggests the complexity and ambiguity with which the individual confronts society. Ghismonda operates with a self-confidence and independence more characteristic of a feudal lord than of a lady. But in a feudal society, woman is relegated to a minor role and is completely impotent in the power structure. Fiammetta, the storyteller, suggests this possible flaw in Ghismonda's otherwise exemplary character: "Era costei bellissima del corpo e del viso quanto alcuna altra femina fosse mai, e giovane e gagliarda e *savia più che a donna per avventura non si richiedea.*" (IV 1,5). Her actions and decisions prove her superiority of mind and will, a superiority that is, however, ineffective in the society in which she lives. This is especially clear in her interaction with her father, who is emotionally the weaker of the two but who has the ultimate power as feudal lord to determine the life and death of his subjects.

Tancredi's weakness is emphasized by his frequent outpouring of tears: he first comes to Ghismonda *"piangendo . . ."* (IV 1,25); in his long speech he *"*bassò il viso, *piagnendo sì forte come farebbe un fanciul ben battuto"* (IV 1,29); when directly confronted with Ghismonda's suicide *"cominciò dolorosamente a piagnere . . ."* (IV 1,59); and finally, at the moment of burial, he still acts only *"dopo molto pianto"* (IV, 1,62). Furthermore, he seems to be uncertain about what to do with Ghismonda: "di te sallo Idio che io non so che farmi" (IV 1,29). And although he recognizes her "grandezza dell'animo," yet he clearly shows a lack of understanding of her depth of feeling for Guiscardo and her firmness of resolution. His violent action against Guiscardo reflects the feudal code which vests total power in the prince — and only in the prince — and makes revenge the only possible retaliation for an offense. Tancredi's words to Ghismonda when he gives her Guiscardo's heart are significant in this light: "'Il tuo padre ti manda questo per consolarti di quella cosa che tu più ami, come tu hai lui consolato di ciò che egli più amava" (IV,1,47). Thus, although Ghismonda acts as if she is in total control of her own destiny and the life and love of others, the power structure of the society in which she must operate cannot afford more than one authority, however weak and ineffectual it might be. Ghismonda, therefore, has no other choice than to die.

Conversely, Rossiglione's wife in IV 9, whose choice of a worthy lover is in perfect harmony with the demands of feudal courtly love, is faced with a jealous husband who opposes the courtly tradition and instead holds a bourgeois view of marriage. She is therefore compelled to choose death rather than accept life with a "disleale e malvagio cavalier" (IV 9,23). In IV 4, two ideological cornerstones of the feudal code, courtly love and honor, are pitted against each other through the male protagonists, Gerbino and his royal grandfather. This *novella* presents an equally catastrophic vision of violent death and irreversible royal "justice."

Throughout the *novelle* of the Fourth Day, social conditions and class status produce the tales' major conflicts. Rich merchants and poor Venetian citizens alike react violently to the hypocrisies and dissimulations of clerics like Frate

Alberto in IV 2. Lisabetta's brothers in IV 5 consider her relationship with Lorenzo a "vergogna" to be eliminated simply because he is of lower social status; there is no other possible motivation for his murder within the *novella*. The social hierarchy plagues Andreuola and Gabriotto in IV 6, as Andreuola fears her fathers' reaction to her love for a man "di bassa condizione," although "di laudevoli costumi pieno e della persona bello e piacevole" (IV 6,8). The same situation occurs in reverse in IV 8, where Girolamo and Salvestra's love affair is doomed because of Salvestra's inferior status. Girolamo's mother sends him away and Salvestra marries a man of her own low station. The lovers, like so many in this day, are reunited only in death.

The protagonists' social status and social milieu are therefore essential to the outcome of dramatic conflicts in the stories of this day. Of the ten *novelle*, four present a situation where the conflict between lovers and society arises out of social imbalance between the lovers: Ghismonda's choice of a socially inferior man is the stated motivation for her father's revenge (IV 1); the same conflict appears in Lisabetta's, Andreuola's and Girolamo's cases. In all these situations, rigid and discriminatory social standards restrict an individual's choices for love and create oppositions that eventually bring death or alienation to one or both of the lovers. Flaws in the judiciary system are suggested in three *novelle*, IV 6,7,and 10. In the sixth, Andreuola is attacked and nearly raped by the chief representative of justice in her city, the *podestà*. In the seventh, Simona, a young woman of humble origin, is unable to defend herself against the murder charges levelled against her by her dead lover's friends. In order to prove her innocence in front of the judge, she is constrained to die. In IV 10, we find a rather unorthodox method of exercising justice in the *stradicò's* instantaneous desire to "attaccar l'uncino alla cristianella di Dio" of messer Mazzeo's servant even before listening to her plea for the liberation of Ruggieri (IV 10,48).

The aggregation of violent social forces — whether relatives, friends, or external authorities — against an individual totally consumed by his love, characteristically takes place in situations where no communication has been established between lovers and their environment. Ghismonda, realizing her father is unwilling to have her remarry, "si pensò di voler avere . . . occultamente un valoroso amante" (IV 1,5-6). The King of Sicily agrees to provide security for the King of Tunis' daughter since "né dello innamoramento del Gerbino aveva alcuna cosa sentita" (IV 4,13). Lisabetta and Lorenzo's love is consumated without her brothers' knowledge or consent, and Andreuola and Gabriotto's is kept hidden from family and friends. Rossiglione keeps "nascoso" his knowledge of his wife's affair with Guardastagno until the moment of his brutal revenge. And although Girolamo's mother is aware of his love for Salvestra, she tries to subvert it and thereby causes his tragic death. While communication does take place between mother and son, it is an unsympathetic process where the depth and power of love are misunderstood. A similar lack of understanding emerges in the episode of pitiful Simona and the poisoned sage bush.

The treatment of certain images or motifs reveals the underlying themes of love and violence, the individual's conflict with society, and the lack of communication and isolation which are typical of this day. In particular, the image of the garden or *locus amoenus* seen in II 6 and 7 and in III 3 and 5 is amply exploited in the Fourth Day, and seems to suggest a personalized justice in direct contrast to a more impersonal social justice. In fact, the "justice" meted out by society in this day hinders the formation of close relationships between its members and works against individuals.[34]

In the *novella* of Ghismonda (IV 1) the garden appears as a frame for the sequence of events leading to the *novella's* tragic outcome. Ghismonda is *"in un suo giardino* con tutte le sue damigelle" (IV 1,17), when her father decides to enter her room, and, while waiting for her to come back he falls asleep by her bed. It is then that Ghismonda, having "lasciate le sue damigelle *nel giardino"* (IV 1,18) comes to her room and makes love to Guiscardo, unaware of her father's presence. Once the lovers have left the room, Tancredi, in order not to be seen, "da una finestra . . . si calò *nel giardino"* (IV 1,21). The garden, then, is used to frame the central scene in which the chain of events leading to the lovers' deaths begins. The garden suggests the social life which exists beyond Ghismonda's room, and juxtaposes this society with the enclosed, personal relationship of the lovers — a relationship closely guarded within Ghismonda's private chambers. While Tancredi immediately reenters the garden after his discovery, Ghismonda is never again seen there, implying that any further social involvement with the courtly world is impossible for her. Guiscardo, on the other hand, is never presented within the *giardino,* but arrives at his tryst with Ghismonda through a hidden underground *grotta.* Clearly his lower social status precludes his participation in the courtly society *giardino* and relegates him to a geographic position commensurate with his social one. The "grotta cavata nel monte," with "uno spiraglio . . . quasi da pruni e da erbe di sopra natevi . . . riturato" (IV 1,9), thus becomes the symbol of Ghismonda and Guiscardo's clandestine love. *Grotta* and *giardino* function as images for the conflicting forces of the *novella:* love based on personal rather than social criteria (the *grotta*) in opposition to a rigidly structured society denying individual freedom of choice (the *giardino*).

In the *novella* of Frate Alberto the *giardino* appears in an ambiguous and highly ironic light. The friar's version of Paradise — that is, of sexual intercourse — is visualized as "uno de' più dilettevoli luoghi che fosse mai . . . tra tanti fiori e tra tante rose . . . ." (IV 2,35). This description suggests a link between sexual fulfillment and the *loco naturale,* a theme which will be amply developed in the *novella* of Andreuola and Gabriotto (IV 6).

In IV 6 the garden signifies the several stages in the development of the love theme. First, initial fulfillment occurs in Andreuola's garden:

> *in un bel giardino* del padre di lei più e più volte a diletto dell'una parte e dell' altra fu menato, E acciò che *niuna cagione mai, se non morte,* potesse questo lor dilettevole amor separare, marito e moglie segretamente divennero.
>
> (IV 6,9)

The isolation of the garden emphasizes the secrecy of love outside the boundaries of society. In this first stage death and social oppression are anticipated.

In the second stage, the premonition of death comes to Andreuola through her dream, which is projected against the same garden background:

> alla giovane una notte dormendo parve in sogno vedere sè essere *nel suo giardino* con Gabriotto e lui con grandissimo piacer di ciascuno tener nelle sue braccia; e mentre che così dimoravan, le pareva vedere del corpo di lui uscire una cosa oscura e terribile . . . e parevale che questa cosa prendesse Gabriotto e malgrado di lei con maravigliosa forza gliele strappasse di braccio e con esso ricoverasse sotterra, né mai più riveder potesse nè l'un né l'altro.
>
> (IV 6,10)

Here death bred in the garden is presented as a force of terror which destroys the unity of the lovers and leaves only solitude and desperation.

The final encounter between the two lovers (third stage) occurs in Andreuola's garden where the rose motif appears for the first time: "la seguente notte *nel suo giardino* il ricevette. E avendo *molte rose bianche e vermiglie* colte, per ciò che la stagione era, con lui . . . a starsi se n'andò" (IV 6,11-12). The rose motif functions later as an extension of the *locus amoenus* physically separate from the garden itself.

At this point, Andreuola shows the anxiety caused by her prophetic dream:

> E come che con lui, abbracciandolo e basciandolo alcuna volta e da lui essendo abbracciata e basciata, si sollazzasse, suspicando e non sappiendo che, più che l'usato spesse volte il riguardava nel volto e tal volta per lo giardin riguardava se alcuna cosa nera vedesse venir d'alcuna parte.
>
> (IV 6,18)

This stage concludes with Gabriotto's sudden death—the actualization of the dream:" . . . Gabriotto, gittato un gran sospiro, l'abbracciò e disse: 'Oimè, anima mia, aiutami, ché io muoio, 'e così detto ricadde in terra sopra l'erba del pratello" (IV 6,19).

The last appearance of the garden occurs with the aftermath of Gabriotto's death, and develops in several narrative steps as well. The first sequence concerns the nurse's suggestions for Gabriotto's burial, either within or near the garden: "'Del sepellirlo è il modo presto qui in questo giardino, il che niuna persona saprà giammai per ciò che niun sa che egli mai ci venisse; e se così non vuogli, mettianlo qui *fuori del giardino* e lascianlo stare'" (IV 6,25). Andreuola then adorns Gabriotto's body with the roses, and exits from the garden with his body:

> postagli la testa sopra uno origliere e con molte lagrime chiusigli gli occhi e la bocca e fattagli una ghirlanda *di rose e tutto da torno delle rose che colte avevano empiutolo* . . . con la fante insieme preso il drappo sopra il quale il corpo giaceva, con *quello del giardino* uscirono . . .
>
> (IV 6,27-31)

Gabriotto's apotheosis occurs in a final scene of honorable public burial. Here the presence of roses again stress the link between love and nature:

> posto nel mezzo della corte il corpo sopra il drappo dell' Andreuola e con *tutte le sue rose,* quivi non solamente da lei e dalle parenti di lui fu pianto ma publicamente quasi da tutte le donne della città e da assai uomini; e non a guisa di plebeio ma di signore, tratto della corte publica, sopra gli omeri de' più nobili cittadini con grandissimo onore fu portato alla sepoltura.
>
> (IV 6,42-43)

The *giardino* thus represents the secret, highly personal love which unites the two young protagonists, and reflects their private world which disintegrates when death enters. Only one of its symbolic elements—the roses—is left to sustain the memory of that former ideal love.

Departure from the garden triggers aggression from the society outside. The women carrying Gabriotto's dead body are first attacked by city guards ("E così andando, per caso avvenne che dalla famiglia del podestà che per caso andava a quella ora per alcuno accidente, furon trovate e prese col morto corpo," (IV 6,31); and later by the *podestà* himself. At the same time, the love nourished within the garden gives Andreuola the strength to defend herself against aggression from the outside: "'niuno di voi sia ardito di toccarmi . . . né da questo corpo alcuna cosa rimuovere, se da me non vuole essere accusato" (IV 6,32), she warns the guards. And the same strength sustains her in her encounter with the mayor:

> (Il podestà) disse, dove ella a' suoi piaceri acconsentir si volesse, la libererebbe. Ma non valendo quelle parole, oltre a ogni convenevolezza volle usar la forza: ma l'Andreuola, da sdegno accesa e divenuta fortissima, virilmente si difese, lui con villane parole e altiere ributtando indietro.
>
> (IV 6,34-35)

Clearly the garden is set in sharp contrast to the city streets and palaces. These opposing environments represent the conflict between individual freedom and social authority which results in aggression against a defenseless individual.

The intermediary between garden and society in this story is the family, represented by Andreuola's father and his friends who intercede for her and stop the *podestà's* attack: "queste cose essendo a messer Negro contate, dolente a morte con molti de' suoi amici a palagio n'andò, e quivi d'ogni cosa dal podestà informato, dolendosi domandò che la figliuola gli fosse renduta" (IV 6,36). The final vision of Gabriotto's honorable burial demonstrates the positive power of such a mediating influence, and presents the vision of a society with all its members—father and daughter, aristocrats and local authorities—reconciled. The eradication of the *locus amoenus* and all that it symbolizes is, however, irreversible. Final reconciliation is made possible only through the death and apotheosis of one of the garden-dwellers. The other, Andreuola, eventually withdraws from society and retires to a convent.

The reconciliation between individual and society is treated with increasing complexity in the following *novella* of Simona and Pasquino (IV 7). There the garden plays yet another significant role. In her introduction to the story, Emilia, the narrator, establishes this new function: "la novella detta da Panfilo mi tira a doverne dire una in niuna cosa altra alla sua simile, se non che, come l'Andreuola *nel giardino* perdè l'amante, e così colei di cui dir debbo" (IV 7,3). Paquino wishes to meet Simona and to be alone with her in a garden: "Pasquino disse alla Simona che del tutto egli voleva che ella trovasse modo di poter venire *a un giardino,* là dove egli menar la voleva, acciò che quivi più a agio e con men sospetto potessero essere insieme" (IV 7,10). He eventually succeeds in his desire: "La Simona . . . *al giardino* statole da Pasquino insegnato se n'andò, dove lui . . . trovò; e . . . a far de' lor piaceri *in una parte del giardin* si raccolsero . . ." (IV 7,11). Up to this point, the *locus amoenus* has provided the background for the fulfillment of love between the two young people. The introduction of a particular element of that garden, "un grandissimo e bel cesto di salvia," (like the roses in the previous *novella*) indicates a change in narrative tone—a change from idyllic to tragic, from love to death:

> Pasquino, al gran cesto della salvia rivolto, di quella colse una foglia e con essa s'incominciò a stropicciare i

> denti e le gengie . . . E poi che così alquanto fregati gli
> ebbe . . . egli s'incominciò tutto nel viso a cambiare,
> e appresso . . . perdè la vista e la parola e in brieve egli
> si morì.
>
> (IV 7,12-13)

Here death is introduced through the *cesto della salvia*.[35] With the death of one of the lovers, aggression by outside society against the other occurs, this time within the garden itself. The first agents of aggression against Simona are Pasquino's friends who twice accuse her of poisoning her lover:

> 'Ahi malvagia femina, tu l'hai avvelenato!' E fatto il
> romor grande, fu da molti che vicini al giardino
> abitavan sentito . . . e . . . fu reputato da tutti che così
> fosse come lo Stramba diceva.
>   Per la qual cosa presola, piagnendo ella sempre
> forte, al palagio del podestà fu menata. Quivi, pron-
> tando lo Stramba e l'Atticiato e 'l Malagevole, compagni
> di Pasquino che sopravenuti erano, un giudice, senza dare
> indugio alla cosa, si mise ad essaminarla del fatto . . .
>
> (IV 7,15-16)

Aggression against the helpless Simona mounts through the impetus of people both aquainted with and unknown to her. Only the judge, as representative of authority, acts objectively to carry out justice:

> . . . non potendo comprendere costei in questa cosa
> avere operata malizia né esser colpevole, volle, lei
> presente, vedere il morto corpo e il luogo e 'l modo da
> lei raccontatogli, per ciò che per le parole di lei nol
> comprendeva assai bene. Fattola adunque senza alcun
> tumulto colà menare dove ancora il corpo di Pasquino
> giaceva gonfiato come una botte, e egli appresso
> andatovi, maravigliatosi del morto, lei domandò come
> stato era.
>
> (IV 7,16-17)

The judge's sense of justice cannot save Simona from the punishment, however unjust, demanded by an aggressive society of outsiders: "niuna altra cosa per lor domandandosi se non che il fuoco fosse di così fatta malvagità punitore" (IV 7,18). Thus Simona must prove her innocence by repeating the fatal actions of Pasquino: "una di quelle foglie di salvia fregatasi a' denti . . . in quel medesimo accidente cadde che prima caduto era Pasquino . . ." (IV 7,17-18). In the same garden where she previously found love, Simona is freed from society's accusations through death. The garden is thus not only linked with love and death of one of the lovers, as in IV 6, but it also serves as the setting for society's aggression against the remaining lover and for the inefficacy of justice. Eventually it is the scene of Simona's death, too. This *novella*, therefore, presents an even bleaker view of the interaction of individual and society than did the previous tale. While in IV 6, Andreuola withdrew to a convent of her own will, here Simona must die before her innocence and love are accepted as genuine. Only after death are she and her lover reunited with their society: "Pasquin cattivello . . . insieme con la sua Simona, così enfiati com'erano, dallo Stramba e dall'Atticciato e da Guccio Imbratta e dal Malagevole furono nella chiesa di San Paolo sepelliti, della quale per avventura erano popolani" (IV 7,23-24). The individual — and especially a lower-class individual — who has privately controlled his own affairs on his own terms, without asking for the approval of society, becomes the victim of that society. Only through imposing personal justice — in this case, death — can he achieve a certain form of approval from society. The garden, then, both provides a background for the themes of the story — love, death, aggression, and final justice — and suggests the opposition between the private world of the individual in love and the outside society. Because it does not conform to social rules and pressures, the private world must suffer at the hands of a hostile society. In both IV 6 and IV 7, the garden as backdrop for drama anticipates a sudden, ruinous event which brings the narrative to a tragic conclusion.

In the *novella* of Ghismonda, *giardino* and *grotta* suggest two worlds in conflict; their clash brings violence and death to Guiscardo and Ghismonda. Their relationship lies outside the accepted rules of Tancredi's feudal court, and therefore must be brutally punished. The *loco naturale* in the Fourth Day thus implies an act of violence — here Guiscardo's seizure and brutal murder — which is perpetrated to vindicate the original act of social rebellion — Ghismonda's involvement with her social inferior. Similarly, in the *novelle* just discussed (IV 6 and 7), as well as in several others of this day, certain members of a well-established social hierarchy feel threatened by the discovery of a situation which deviates from those social laws by which they must abide in order to survive. Once they discover this socially unacceptable situation, these representatives of society are compelled to eradicate the imbalance by any means necessary.

In IV 5, Lisabetta's brothers seek out the natural environment as a place to rectify her social breech, for society's laws are least felt there. Enraged by Lisabetta's affair with her social inferior, Lorenzo, her brothers find a "luogo molto solitario e rimoto" and murder him. While the love scenes in this *novella* take place inside Lisabetta's home, the natural background is used to emphasize the brothers' foul aggression against Lorenzo:

> sembianti faccendo d'andare fuori della città a diletto
> tutti e tre, seco menaron Lorenzo; e pervenuti in *un
> luogo molto solitario e rimoto*, veggendosi il destro,

> Lorenzo, che di ciò niuna guardia prendeva, uccisono e sotterrarono in guisa che niuna persona se n'accorse.
> (IV 5,8)

The same *luogo* reappears two times in the narrative: first in Lisabetta's dream, pointed out by Lorenzo's ghost — "E disegnatole *il luogo* dove sotterato l'aveano . . . disparve" (IV 5,13), and again when she visits the place: "e tolte via foglie secche che *nel luogo* erano, dove men dura le parve la terra quivi cavò; né ebbe guari cavato, che ella trovò il corpo del suo misero amante . . ." (IV 5,15). The *loco naturale* is thus strictly connected with violence, death, and sorrow. These last two connotations are amplified with the introduction of another natural element, the "bellissimo bassilico salernetano" planted by Lisabetta in the same pot in which she has buried Lorenzo's head. This macabre combination of natural and human elements again stresses the strict correlation between the natural background and a solitary existence. Here the *basilico* represents Lisabetta's decision to spend her whole life in devoted mourning for her beloved Lorenzo:

> E per usanza aveva preso di sedersi sempre a questo testo vicina e quello con tutto il suo disidero vagheggiare, sì come quello che il suo Lorenzo teneva nascoso: e poi che molto vagheggiato l'avea, sopr'esso andatasene cominciava a piangere, e per lungo spazio, tanto che tutto il basilico bagnava, piagnea.
> (IV 5,18)

The final act of violence perpetrated by Lisabetta's brothers against her is the removal of her "testo di bassilico [sic]";[36] Lisabetta is deprived of her last reason for existence, and through her own choice, "piagnendo si morì" (IV 5,23). Once more, the lonely, defenseless individual is victimized by society's violence, and she escapes that violence by retreating into a private world which can only lead her to death. As in other *novelle* of Day IV, the private world is symbolized by an image from nature (the *basilico*) whose destruction or disappearance signifies the defeat and destruction of the individual. In this *novella* as in the *novella* of Ghismonda, aggression against a self-reliant individual is performed by members of her own family.

This same pattern is repeated in the story of Gerbino (IV 4). Gerbino's self-imposed justice based on the laws of his noble love is countered by an act of royal "justice" performed by his grandfather, the king, who punishes Gerbino's civil disobedience with death. Here the natural element which serves as backdrop for Gerbino's actions is the sea, which, as noted in Day II, underscores with its fluctuations the alternating hopes and disappointments of the lovers. The girl's death and burial on the island of Ustica is followed quickly by the act of royal justice in Palermo which results in Gerbino's death:

> . . . il re Guiglielmo turbato forte, né vedendo via da

> poter lor giustizia negare, ché la dimandavano, fece
> prendere il Gerbino; e egli medesimo, non essendo
> alcun de' baron suoi che con prieghi da ciò si sforzasse di
> rimuoverlo, il condannò nella testa e in sua presenzia
> gliele fece tagliare, volendo avanti senza nepote
> rimanere che esser tenuto re senza fede.
>
> (IV 4,26)

The sea suggests Gerbino's personal form of justice, a justice founded on love, which tragically causes the death of his lady. The city of Palermo, instead, represents the more general and impersonal form of justice which destroys any socially unacceptable act of individual rebellion.

A similar attempt to repress the personal right to love is seen in the *novella* of Rossiglione and Guardastagno (IV 9), where a husband murders his wife's lover in unchivalric ambush and feeds her his heart.[37] The action of the *novella* proceeds according to courtly laws of loyalty and love. The theme of friendship and unity dominates the tone of the narrative in its first sequence, where the analogical relationship of the two knights eventually becomes homological:

> . . . in Provenza furon già due nobili cavalieri, de' quali
> ciascuno e castella e vassalli aveva sotto di sè; e aveva
> l'un nome messer Guiglielmo Rossiglione e l'altro messer
> Guiglielmo Guardastagno. E perciò che l'uno e l'altro
> era prod'uomo molto nell'arme, s'armavano assai e in
> costume avean d'andar sempre a ogni torneamento o
> giostra o altro fatto d'arme insieme e vestiti d'una assisa.
>
> (IV 9,4-5)

The linguistic texture of this passage defines the motif of unity by means of sentence constructions and figurative devices that stress parallelism and harmony while eliminating differentiation and plurality.[39] The use of hyperbaton arranges the phrase "de' quali ciascuno e castella e vassalli aveva sotto di sé" so that the elements of plurality "castella e vassalli" are contentrated in the middle of the sentence — the weakest part — and are preceded by a singular subject "ciascuno" and followed by a singular verb "aveva." Further, polysyndeton links the plural elements in a harmonious parallel construction that emphasizes Rossiglione and Guardastagno's equality in possessing "e castella e vassalli." The similarity of the two men is emphasized still further through the repetition of similar sounds in each succeeding pair of words: *ciascuno-castella; vassalli-aveva; sotto-sé*. This pattern continues in the next sentence, which has as its subject the communal "l'uno e l'altro," in contrast to the previous "ciascuno."

The two knights are thus fused through the use of a singular verb which stresses their common sentiment and action. An even more striking parallel is seen in their shared name: Guiglielmo. This detail, not found in any of the possible sources of the *novella*,[39] merges the identities of the two friends to such an extent that it becomes nearly impossible to conceive of the two as single individuals. Moreover, their full names, besides being equal in syllables, are rhythmically identical, each representing a *cursus trispondaicus*: Guiglielmo Rossiglione, Guiglielmo Guardastagno. With "insieme e vestiti d'una assisa," the passage closes on a final note of fraternal unity which extends the identity of the two friends from the linguistic realm to the physical. The term *una*, echoing the previous *insieme*, is the key word of the clause, suppressing any notion of plurality and culminating in the fusion of the identities of the two men. Thus this brief passage forcefully presents the motif of unity—a matter of no small consequence since this motif forms a basis for the dynamics of the whole *novella* and paradoxically brings about its tragic conflict. Indeed, all the passions in this tragic story can be traced back to the original state of unity. Specifically, the unity motif gives rise to love, for it follows that as soon as the identity of the two men has been established, the woman's affection for the one will inevitably draw her to the other. Hate is catalyzed, in turn, by the loss of identity of the two knights: when Rossiglione becomes aware of the love between his wife and Guardastagno, he asserts his individuality as a jealous husband, thus distinguishing himself from the other man through a new emotional response. Rossiglione's hate grows in direct proportion to the love he previously felt for Guardastagno, and thus his feelings of friendship are nullified. The distance is short from hate to murder, and Rossiglione inevitably commits the brutal act. Guardastagno, on the other hand, is never aware of his loss of identity with Rossiglione. His actions and feelings remain as they were during the first narrative moment, and his passive role in the narrative proceeds from this ignorance. The woman's suicide and Rossiglione's ultimate isolation result from their eventual recognition of disunity.

The *loco naturale* of the forest, "forse un miglio del suo castello" (IV 9, 10), provides the background for Rossiglione's murder of Guardastagno, as well as for the mutilation of his dead body: "Il Rossiglione, smontato, con un coltello il petto del Guardastagno aprì e con le proprie mani il cuor gli trasse. . ." (IV 9, 13). The natural background of the forest heightens the savagery and violence of Rossiglione's attack against his dearest friend—a knight who chose to live by the code of courtly love.

From the previous considerations we may draw the following conclusions about the function of the garden or *loco naturale* in the *novelle* of the Fourth Day:

1) The garden, or *locus amoenus*, may be the narrative correspondent of love and/or the fulfillment of love, and in this sense, it has positive connotations: the *grotta* is the means by which Guiscardo reaches Ghismonda's room, where the two can fulfill their love (IV 1), Frate Alberto's "paradiso" is "uno de' più dilettevoli luoghi che fosse mai. . . tra tanti fiori e tante rose. . ." (IV 2), the *giardino*

is the site of rendezvous for Andreuola and Gabriotto's amorous encounters (IV 6), and it is the only place where Simona and Pasquino can meet and fulfill their love (IV 7). In all these cases, natural enclosures reflect love on an individual basis, beyond society's limits. Through their precisely described boundaries, they suggest a secluded relationship removed from the laws of the urban or courtly world to which the individual belongs as a social being.

2) In a second moment, the *loco naturale* becomes the narrative correspondent of aggression and/or destruction: the *grotta* becomes a trap for Guiscardo, where he is subjected to violence and imprisonment, and the *giardino* now represents the courtly society from which the two lovers are excluded once their secret relationship is discovered (IV 1); the beautiful garden with "molte rose bianche e vermiglie" becomes the scene of Gabriotto's sudden death (IV 7); the sage bush is the instrument of violent and disfiguring death for both Simona and Pasquino.

3) In yet other situations, the natural environment is treated only negatively, and functions exclusively as the objective correlative of violence and death: Lorenzo's murder occurs in the "luogo molto solitario e rimoto" (IV 5); Gerbino attempts to capture his beloved at sea and causes her death (IV 4); and Guardastagno is murdered in the *bosco* (IV 9). In its negative roles the *loco naturale* becomes the narrative correspondent for the retaliation of a violent society against individuals who tried to isolate themselves and ignored its laws. Thus its function in this day is understandably ambiguous, suggesting at once the individual's need to obey his own sense of justice and moral law and his duty to obey the laws and mores imposed by the society in which he lives.

In conclusion, the Fourth Day conveys a rather complex view of the Decameronian world. Human resourcefulness and awareness, qualities shared by the day's most able characters—Ghismonda, Gerbino, Andreuola, Girolamo, and the wife of Rossiglione—are still highly valued. And yet, even such capable individuals cannot stem the inevitable tragedies which undo them. Love is seen as a powerful force that the individual willingly accepts in order to create a natural and authentic relationship with another human being. Yet the lovers of this day are constantly faced with violence, death and/or isolation when their affairs come into conflict with society's rigid behavioral codes. The complexity of human relationships in this day suggests that caution must be exercised in matters of love and social interaction; that above all, lovers should beware of shutting themselves off from society at large. The dynamic interaction of individuals with their social environments will be of primary concern in the *novelle* of Day V and of each of the following days.

6. Day V: Love, Nature, and Society: Towards a Harmonious Solution

In Day V, the individual still finds himself involved in personal affairs which are at odds with a complex and limiting social structure around him. Here, however, contrary to Day IV, the individual manages to control his own situation and creates ways to communicate with his society, thus building up connections which allow for mutual final acceptance and understanding. The individual is able to fulfill his needs, and yet he acknowledges his duties towards the laws of his society which, in turn, accepts his right to personal experience and freedom.

The topic of the Fifth Day's *novelle* contrasts with that of the Fourth, which was based upon "coloro li cui amori ebbero *infelice fine*" (III Conclusion, 6). Fiammetta, in accepting her nomination as queen of the day, makes pointed reference to the change in tone:

> "Filostrato, e io la prendo volentieri; e acciò che meglio t'aveggi di quel che fatto hai, infino a ora voglio e comando che ciascun s'apparecchi di dover doman ragionare di ciò che a alcuno amante, dopo alcuni fieri o sventurati accidenti, *felicemente avvenisse'*."
>
> (IV Conclusion, 5-6)

With the substitution of Fiammetta's "felicemente avvenisse" for Filostrato's "infelice fine," the action of each *novella* of the Fifth Day proceeds to the happy ending so outspokenly solicited by the new queen. The similar closing statements of the *novelle* create a repetitive pattern as each *novellatore* carefully spells out the marriage vows and everlasting happiness that constitute the ideal resolution of his or her tale.[40] Such happiness is not easily attained, however, for each of the protagonists undergoes ordeals and afflictions in the course of his or her quest for fulfilled love.

The social milieu of the characters is usually of the high (V 1,3,4,6,7,8, and 9) or middle class (V 2,5, and 10) in a late *Duecento*-early *Trecento* historical context (V 1 and 7 are the only exceptions). The setting varies in each *novella*: a southern environment appears with the Mediterranean islands of Cyprus and Rhodes in V 1 and Lipari in V 2; we move north to Rome in V 3, and to Romagna in V 4 and 5; back south again to Ischia in V 6 and Trapani in V 7, only to set out north again to Romagna in V 8, Florence in V 9, and Perugia in V 10.

As in the Fourth Day, narrative action derives from the threat posed to a love affair by societal or other extrinsic forces. Here, however, lovers seem to have the power to reverse their ill fortunes and achieve not only personal happiness but society's recognition and acceptance. In most cases, protagonists depart from their familiar environments to conduct quest-like adventures in unfamiliar and often hostile surroundings. Thus, contrary to Day IV and reminiscent of Day III—the spatial framework within each *novella* is constantly subject to change, usually through a move from urban to natural environments. Shifts in location allow characters to use their new surroundings to eliminate obstacles that hinder their quest for fulfilled love. In many *novelle*, such shifts between urban and natural environments underscore changes in the relationships between individuals and society.

In this day, both city and country settings present an initial condition of social or personal uneasiness. Such is the case for Cimone (V 1), who is banned from the city and sent to the *contado* because of his uncouthness; for Pietro and Agnolella (V 3), who leave Rome because of familial opposition to their love and find themselves in the violent world of the forest; for Reparata, who is kidnapped from her home town and is imprisoned in the King of Sicily's "case bellissime d'un suo giardino," called "la Cuba" (V 6); for Nastagio degli Onesti, who leaves an unhappy city life to retire near the *pigneta* of Chiassi, where he witnesses a terrifying *caccia infernale* (V 8); or for Federigo degli Alberighi, who because of his inability to "essere cittadino" any longer, must leave Florence and retire to his "poderetto piccolo" (V 9).

After these negative moments, however, the experience undergone in the natural environment produces a positive resolution for each adventure. In Cimone's case, for instance, the *villa* or *contado* to which he is relegated by his father at first represents a form of existence inferior to that in the city:

> gli comandò che *alla villa n'andasse* e quivi co' suoi lavoratori si dimorasse; la qual cosa a Cimone fu carissima, *per ciò che i costumi e l'usanza degli uomini grossi gli eran più a grado che le cittadine.*
>
> (V 1,5)

On the other hand, the city in this first narrative moment is seen as a center of courtesy, refinement, and nobility from which Cimone is ostracized because of his uncouth and gross nature. The *villa* implicitly is the suitable location for one so little civilized. Cimone, however, soon finds himself in a *locus amoenus*, amidst "un boschetto bellissimo" with "un pratello d'altissimi alberi circuito . . . nell'un dei canti del quale era una bellissima fontana e fredda" (V 1, 6-7). In the midst of this perfected natural world, a sudden apparition of feminine grace and beauty strikes Cimone's sight and awakens his dormant intellect:

> La quale come Cimon vide, non altramenti che se mai più forma di femina veduta non avesse, fermatosi sopra il suo bastone, senza dire alcuna cosa, con ammirazion grandissima la incominciò intentissimo a riguardare; e

> *nel rozzo petto, nel quale per mille ammaestramenti non era alcuna impressione di cittadinesco piacere potuta entrare*, sentì destarsi un pensiero il quale nella materiale e grossa mente gli ragionava costei essere la più bella cosa che già mai per alcun vivente veduta fosse.
>
> (V 1,8)

Beauty, viewed in a natural background, performs the miracle of love on the uncouth young man, with the *locus amoenus* playing an essential role in his transformation. Cimone's love for Efigenia, born amidst perfected nature, compels his metamorphosis from a *uom selvatico*—worth only of life in *villa*—to a civilized human being who returns to the city longing for culture, conversation, and recognition—and achieves them all:

> Essendo adunque a Cimone nel cuore, nel quale niuna dottrina era potuta entrare, entrata la saetta d'Amore . . . in brevissimo tempo, d'uno in altro pensiero pervenendo, fece maravigliare il padre e tutti i suoi e ciascuno altro che il conoscea . . . con grandissima ammirazione d'ognuno, in assai brieve spazio di tempo non solamente le prime lettere apparò, ma valorosissimo tra' filosofanti divenne . . . E in brieve . . . egli riuscì il più leggiadro e il meglio costumato e con più particulari virtù che altro giovane alcuno che nell'isola fosse di Cipri.
>
> (V 1, 16-20)

With Cimone's return to the city, the first narrative sequence is complete; he moves away from and back to the city through his experience in the natural world. While the city maintains its positive connotation of refined and noble existence, the country is seen in two lights: first as the seat of gross and unrefined life; then as the perfected *locus amoenus* where Cimone's enlightenment begins. Nature, as a composite image, would seem to represent the life experiences which allow an individual to discover himself.

In the second part of the narrative, Cimone again moves away from and then returns to Cyprus, now playing an extremely active role in his pursuit of Efigenia. The sea replaces the *villa* as natural setting for Cimone's adventures, and, as in Day II, its movement underscores the vicissitudes of his fortunes. Cimone pursues Efigenia at sea, wins her in battle, and, by a stroke of ill luck, loses her and is taken prisoner in Rhodes. Rhodes as an urban center is seen in an ambiguous light: where Cyprus is home of all that is civilized and refined, it is in Rhodes that Cimone, paragon of all Cyprian virtues, is imprisoned and sentenced to death. Furthermore, it is the traitorous Rhodian, Lisimaco, who is primarily responsible for planning the kidnapping of Efigenia and Cassandra.

The kidnapping turns a wedding feast into a blood bath and presents a final vision of Rhodes "piena . . . di sangue, di romore e di pianto e di tristizia" (V 1, 69). In this second part of the *novella*, the city plays an ambiguous role and seems to suggest the dangers inherent in the uncontrolled individual will bent on fulfilling its own desires in total disregard for social restraints.

This second movement relates the *novella* to the basic dramatic conflict of the previous day—individual versus society. In Day IV the individual became the victim of a repressive society which he had tried to ignore or defy. In Cimone's case, we find the same basic contrast between individual and society, but with a subtle twist: Cimone attacks and severely damages a *foreign* hostile environment in order to accomplish his ends and he eventually succeeds. The careful emphasis on Cimone's everexpanding list of accomplishments, his idealized refinement and seeming perfection, create a wholly positive view of the character, thus foreshadowing his ultimate achievements. Our predisposition to admire Cimone, Lisimaco's presence as the true "heavy" of the piece, Cimone's foreign origin, and his desire to win the woman who initiated his spiritual rebirth, all seem to mitigate his culpability in committing violence against an unfamiliar society which seeks to deny him love.

At the same time, the role played by Efigenia is essential to the positive outcome of the lovers' fortunes and to their eventual reintegration into Cyprian society. Contrary to the lady lovers of the Fourth Day, Efigenia follows the dictates of her society and opposes Cimone's self-oriented love. She is thus the link between Cimone and the society he seeks to defy. On the one hand, she is the exclusive object of Cimone's asocial desires; on the other, she represents the social order in her devoted commitment to her family's will. She thus foreshadows the other heroines of this and the following days who are much more socially concerned than their counterparts in the Fourth Day.

The *novella* of Pietro and Agnolella (V 3) develops in a pattern similar to V 1, but, with its more compressed time span—one day, one night, and the following morning—dramatizes its action at a high level of narrative intensity. Day, night, and early morning, in fact, alternate to accentuate the three basic narrative moments of the story: 1) escape from family and city, separation and aimless wandering in the forest; 2) danger of death in the forest; 3) denouement and reunion in the castle at the rim of the forest. In the early morning of the first day, the lovers leave Rome, "coda . . . del mondo," and enter the countryside a few miles from the city. There they become separated and wander about the forest in fruitless pursuit of each other from midday to sunset. The narrative tone of this first movement is a composite one deriving from the different experiences of the protagonists: their happiness at being together; fear of pursuit by relatives and friends; anxiety over the threat to Pietro's life at the hands of the *fanti*, and anxious sorrow at being separated. Night brings an even darker mood with its terrifying ordeals for each of the lovers. Only in the early morning of the next day do relief and assistance ease the night's woes as the lovers arrive separately at the Orsini castle on the forest's outer edge. This circadean cycle from one morning to the next brings with it a complete cycle in the moods of the two protagonists: from happiness slightly marred by fear, through fear and anxiety to sorrow, and finally to complete happiness. These emotions correspond to their adventures from an initial moment of togetherness away from antagonistic society, through separation and isolation, to a final reunion within a favorable environment.

The narrative sequences conveying the separate adventures of the lovers in the forest alternate in an "ad incastro" pattern.[41] When a group of armed soldiers falls upon them, Agnolella takes to flight and disappears in the forest while Pietro is taken prisoner. The narrative follows Pietro's adventures from the time when, having regained his freedom, he searches through the forest for Agnolella without success and ends up lost in the "selva":

> Andò adunque questo Pietro sventurato tutto il giorno per questa selva gridando e chiamando, a tal ora tornando indietro che egli si credeva innanzi andare; e già, tra per lo gridare e per lo piagnere e per la paura e per lo lungo digiuno, era sì vinto, che più avanti non poteva. E vedendo la notte sopravenuta . . . trovata una grandissima quercia . . . sù vi montò . . .
> (V 3, 17-18)

At this point the narrative takes up Agnolella's adventures, stepping back to the time of her narrow escape from the band of soldiers: "La giovane fuggendo, come davanti dicemmo . . ." (V 3,20). She wanders at length in the forest, finds refuge for the night in a poor hut where she miraculously escapes rape and death, and in the morning is led to the Orsini castle. The continuation of Pietro's adventures follows then from the time he climbed the tree, through his terrifying night, hunted by wolves and tortured by bitter cold and fear, to his encounter with the shepherds the next morning, and finally to his reunion with Agnolella at the Orsini castle. With the "ad incastro" technique, the suspense of the story is intensified: one character's terrifying adventures in the forest intimate that equally frightening experiences are in the making for the other. We therefore, as audience and readers, have a double reaction to each narrative sequence: one in response to a character's actual experience, and one in response to what is foreseen and feared.

The natural background plays an intriguing role in this *novella*, since most of the narrative action takes place in the "selva," a fictional element which, while it usually symbolizes evil, here represents the dangers an individual must face when isolated from his own society. When attacked by armed men, Agnolella runs away "verso una selva grandissima" and loses her way there:

> La giovane fuggendo . . . non sappiendo dove andarsi . .
> . si mise tanto *fralla selva,* che ella non poteva vedere il
> luogo donde in quella entrata era: per che . . . tutto il dì,
> ora aspettando e ora andando e piagnendo e chiamando
> e della sua sciagura dolendosi, *per lo salvatico luogo*
> s'andò *avvolgendo"*
>
> (V 3,20)

The "selva" clearly presents total solitude, confusion, fear, and sorrow. The expressions "si mise tanto *fralla* selva" and "per lo salvatico luogo s'andò *avvolgendo"* suggest the closure that the "selva" brings to the isolated human being entangled there. Pietro encounters a similar plight. When free of his abductors, he tries unsuccessfully to trace Agnolella's whereabouts, and eventually he too loses his way in the "selva":

> Ma non vedendo *per la selva* né via né sentiero, né
> pedata di caval conoscendovi . . . non ritrovando la sua
> giovane, più doloroso che altro uomo cominciò a
> piagnere e a andarla or qua or là *per la selva* chiaman-
> do; ma niuna persona gli rispondeva, e esso non ardiva
> a tornare adietro e andando innanzi non conosceva
> dove arrivar si dovesse; e d'altra parte delle fiere che
> nelle selve sogliono abitare aveva a un'ora di se stesso
> paura e della sua giovane, la qual tuttavia gli pareva
> vedere o da orso o da lupo strangolare.
>
> (V 3, 15-16)

In Pietro's case, the "selva" brings not only the confusion and sorrow Agnolella experienced, but adds, with the "fiere," implications of violence and death. These eventually materialize in the wolves' deadly attack on Pietro's "ronzino" and in Agnolella's close escape from the "gran brigata di malvagi uomini" (V 3,32).

Only at dawn, the time usually associated with regeneration and rebirth, are the evils of the forest conquered. Both young people find a hospitable environment in the castle on the outskirts of the "selva." In this *novella* the natural setting of the "selva" suggests the dangers and evils that an individual may face when he severs all ties from society and must rely wholly upon his own resources. Both Agnolella and Pietro demonstrate their potential for survival by successfully facing the different situations which confront them at the end of their first day in the "selva": Pietro decides to spend the night in a tree out of reach of wolves and other wild animals, and Agnolella quickly hides in the hay from the "malvagi uomini" who attack the hut where she is spending the night. Thus these two individuals, by conquering confusion and fear and by foreseeing and thus escaping violence and death, are able to counter the evils of the forest and to reach the castle where they are reunited in a secure environment. The castle would then seem to represent the power of the social self which succeeds in effectively eliminating the "selva"'s negative influences. The return to the city after experiencing forest and castle suggests the need for an individual to return to his own society in order to exercise his newly acquired personal and social skills. skills.

A similar view of the challenge confronting an individual in a natural background and its effects on his personal and social situation can be found in another story of the same day, that of Nastagio degli Onesti in the "pigneta" near Ravenna (V 8).[42] Here too, the city appears at the beginning of the narrative and plays an important role in the protagonist's plight. Despite his nobility and wealth, Nastagio is miserable. His passionate love for a girl from the even wealthier Traversari family is unreciprocated. His unhappiness is unbearable, and leads him to suicidal tendencies: "La qual cosa era tanto a Nastagio gravosa a comportare, che per dolore più volte dopo essersi doluto gli venne in disidero d'uccidersi" (V 8,7). Departure from the city seems the only remedy for his situation. The place chosen for his self-imposed exile is just on the outskirts of the pine forest near Chiassi: un luogo fuor di Ravenna forse tre miglia, che si chiama Chiassi" (V 8,10). This pine forest recalls the well-known Dantesque "pineta in sul lito di Chiassi" (Purgatorio XXVIII,20) to which Dante compares the Garden of Eden at the top of Purgatory, "la divina foresta spessa e viva" (Purgatorio, XXVIII,21). Nastagio's forest, then, through its connection with Dante's text, suggest the potential for spiritual regeneration. On the other hand, as a forest, it also carries those negative connotations associated with the *selva* in V 3. The development of the narrative against the backdrop of this "pigneta" confirms both its negative and positive inferences conveyed at this point of the story.

Nastagio's first walk in the "pigneta" is described in these terms:

> Ora avvenne che, venendo quasi all'entrata di maggio . . . piede innanzi piè se medesimo *trasportò* pensando infino *nella pigneta.* Ed essendo già passata presso che la quinta ora del giorno e esso bene un mezzo miglio per *la pigneta* entrato, non ricordandosi di mangiare né d'altra cosa . . .
>
> (V 8, 13-14)

The visionary mood of Nastagio's early morning walk into the forest in the spring and on a Friday, as the protagonist of the *caccia infernale* remarks, is a perfect combination of classical and Christian symbology which suggests a spiritually regenerative quest. Again Dante's experience in Purgatory is called to mind by the motif of the slow walk taken into the forest: "Già m'avean trasportato i lenti passi/dentro alla selva antica . . ." (Purgatorio XXVIII,22-23). The relationship between Nastagio's "pigneta" and Dante's "selva antica" is underlined by the use of the verb "trasportare" in both passages. This beatific mood created by the implied reference to the Earthly Paradise changes when the narrative focuses on a smaller section of the "pigneta," "un boschetto assai folto d'albuscelli e di pruni" (V 8,15), where Nastagio:

> vide venire . . . correndo verso il luogo dove egli era, una bellissima giovane ignuda, scapigliata e tutta graffiata dalle frasche e da' pruni, piagnendo e gridando forte mercè; e . . . a' fianchi due grandi e fieri mastini, li quali duramente . . . la mordevano; e . . . sopra un corsier nero un cavalier bruno, forte nel viso crucciato, con uno stocco in mano, lei di morte con parole spaventevoli e villane minacciando.
>
> (V 8, 15-16)

The scene's violence reaches its climax with the killing, dismemberment, and reconstitution of the young woman's body before Nastagio's appalled eyes. The connotation of evil and death frequently linked with the image of the forest is amply exploited by this dramatic *caccia infernale*, which symbolizes the violence of hate, the physical dangers of love, and the constant threat of death. At the same time, more Dantesque references surface to create a parallel between the "boschetto assai folto d'albuscelli e di pruni" and the "dolorosa selva" of Dante's suicide victims in Inferno XIII. There Dante breaks off "un ramicel da un gran pruno" and later witnesses the flight of "due . . . nudi e graffiati" from "nere cagne, bramose e correnti" who later dismember one of the two escapees. These obvious references to Dante's episode add a spiritual dimension to the dangers of unbridled love and suggest the spiritual peril of the brokenhearted Nastagio's suicidal tendencies. And yet, the positive connotation of the reference to the Garden of Eden at the beginning of the forest scene suggests a satisfactory outcome for Nastagio's experiences in the "pigneta." Nastagio, in fact shows his "resourcefulness" by turning the infernal hunting scene to his own advantage. He invites a large group of his Ravenna friends and social equals (including his cruel lady and her family) to dine at a banquet in that same spot in the *pigneta*. There they take part in his clever plan to convince the "donna amata" to reciprocate his love. In this new context, the repetition of the infernal hunt loses much of its violent impact and conveys instead the theme of regenerative love which counteracts death and infernal suffering. The second performance of the "caccia infernale" employs an obvious *travestissement* device to equate the participants in the infernal hunt with Nastagio and his company: the "cavalier bruno" is a projection of Nastagio, and the "bellissima giovane, ignuda e scapigliata" a projection of the girl he loves. It is the unsubtle suggestion of similar fates for the "bellissima giovane" and the Travesari girl that brings a happy ending to Nastagio's amorous adventures.

The sources of this *novella* contain no mention of a forest either in supposed direct influences, such as Vincent de Beauvais' *Speculum Historiale* or the *Alphabetum Narrationum*, or in the analogous episode in Jacopo Passavanti's *Specchio di Vera Penitenza*, a work contemporary to the *Decameron*. The presence of the forest exclusively in the Decameronian version of the story, where it is the setting for both hero's enlightenment and the transformation of suffering and death into personal satisfaction and love, throws a significant light on the role of the natural world in this work. The forest, as in the *novella* of Pietro and Agnolella, is again strictly connected with the experience of an isolated individual who must prove himself in a hostile environment and must rely wholly on his own resources to do so.

Nastagio's banquet brings together two of the most powerful forces controlling an individual's existence: 1) the city society, with its rules and traditions which tend to absorb the individual into his/her social group, and 2) the isolated natural environment which, with its inherent dangers, challenges an individual's strength and self-sufficiency. By planning the banquet in the forest, Nastagio succeeds in overcoming the dangers to be found in nature. At the same time, he makes his urban society aware of the forest's perilous incidents. By doing so, he also arouses fear in his recalcitrant woman, the only element of his society still alien and contrary to him and to love, and through fear he brings her to accept the traditional social order of matrimony.

Because Nastagio succeeds in transforming the dangerous world of nature to his own advantage, his experience in the forest is different from either Pietro's or Cimone's. Both of these characters faced a menacing natural environment, but, although they offered valid resistance, they were unable to conquer it. Rather, they had to abandon it in order to derive value from the strength and intelligence which allowed them to survive.

The dangers that Nastagio overcomes in the forest, because of their Dantesque references, appear to be spiritual rather than physical. Nastagio then goes one step beyond Pietro and Cimone: he succeeds not only in turning these dangers to his own advantage within the forest itself, and in fulfilling his quest for love, but he also learns a moral lesson on the spiritual dangers of suicide.

The *novella* of Federigo degli Alberighi (V 9)[43] provides a comparable, although slightly dissimilar, treatment of city and countryside. As in the preceding *novella*, the city plays a primary role and is introduced at the beginning of the story. The close ties between the splendid traditions of the Florentine past and the noble and chivalrous character of Federigo are suggested by Fiammetta, the narrator of the story, at the outset:

> in Firenze fu già un giovane, chiamato Federigo di messer Filippo Alberighi, *in opera d'arme e in cortesia pregiato* sopra ogni altro *donzel* di Toscana.
> (V 9,5)

Federigo, who lives wholly by the dictates of courtly love, is a prime representative of the chivalric way of life:

> Il quale, sì come il più de' gentili uomini avviene, d'una gentil donna chiamata monna Giovanna s'innamorò . . . e acciò che egli l'amor di lei acquistar potesse, giostrava, armeggiava, faceva feste e donava, e il suo senza alcuno ritegno spendeva . . .
>
> (V 9,6)

Monna Giovanna is, on the other hand, solidly entrenched in the rich, bourgeois family tradition of communal Florence, as her chaste response to Federigo's advances would indicate: "ma ella, non meno onesta che bella, niente di queste cose per lei fatte né di colui si curava che le faceva" (V 9,6).

Federigo must go from the city to the *contado* when, having pressed his courtly values — which are in direct opposition to monna Giovanna's — to their limit, he depletes his entire fortune and can no longer afford to live in Florence as a "cittadino":

> Spendendo adunque Federigo oltre a ogni suo potere molto e niente acquistando . . . le ricchezze mancarono e esso rimase povero, senza altra cosa che un suo poderetto piccolo essergli rimasa . . . e oltre a questo un suo falcone de' miglior del mondo. Per che, amando più che mai *né parendogli più potere essere cittadino come disiderava,* a Campi, là dove il suo poderetto era, se n'andò a stare.
>
> (V 9,7-8)

When Federigo leaves the city and monna Giovanna remains there, secure in her family position and financial ease, the city seems to be a place in which nobility without riches cannot survive. But Federigo's nobility outlasts his departure from the city, and in symbolic form is present *in contado* in the image of his beloved falcon: "Quivi, quando poteva uccellando e senza alcuna persona richiedere, pazientemente la sua povertà comportava" (V 9,8). Later, monna Giovanna also loses her position in the city when her husband, the central element of her solid family life, "infermò e . . . morissi" (V 9,9). She too then exits from the city and retires with her son "in contado" for the summer: "con questo suo figliuolo se n'andava in contado a una sua possessione assai vicina a quella di Federigo" (V 9,10). The child is the symbol of monna Giovanna's family-centered existence: "la madre . . . come colei che più no' n'avea e lui amava quanto più si poteva" (V 9,12). He is the center of her life in the same way that the falcon is the center of Federigo's. A strange bond develops between the child and the falcon against the backdrop of the *contado:* "questo garzoncello . . . avendo veduto molte volte il falcon di Federigo volare e *stranamente* piacendogli, forte disiderava d'averlo" (V 9,11). For the first time, through the child's attraction to the falcon, there exists a potential connection between Federigo's courtly values and the bourgeois ideals of monna Giovanna. A rapprochement between these two extremes, however, can occur only under extraordinary circumstances. When her son falls ill and requests the falcon, monna Giovanna goes to Federigo. He, in order to entertain her, sacrifices his cherished falcon for her supper, and she eats it unwittingly before she can make her request. In consequence, monna Giovanna's inconsolable son perishes. Thus both falcon and child, the symbols of the different ideals of the two main characters, are lost "in contado". These losses seem to suggest that both characters must sacrifice their ideological frames of reference before they can accept each other. Federigo surrenders his courtly ideals, and attains, through marriage to the wealthy Giovanna, bourgeois contentment; monna Giovanna loses her husband and son but learns to appreciate her suitor's aristocratic ideal of love, preferring "avanti uomo che abbia bisogno di ricchezza che ricchezza che abbia bisogno d'uomo" (V 9,42)

Thus, here as in V 1,3, and 8, survival in an isolated realm beyond the city allows an individual to better himself and to build stronger ties with his urban society, thus enabling him to return to the city in triumph. By fleeing a hostile urban environment where life has become insupportable spiritually (V 8) or financially (V 9), the individual may find refuge and a means of return to the city through nature.

Several other stories of this day, such as the *novelle* of Martuccio and Gostanza (V 2), and Reparata and Gianni da Procida (V 6), portray individuals who leave their familiar social milieus, face dangerous situations in foreign lands, overcome them, and eventually return to their homes. In V 2, Martuccio, having been rejected by Gostanza's family, resentfully turns from his hostile society to the sea, where he hopes to make his fortune. Martuccio is believed to have been killed, a victim of pirate raid, but instead has been taken prisoner in a foreign land. The news of Martuccio's death triggers Gostanza's desperate decision to abandon her society in the hope that she will be reunited with her lost lover in death. She casts herself adrift, oarless and alone, hoping to drown. But for Gostanza as well as for Martuccio, the sea foils human expectations: although she is believed dead at home, Gostanza lands safely in Barbery. In this *novella*, as in the tale of Pietro and Agnolella, the narrative alternately follows one and then the other lover's adventures: first Martuccio's capture at sea and imprisonment in Tunis are recounted; the focus then shifts to Gostanza's attempted suicide and fortuitous arrival in Barbery, where she is cared for by a "bonissima donna saracina"; we switch back to Martuccio once again as he cleverly advises the King of Tunis to defeat his opponent from Granada by using "corde molto più sottili agli archi de'vostri arcieri che quelle che per tutti comunalmente s'usano" (V 2,32). Martuccio's successful plan not only wins him his freedom, but the friendship of the king and renown throughout the kingdom as well. Gostanza consequently learns that he is still alive and their reunion follows swiftly thereafter.

Martuccio's resourcefulness not only delivers him from personal distress, but also improves the affairs of a whole kingdom. The fortunes of the two lovers also improve as Martuccio and Gostanza are finally reunited in a favorable foreign milieu. Their experience in Tunis, following their respective incidents at sea, offers the lovers a suitable environment in which to test their potential for survival and success. Once this potential has been realized in Tunis, no obstacles remain for them in their native Lipari.

A similar pattern of events occurs in the *novella* of Gianni and Reparata (V 6), although their initial departure from their homes is not provoked by a society hostile to their love. Rather, a band of "giovani ciciliani" lands on Ischia and they kidnap Reparata to take her back to Sicily for their king. Here again, the sea underscores the unstable fortunes of the story's protagonists. Gianni sets off in search of Reparata and finds her ensconced in the king's "giardino, il quale chiamava la Cuba" (V 6,9). The garden around the palace in which Reparata is held is solitary and well-fortified, but Gianni, "aggrappatosi *per parti che non si sarebbono appiccati i picchi,* nel giardin se n'entrò" (V 6,15). This image of the garden, and the careful attention given to Reparata's loss of "onore," suggest the intimate and forbidden relationship between the lovers and its implicit dangers. When they are discovered together the danger becomes explicit: they are bound naked in the public *piazza* to be burned at the stake. Good fortune intervenes, however, when the king's admiral recognizes Gianni and Reparata and persuades the monarch to restore them to life, honor, and love.

The settings for the major incidents of the *novella* fall into a pattern: clandestine activities occur in secluded natural environments—Reparata is kidnapped on an isolated beach, and the lovers have their illicit reunion in the tower in the *giardino*—while the public parallels to these events occur within the city—Reparata and Gianni are bound in the *piazza* of Palermo and are finally married and reintegrated into society in the king's palace. This contrasting use of natural and urban elements again serves to underline the innate conflict between the individual—whose solitude and struggle for survival are suggested by the natural background—and society, which functions optimally within an urban setting. That final reconciliation of individual and society occurs in the city suggests the inevitably public role that a successful member of society must play.

If we compare this *novella* with the "Torre dell'Arabo" episode in the *Filocolo*, which is its most direct source, we see that the Decameronian characters are much more resourceful and self-reliant than those in the earlier work.[44] All superhuman intervention disappears from the *novella*, and the main characters face their ordeals without external aid. Considering the female protagonists of the two works-Biancifiore in the *Filocolo* and Reparata in the *Decameron*-their roles in their respective narratives seem to be equally passive. And yet, Reparata changes at the crucial time of her potential liberation from captivity, a change which is not visible in Biancifiore. In the first sequences of the *novella*, Reparata plays a passive role as the object of Gianni's passion and the *giovani ciciliani's* aggressions. When she arrives in Palermo, the king "comandò che fosse messa in certe case bellissime d'un suo giardino . . . e quivi servita" (V 6,9). Again she is the passive object imprisoned according to the king's whim. With all these misfortunes befalling her, Reparata's reactions — aside from her screams when she is kidnapped-never enter the narrative context. Her passivity ends, however, when she sees Gianni and perceives the possibility of escape through his intervention. Taking the initiative, she tells him how to reach her and plans to give herself to him willingly as an inducement to help her escape. "La giovane . . . pensando a niuna persona più degnamente che a costui potersi donare e avvisando di poterlo inducere a portarla via, seco aveva preso di compiacergli in ogni suo disidero . . ." (V 6,16). Thus, through her ordeals, Reparata changes from a helpless and passive character to one with a clear perception of her precarious situation and the means at her disposal to alter it for the better.

Other significant modifications in the material from the *Filocolo* appear in the character of the male protagonist. In the *Filocolo*, Florio is constantly aided by supernatural interventions. In the *novella*, instead, Gianni must get by on his own brains and stamina in order to be reunited with Reparata. Once he finds her, nothing holds him back — neither fear of royal power, "a Palermo . . . trovato che la giovane era stata donata al re . . . fu forte turbato e quasi ogni speranza perdé . . . Ma pur, da amor ritenuto . . . si stette . . ." (V 6, 12-13), nor the seemingly unassailable physical obstacles that separate him from Reparata, "aggrappatosi per parti che non vi sarebbono appiccati i picchi, nel giardin se n'entrò . . ." (V 6,15). On these two occasions, Gianni demonstrates that his personal convictions enable him to overcome social constraints and physical obstacles without any outside assistance.

When the king discovers Gianni's audacious incursion into "la Cuba," the lovers can no longer rely on their own wits to save them. Aid comes not from a supernatural source, however, but from a character drawn from history, the Admiral Ruggieri de Lauria. While the admiral in the *Filocolo* is an archetype of evil transformed by supernatural forces into a benevolent father-figure, Ruggieri is a character of historical consequence who actually served under the King of Sicily in 1296 or 1297, and who would have known both Giovanni da Procida, Gianni's uncle, and Marino Bulgaro, Reparata's father. The *novella's* audience and narrators, would recognize the historical probability of its conclusion, since the King of Sicily did, indeed, depend on da Procida and Bulgaro to maintain his power, and would not have wanted to offend them. By using historical personalities rather than the mythicized characters of the romance, Boccaccio steadfastly upholds the true-to-life dictates of the *novella* genre. He also increases the participatory role of inner and outer audiences who are easily stirred by events and characters with whom they are well-acquainted. The *novella* version of the tale strengthens the social dimension of the work by underscoring the conflict between individual and authority within a historically accurate context. Again, the protagonist is faced with a conflict between social obligations and personal rights. Gianni, as a faithful subject of the king, is aware of the proscription against interfering with the king's possessions. At the same time, his personal right to love overcomes his sense of feudal duty. The king, on the other hand, is so incensed about the breech to his royal prerogatives that he takes revenge on Gianni and Reparata without waiting to discover their identities. He thus commits an error in royal judgment by failing to uphold his feudal obligation to da Procida and Bulgaro. Through Ruggieri's intervention, however, the king at last reconciles his royal prerogatives and obligations with the lovers' right to express their love for each other. The conflict between social and personal rights and responsibilities is solved through Admiral Ruggieri's role as enlightened intermediary between the king and his subjects. The changes introduced in the *novella* thus stress the bond of reciprocal responsibilities between ruler and ruled, and the social conscience that must guide the one, while resourcefulness aids the other.

It is through resourcefulness that many characters of the Fifth Day are able to satisfy their amorous desires. More precisely, they succeed because they cleverly use their environments to their own advantage. Like Nastagio, Caterina in V 4, makes use of nature so that she may be united with her lover, Ricciardo. With the excuse of "soperchio caldo," Caterina convinces her parents to prepare her bed "in sul verone che è presso al giardino" (V 4,12) where she may fall asleep "udendo cantare l'usignuolo" (V 4,21). She then welcomes Ricciardo to her "letticello" over the garden and "quasi per tutta la notte diletto e piacer presono l'un dell'altro, molte volte faccendo cantar l'usignuolo" (V 4,29). When Caterina's father discovers his daughter sound asleep, holding her lover "per quella cosa che voi tra gli uomini più vi vergognate di nominare" (V 4,30), his good-humored reaction reveals with innuendo the lighthearted mood of the day: "Vieni a vedere," he says to his wife, "che tua figliola è stata sì vaga dell' usignuolo, che ella l'ha preso e tienlosi in mano" (V 4,33). Conflict between lovers and their families or society, seen in many *novelle* of this and the previous days, is non-existent here. Instead, Caterina's parents show appreciation for the lovers' resourcefulness. Through double entendre the image of the "usignolo" suggests the harmony and good humor which culminates in Caterina's marriage to Ricciardo, who "si troverà aver messo l'usignuolo nella gabbia sua e non nell'altrui" (V 4,38).[45]

Conflict between lovers and family does reappear in the *novella* of Violante and Teodoro (V 7), where Violante's father is outraged by her affair with a socially inferior man. He commands that Teodoro "per la terra frustrato fosse e poi appiccato per la gola" (V 7,29), then offers Violante a choice between "due morti, o del veleno o del ferro" (V 7,30), and for the *sine qua non* of parental vengeance, orders his servant to dispose of his new-born grandson: "percossogli il capo al muro, il gitta a mangiare a' cani" (V 7,30). Social considerations are of primary importance here in understanding so violent a reaction to a daughter's choice of lover, especially in light of messer Lizio's benign behavior in the previously discussed fourth *novella* of the day. There the story concerned a late thirteenth century northern upper class family in Romagna. Here instead, the tale is set in Sicily during the reign of "il buon re Guglielmo," (*i.e.* from 1166-1189), and concerns a powerful feudal family headed by Amerigo Abata da Trapani. Clearly these spatial and temporal differences suggests that it is possible for young people to express love and self-fulfillment with far greater ease in a northern communal setting than in the feudal south. We need only recall the tragic outcome of the *novella* of Guiscardo and Ghismonda, also set in the feudal Kingdom of Sicily, for further proof of that society's repressive atmosphere.

The prescribed theme of the day dictates that good fortune must prevail, however, and a *deus-ex-machina*—who turns out to be Teodoro's long-lost father—enters to bring the tale its happy denouement. With Fineo's recognition of Teodoro as "libero uomo e mio figliuolo" (V 7,42), Amerigo rescinds the death sentences and the conflict between lovers and family is resolved in total harmony: "Così adunque in concordia fatta sposare la giovane, festa si fece grandissima con sommo piacere di tutti i cittadini" (V 7,51).

In V 5, conflict stems not from family disharmony or class differences but from two young men's love for the same girl. War, conflagration, and coincidence work together to bring a presumed orphan back to her native Faenza, where one of her suitors turns out to be her brother. She marries the other, but only after a confusing knot of circumstances is untied and the two young men are first arrested and then freed for attempting to kidnap her. Shifts in setting and the breakneck pace of the narrative are reminiscent of the Second Day where characters are tossed about by fortune. Personal interests and social laws are thrown into confusion until Agnesa's identity is discovered, but here too, harmony is restored and all ends happily.

In V 10, Dioneo's tale, a socially awkward situation stands at the core of the *novella*, yet its conclusion is surprisingly harmonious. Dioneo introduces his tale by inviting his female narratees to approach it in the same way they would a rose; "'innamorate donne,'" says Dioneo to the women of the *lieta brigata*,

> "'voi, ascoltandola, quello ne fate che usate siete di fare quando *ne' giardini* entrate, che, distesa la dilicata mano, cogliete *le rose* e lasciate *le spine* stare: il che farete lasciando il cattivo uomo con la mala ventura stare con la sua disonestà e liete riderete degli amorosi

inganni della sua donna . . . '"
(V 10,5)

Not only does Dioneo reinforce the constant connection between women, the *giardino*, and love, but with his "spine" image he suggests the possible tribulations connected with amorous relationships. Thus within his brief introduction, Dioneo makes certain that the theme of the previous *novelle* is not lost to his audience, and at the same time looks ahead with "gli amorosi inganni della sua donna," to the theme of the Seventh Day, in which he will rule.

As for the "inganni" of Pietro's wife, they seem to reveal an awareness and resourcefulness common to all characters of this day. If one compares this *novella* with its primary source, two innovations come to light which suggest a view of society different from Apuleio's.[46] The more important of the two is Pietro's homosexuality, which functions here as the catalyst for the wife's "inganni," just as jealousy, old age, and stupidity do in the *novelle* of the Seventh Day. Homosexuality is not viewed sympathetically: throughout the narrative, Pietro is "il cattivo uomo" to the narrator and "il cattivo marito" to his wife, his sexual bent "disonestà" or "cattività," and the topic of the *novella* "cattive cose." At the story's end, however, there is no suggestion of moral condemnation in the curious but harmonious *mènage-à-trois* formed by Pietro, his wife, and her lover. The second innovation, the wife's soliloquy on her husband's "cattività," creates an opposition between the natural correlation of marriage and sexual relations and the unnaturalness of homosexuality: "'se io non avessi creduto ch'e' fosse stato uomo, io non l'avrei mai preso. Egli che sapeva che io era femina, perchè per moglie me prendeva se le femine contro all'animo gli erano? Questo non è da sofferire" (V 10, 10-11). The woman thus decides to "dilettare di quello che egli si diletta. Il quale diletto fia a me laudevole, dove biasimevole è forte a lui: io offenderò le leggi sole, dove egli offende le leggi e la natura" (V 10,13). Both innovations underscore a belief in the natural law of love that the Narrator has thus far stressed in the general Introduction and in the Introduction to the Fourth Day, as have the storytellers in most of the *novelle* of the Third, Fourth, and Fifth Days. By presenting the male character as a homosexual, the exclusively negative Apuleian view of women is diminished. The narrative focuses on the woman's resourcefulness in remedying her matrimonial predicaments rather than on moral issues. The verbal agility that helps her throughout her ordeal—and Pietro well knows that "le parole non eran per venir meno in tutta notte" (V 10,59)—makes Pietro's wife the precursor of the Sixth Day's protagonists, each of whom "o con pronta risposta o avvedimento fuggì perdita o pericolo o scorno" (V Conclusion, 3).

The function of nature throughout the Fifth Day also anticipates Day VI. We have seen in most Day V *novelle* that characters were forced to leave the city and find strength and self-fulfillment in a natural setting in order to be successfully reintegrated into urban society. In the Sixth Day, characters appear almost exclusively in urban settings, especially in Florence, the city *par excellence*. The Fifth Day is thus a step in the progression from city to country and back to city which reflects not only the settings for the Day VI *novelle*, but the storytellers' setting as well. The Tenth (and last) Day corresponds rhythmically, thematically, and structurally to the Fifth (and central) Day. It presents the same narrative play on urban and natural settings as the Fifth and concludes when the storytellers (who, as we shall see, feel closely connected with the fictional characters of the Sixth) decide to return to Florence after their two-week sojourn in the countryside. Thus the pivotal Fifth Day not only prepares its audiences for the settings and action of the Sixth, but anticipates the Conclusion to the entire *Decameron* as well

To summarize, we may say that the Fifth Day's *novelle* present a world far better than that which confronts the fictional characters in any of the previous days of storytelling. As in the Second Day, the natural environment plays a crucial role in the development of the *novelle*. But where nature was often a hostile force in Day II, in Day V it plays an essential role in bettering the lives of the protagonists. It seems, indeed, that nature plays a role for the protagonists of the *novelle* similar to the one it has played all through the *cornice* for the storytellers, after their exit from the city. In fact, in both cases it represents the essential human experience of self-realization which helps to form a socially better human being. After initial sequences in which irrational forces (as in Day II) or antagonistic situations (as in Days III & IV) create difficulties for many characters, it is the characters' resourcefulness and clever maneuvering which lead to blissful denouements. These Day Five characters, like those in the Third and Fourth Days, are capable and active individuals. Yet, unlike their counterparts, they are able to overcome unfamiliar surroundings and familial and societal opposition, and they end their adventures in harmony with their environment.

These first Five Days of the *Decameron* have shown an increasing desire to make the individual a functional element in his society. Although this concern for the individual in society was apparent even in the First Day, there, emphasis was placed on a moralistic and negative view of society. Such is the obvious case in the *novella* of Ser Ciappelletto. The dangers of an unstructured environment devoid of behavioral restrictions are treated in most *novelle* of the Second Day. In the Third Day, the individual succeeds in controlling his limited environment through resourcefulness and awareness. In the Fourth Day, this limited environment expands into a complex social structure that functions oppressively against the individual. Often he is unaware of the demands made on him by his social milieu, and therefore, he must suffer harsh consequences. In Day V, the individual still finds himself involved in a personal love affair at odds with the complex social structure around him that attempts to limit his freedom of choice. Here, however, contrary to Day IV, the individual manages to control his own situation and finds ways to communicate with others in society. He thus establishes connections which allow mutual acceptance and understanding. In this Day, a clear pattern of satisfactory interconnections between individual and society is sketched. Not only is the individual able to fulfill his own needs, but he accepts his responsibilities to society. This relationship improves through the following days of storytelling until, in the last Day, a perfected ideal of life is achieved.

In the next chapter, our analysis of Days VI through X will, therefore, consider each day's additions to the steadily improving and increasingly complex relationships between the individual and society.

NOTES

1. The chart provided by Pamela Stewart in her essay "La novella di madonna Oretta e le due parti del *Decameron*" in *Yearbook of Italian Studies* (1973-5), 27-40, is enlightening on this subject.

2. Stewart, pp. 38-39. See also Umberto Bosco, *Decameron (Rieti, 1929)*, C. Muscetta, *Boccaccio* (Bari, 1972), F. Neri, "Il disegno ideale del *Decameron*," in *Storia e Poesia* (Torino, 1936), J. Ferrante, "Narrative Patterns in the *Decameron*," in *Romance Philology*, XXXI (May 1978), 585-604, on this approach to the *Decameron*.

3. See Vittore Branca, "Le nuove dimensioni narrative," in *Boccaccio medievale*, 165-87, and especially 169-70. In addition to Branca, I would like to acknowledge the Italian critics to whom I owe many of my ideas and who have been essential to my work on Boccaccio: Mario Baratto, *Realtà e stile nel Decameron* (Vicenza: Neri Pozza, 1970); Giovanni Getto, *Vita di forme e forme di vita nel Decameron* (Torino: Petrini, 1966²); Carlo Grabher, *Boccaccio* (Torino: UTET, 1941); Carlo Muscetta, *Giovanni Boccaccio* (Bari: La Terza, 1972); Giorgio Padoan, "Mondo aristocratico e mondo comunale nell'ideologia e nell'arte di Giovanni Boccaccio," in *Il Boccaccio, le Muse, il Parnaso e l'Arno* (Firenze: Olschki, 1978), 1-91; Giuseppe Petronio, "La posizione del Decameron," in *La Rassegna della letteratura italiana*, 61 (1957), 189-207.

4. I have dealt with this topic in "Saggio di lettura della prima giornata del *Decameron*," in *Teoria e critica*, 1 (1972), 111-38.

5. On this *novella* (1 3) see Mario Penna, *La parabola dei tre anelli e la tolleranza nel medioevo* (Torino: Rosenberg, 1953).

6. On *novella* 1 7 see G. Vinay, "Ugo Primate e l'archipoeta," in *Cultura neolatina*, 9 (1949), 5-40.

7. On *novella* 1 4 see Guido Almansi, "Il monaco e l'abate," in *L'estetica dell'osceno* (Torino: Einaudi, 1974), 131-42; Mario Baratto, *Realtà e stile* nel *Decameron*, 230-34; C. Kleinhenz, "Stylistic Gravity: Language and Prose Rhythms in the *Decameron* I,4," in *The Humanities Association Review*, 26 (1975), 289-99.

8. See Louis Green, *Chronicle Into History*, p. 72.

9. See Gene Brucker, *Renaissance Florence*, p. 90.

10. On *novella* 1 5 see Baratto, *Realtà e stile nel Decameron*, 331-32. I discuss the use of the adjectival form "onest" in my "Saggio di lettura della prima giornata . . ." p. 127.

11. Emilia again mentions clerical hypocrisy in VIII 4 and feminine presumptuousness in VI 8 and IX 9, while Pampinea strikes at women's stubborness again in IX 7.

12. On I 6 see G. Biscaro, "Inquisitori ed eretici a Firenze," in *Studi medievali*, NS 2 (1929), 347-75; NS 3 (1930), 266-87; NS 6 (1933), 161-99.

13. Pampinea repeats this statement in similar words at the end of her other story concerning woman's presumptuousness vis-à-vis a wise man—VIII,7—in which a foolish widow tries to trick a *scolare*. He revenges himself in a much crueler way than did maestro Alberto. Pampinea then comments to the female narrators, "E per ciò guardatevi, donne, del beffare, e gli scolari spezialmente" (VIII 7,149).

14. On I 1 see Luigi Fassò, *Studi e ricerche di storia letteraria* (Milano: Marzorati, 1947); F.L. Mannucci, "La figura di Ser Ciappelletto nella prima novella del Decameron," in *Miscellanea storica della Valdelsa*, 33 (1925), 105-7; Millicent Marcus, "Psuedo-Saints and Storytellers: The Tale of Ser Ciappelletto" in *An Allegory of Form: Literary Self-Consciousness in the Decameron*, Stanford French and Italian Studies, Volume XVIII, (Stanford University Press, 1979), 11-26.

15. I discussed Ciappelletto's "evil" in "Ser Ciappelletto or 'Le Saint Noir': A Comic Paradox," in *An Anatomy of Boccaccio's Style* (Napoli: Cymba, 1968), pp. 23-51, and in "Saggio di lettura della prima giornata . . .," *Ibid*, 130-37.

16. Or, what C. Cazale-Bernard calls "Le sens de l'aventure dans le *Decameron*," in *Revue des études italiennes*, 19 (1973), 102-23; hereafter cited as *REI*. See also Millicent Marcus's "Spinning the Wheel of Fortune" in her *Allegory of Form . . .*, 27-43.

17. The sea is interpreted differently at different points in G. Almansi's "Lettura della novella di Alatiel," in *Paragone*, 22 (February 1971), 26-40. See especially: p. 31, "Nel *Decameron* il mare è . . . narrativamente e poeticamente inerte" vs. p. 27, in II 4 "il mare . . . è strettamente funzionale . . ."; or p. 28, "Ma il mare è . . . una didascalia spaziale, più che una presenza letteraria" in II, 10, vs. p. 32, "il mare di Alatiel . . . è oberato di segni e dettagli che sembrano suggerire un sistema simbolico o allusivo." In *Vita di forme*, p. 194, Giovanni Getto sees the sea as one of the *Decameron's* "spazi geografici . . . più vivi."

18. On *novella* II 2 see Arturo Graf, "San Giuliano nel *Decameron* e altrove," in *Miti, leggende, e superstizioni del Medioevo* (Torino: Loescher, 1893), Vol. 2, 205-14; B. Gaiffer, "La legende de S. Julien," in *Analectica bollandiana*, 63 (1945), 145-219; M. Oberziner, "Il paternostro di S. Giuliano," in *Lares*, 4 (1933), 10-25; G. Petronio, "Rinaldo d'Asti e il paternostro di San Giuliano," in *La Rassegna*, 39 (1931), 333-38; G. Pitré, "Il paternostro di San Giuliano," in *Archivio per lo studio delle tradizioni popolari*, 21 (1902), 3-10.

19. On II 7 see Almansi, "Lettura della novella di Alatiel"; S. Deligiorgis, "Boccaccio and the Greek Romances," in *Comparative Literature*, 29 (1967), 97-113, and *Narrative Intellection in the Decameron* (Iowa City: University of Iowa Press, 1975), 36-40; C. Segre, "Comicità strutturale nella novella di Alatiel," in *Le strutture e il tempo* (Torino: Einaudi, 1974), 145-59.

20. I have discussed the role of the *locus amoenus* in my article "La funzione narrativa del 'giardino' o 'locus amoenus' nel *Decameron*," in *Teoria e critica*, 2 (1973), 1-22.

21. On novella II 5 see Benedetto Croce, *La novella di Andreuccio da Perugia* (Bari: La Terza, 1911), and more recently, F. Cerreta, "La novella di Andreuccio: problemi di unità e d'interpretazione," in *Italica*, 47 (1970), 255-64; G. Lucente, "The Fortunate Fall of Andreuccio da Perugia," in *Strumenti critici*, 20 (1973), 1-51.

22. This up and down rhythm, noticed by Croce, *op. cit.*, and by V. Branca in *Boccaccio medievale*, p. 117, has been amply discussed by Getto in "La composizione della novella di Andreuccio," in *Vita di forme*, 78-94.

23. See Almansi's "Lettura della novella di Bernabò e Zinevra (II 9)," in *Studi sul Boccaccio*, 7 (1973), 125-40. He considers this *novella* to be particularly important because of its position "al culmine di un gruppo tematico di particolare tensione morale e ideologica" (p. 127).

24. Tzvetan Todorov speaks of the "due livelli di rapporti, quello dell'essere e quello dell'apparire," in "Le categorie del racconto letterario," in *L'analisi del racconto* (Milano: Bompiani, 1969), p. 244.

25. This is the terminology used by Roland Barthes in "Introduzione all'analisi strutturale dei racconti" in *L'analisi del racconto* (Milano: Bompiani, 1969), 28-29.

26. In her unpublished essay, "Love's Labors Rewarded and Paradise Lost: *Decameron* III 10," Victoria Kirkham intelligently discusses the role of "bad" lovers as losers in the metaphorical context of the other world, particularly in III 4, where we find "frate Puccio . . . in Paradiso"; in III 8, where Ferondo ends up "in Purgatorio"; and in III 10, where Rustico succeeds in his attempts to "rimettere il diavolo in inferno."

27. On this topic see P. Toldo's "Les morts qui mangent," in *Bulletin italien*, 5 (1905), 291-97. For a more general treatment of the *novella* see V. Bramanti, "Il purgatorio di Ferondo: Decameron III, 8," in *Studi sul Boccaccio*, 7 (1973), 178-87.

28. Roland Barthes speaks of "una relazione parametrica" for those narrative units called "indizi", *op. cit.*, p. 21: H. Cole discusses III,9 in the context of Day III in "Dramatic Interplay in the *Decameron*: Boccaccio, Neifile and Giletta da Nerbona, " in *Modern Language Notes*, 90 (1975), 38-57; p. 39.

29. Barthes, *op. cit*, 17-22.

30. J. Wheelock speaks of this *novella's* semantic irony in "The Rhetoric of Polarity in Decameron III 3," in *Lingua e stile*, 9 (1974), 257-74.

31. C.L. Perrus has studied the relationship between narrative sequence and ideology in this *novella* in "Lecture de la nouvelle III 5 du Decameron," in *REI*, 23 (1972), 235-44.

32. See G. Padoan, "Sulla genesi del *Decameron*," in *Boccaccio: Secoli di Vita*, ed. Marga Cottino-Jones and Edward F. Tuttle (Ravenna: Longo, 1977), 143-76, for a discussion of this *novella* and its relation to X 4.

33. See. G. Getto, "La novella di Ghismonda e la struttura della quarta giornata," in *Vita di forme*, 95-138; G. Almansi, "Tancredi e Ghismonda," in *L'estetica dell'osceno*, 161-82; M. Baratto, *Realtà e stile*, 180-95; M. Marcus, "Tragedy as Trespass, The Tale of Tancredi and Ghismonda," in *An Allegory of Form: Literary Self-Consciousness in the Decameron*, 44-63.

34. I discussed this point in my article "La funzione narrativa del

giardino," especially 9-17.

35. On this *novella* see A. Pace, "Sage and Toad: A Boccaccian Motif (and a Misinterpretation by Musset)," in *Italica*, 48 (1971), 187-99; M. Pastore Stocchi, "La salvia avvelenata (Dec. IV, 7)," and "Un epifonema per Simona e Pasquino," in *Studi sul Boccaccio*, 7 (1973), 192-6; 196-200.

36. See D. Devoto, "Quelques notes au sujet du 'pot de basilic'," in *Revue du litterature comparée*, 37 (1963), 430-6; and E. Valori, "Il vaso di basilico e la novella di Lisabetta da Messina," in *Rivista delle bibiloteche e degli archivi*, 19(1909), 193-8; and 20 (1910), 11-15.

37. On this topic, see Henri Hauvette, "La 39 ^{e} nouvelle du *Décameron* et la legende du 'coeur mangé'," in *Études sur Bocace* (1894-1916), (Torino: Bottega d'Erasmo, 1968), 127-49.

38. The following discussion is derived partially from my essay "Tragedy in Chiaroscuro Effect: Rossiglione and Guardastagno," in *An Anatomy of Boccaccio's Style*, 121-47; On the subject of suicide, see D. Rolfs, "Dante, Petrarch, Boccaccio and the Problem of Suicide," *The Romanic Review*, LXVIII, 3 (May, 1976), 200-225.

39. In all the renderings of the "vida," Rossiglione's name is "Raimon a Raimons." See *Biografies des Troubadours: Textes provencaux des XIIIe et XIVe siècles* (Paris: Jean Boutière et A.H. Schultz, 1950), 154-72; A. Langlois, "Le troubadour Guilhem de Cabestahn," in *Annales du Midi*, 26 (1911), 5-51; 189-225; 349-56. In *novella* LXII of the *Novellino*, which deals with the same topic, the protagonists are nameless.

40. In V I, Panfilo says of the four protagonists: "E pervenuti in Creti, quivi da molti e amici e parenti lietamente ricevuti furono: e sposate le donne e fatta la festa grande . . . Cimone con Efigenia lieto si tornò in Cipri e Lisimaco similmente con Cassandra ritornò in Rodi; e ciascun lietamente con la sua visse lungamente contento nella sua terra." (V,1,70,71).

In V 2, Emilia concludes: ". . . a Lipari ritornarono, dove fu sì grande la festa, che dire non si potrebbe giammai. Quivi Martuccio la sposò e grandi e belle nozze fece; e poi appresso con lei insieme in pace e in riposo lungamente goderono del loro amore." (V,2,47-48)

In V 3, Elissa concludes: "Pietro lietissimo, e l'Agnolella più, quivi si sposarono; e come in montagna si potè, la gentil donna fé loro onorevoli nozze, e quivi i primi frutti del loro amore dolcissimamente sentirono . . . e esso con molto riposo e piacere con la sua Agnolella infino alla lor vecchiezza si visse." (V,3,53-54)

In V 4, Filostrato says: "Ricciardo . . . in presenza degli amici e de' parenti da capo sposò la giovane e con gran festa se ne la menò a casa e fece onorevoli e belle nozze; e poi con lei lungamente in pace e in consolazione uccellò agli usignuoli e di dì e di notte quanto gli piacque." (V,4,49)

In V 5, Neifile ends: ". . . a Minghino con gran piacer di tutti i suoi parenti diede per moglie la giovane, il sui nome era Agnesa . . . E Minghino appresso lietissimo fece le nozze belle e grandi, e a casa menatalasi, con lei in pace e in bene poscia più anni visse."
(V,5,39-40)

Pampinea concludes V 6: ". . . a Gianni fece la giovinetta sposare. E fatti loro magnifichi doni, contenti gli rimandò a casa loro, dove con festa grandissima ricevuti lungamente in piacere e in gioia poi vissero insieme." (V,6,42)

Lauretta concludes the seventh *novella:* " . . . egli . . . con grandissima festa e allegrezza fatte fare le lor nozze . . . E dopo alquanti dì il suo figliuolo e lei e il suo picciol nepote, montati in galea, seco ne menò a Laiazzo, dove con riposo e con pace de' due amanti, quanto la vita lor durò, dimorarono." (V,7,52-53)

V 8, concludes with Filomena's comments: "E la domenica seguente Nastagio sposatala e fatte le sue nozze, con lei più tempo lietamente visse." (V,8,44)

Filomena, the day's queen, concludes V 9 similarly: "Li fratelli . . . lei con tutte le sue ricchezze gli donarono. Il quale, così fatta donna e cui egli cotanto amata avea per moglie vedendosi, e oltre a ciò ricchissimo, in letizia con lei, miglior massaio fatto, terminò gli anni suoi." (V,9,43)

41. Roland Barthes, *op. cit.* p. 41.

42. On V 8 see M. Giacon, "La novella di Nastagio e la canzone delle visioni," in *Studi sul Boccaccio,* 8 (1974), 215-249; G. Kamber, "Antitesi e sintesi in 'Nastagio degli Onesti'," in *Italica* XLIV, (1967); C.L. Perrus, "La nouvelle V,8 du *Decameron:* Deux experiences de lecture," *REI* 21 (1975), 209-48.

43. On V 9 see Licurgo Cappelletti, "Commento sopra la IX novella della V Giornata del *Decameron,*" in *Propugnatore* 8 (1878), parte 2, p. 309.

44. Giovanni Boccaccio, *Filocolo,* in *Tutte le opere di Giovanni Boccaccio,* ed. Vittorio Branca (Verona: Mondadori, 1967), vol. I, 61-675.

45. See Cesare Segre, "Da Boccaccio a Lope de Vega: derivazioni e trasformazioni," in *Boccaccio: Secoli di Vita,* 225-237; 234-235.

46. See Laura Sanguineti White, *Apuleio e Boccaccio* (Bologna: Edizioni Italiane Moderne, 1977), 51-59; 71-154.

PART II

Order Within Reach: Days VI-X

Through Days VI to X the individual-society relationship develops in a crescendo of thematic complexity and broadening perspective. In this section the world of the tales and that of the *onesta brigata* draw closer together, for the storytellers more frequently enter the tales they narrate and they increasingly share similarities in world view and social situation with their *novelle* characters. And, in Days VI-X, we see the *novella* characters striving to manage their world as intelligently and successfully as the storytellers have managed theirs since they left Florence.

Structurally, there are striking correspondences between these last days and the previous five. Day VI officially reconsiders the virtues of verbal wit, a topic which tacitly controlled the themeless First Day. Days VII and VIII amplify the theme of individual ingenuity and resourcefulness, as did Days II and III; in the later days the narrators stress the potential good that gifted individuals can do in unrestricted social environments. The themeless Ninth Day relates back to Day I; at the same time, the narrative tone of most of its *novelle* creates a sombre mood based upon a rather bleak view of human relationships. Such a view is close to that of the Fourth Day, the Ninth Day's counterpart in the *Decameron's* first sequence. By contrast, the Tenth and final Day emphasizes those qualities which created the happy situations in the Fifth Day. In the *novelle* of the Tenth Day we see superior individuals in situations which become models for a perfected society.

1. Day VI: Wit and Success

The *novelle* of Day VI, as several critics have pointed out, consider many themes and situations previously formulated in Day I.[1] Narrators' tendencies to find connections between their own situations and the experiences undergone by *novelle* characters are intensified either at the opening or closing of each *novella*. Displays of verbal wit and storytelling skill occur throughout this day, as they did in Day I, and the *novelle* deal most frequently, as in the First Day, with human shortcomings.[2] The similarities with Day I culminate in Filomena's exordium to VI 1, which is almost a verbatim repetition of Pampinea's preamble to I 10:[3]

Filomena, VI 1,2-4

Giovani donne, come ne' lucidi sereni sono le stelle ornamento del cielo e nella primavera i fiori de' verdi prati e de' colli i rivestiti albuscelli, così de' laudevoli costumi e de' ragionamenti belli sono i leggiadri motti; li quali, per ciò che brievi sono, tanto stanno meglio alle donne che agli uomini quanto più alle donne che agli uomini il molto parlar si disdice. È il vero che, qual si sia la cagione, o la malvagità del nostro ingegno o inimicizia singulare che a' nostri secoli sia portata da' cieli, oggi poche o non niuna donna rimasa ci è la qual ne sappia ne' tempi oportuni dire alcuno o, se detto l'è, intenderlo come si conviene: general vergogna di tutte noi. Ma per ciò che già sopra questa materia assai da Pampinea fu detto, più oltre non intendo di dirne.

Pampinea, I 10,3-5

Valorose giovani, come ne' lucidi sereni sono le stelle ornamento del cielo e nella primavera i fiori ne' prati, così de' laudevoli costumi e de' ragionamenti piacevoli sono i leggiadri motti; li quali, per ciò che brievi sono, molto meglio alle donne stanno che agli uomini, in quanto più alle donne che agli uomini il molto parlare e lungo, quando senza esso si possa far, si disdice, come che oggi poche o niuna donna rimasa ci sia la quale o ne 'ntenda alcun leggiadro o a quello, se pur lo 'ntendesse, sappia rispondere: general vergogna è di noi e di tutte quelle che vivono.

This day's reformulation of the themes, situations, and narrative points of view treated in the Day I *novelle* seems to demonstrate not only the author's technical virtuosity in the use of *variatio*, but also his bold suggestion that resourceful and intelligent individuals can actually remold their society into a happier and more harmonious world. With its vigorous verbal play, the Sixth Day moves a step closer to the ideal world at which the *Decameron* seems to aim. Even in the opening scenes of the day, verbal pleasantry takes center stage as the servants quarrel over woman's participation in premarital and adulterous sex. A playful tone is thus established at the outset of the Sixth Day, while at the outset of Day I, the description of the Black Plague and its effects created a dark and pessimistic mood which influenced the narrative attitude of the entire day. Day VI's playful introductory sequence, on the other hand, extends throughout the day's *novelle* as characters rely upon verbal skill and wit in overcoming the pitfalls of everyday life.

Although their urban background is the focus of the *novelle*, only half of the tales take place exclusively in the city (VI 2,3,7,8, and 9). The remainder—the opening, central, and closing tales—unfold either wholly or partially in the country (VI 1,4,5,6, and 10), suggesting by their position the importance of nature even in the day dedicated to the city. It should be noted at once that the country scenes all take place in the *contado* surrounding Florence.

The settings in the Florentine *contado* not only underscore the centrality of Florence in the *novelle*, but link the *novelle* and *cornice* characters, who continually remark upon this connection. Filomena, for instance, presents Madonna Oretta as "moglie di messer Geri Spina . . . per avventura essendo *in contado, come noi siamo* . . ." (VI 1,6). Almost every succeeding *novellatore* makes a similar observation: Cisti is presented as *"nostro* cittadino" (VI 2,3); monna Nonna de' Pulci as "una giovane, la quale *questa pistolenzia presente ci ha tolta donna . . .* cui *voi tutte* doveste conoscere . . ." (VI 3,8); Currado Gianfigliazzi as "sempre della *nostra città* . . . notabile cittadino, liberale e magnifico" (VI 4,4); messer Forese and Giotto as "due *nostri* cittadini" (VI 5,4); Michele Scalza as living "nella *nostra* città" (VI 6,4), while the Baronci, who provide the topic of discussion for the same *novella,* are introduced as acquaintances of Panfilo: "i Baronci . . . li quali per avventura *voi non conoscete* come fa egli (Panfilo)" (VI 6,3). Guido Cavalcanti, too, is introduced as living "nella *nostra* città" where "ne' tempi passati furono . . . assai belle e laudevoli usanze" (VI 9,4); and finally Certaldo is "un castel di Val d'Elsa posto nel *nostro* contado" (VI 10,5). Such emphasis on the adjective "nostro" in relation to Florence places a resultant stress on the relationship between the *novelle* of this day and the *cornice* characters. Thus the outcome of the protagonists' experiences in these *novelle* and the influence they have on their own society, may reliably foreshadow the storytellers' own outcome and influence on their own society upon their return from the *contado.*

Another connection between the *novellatori* and the protagonists of this day's tales is conveyed through the importance placed on the art of speaking and telling stories by the protagonists themselves. Such emphasis is visible in the first *novella* of the day,[4] when one of the *cavalieri* in madonna Oretta's company decides to make use of storytelling to pass the time during their retreat in the country: "'Madonna Oretta,'" says the *cavaliere,* "'quando voi vogliate, io vi porterò, gran parte della via che a andare abbiamo, a cavallo con una delle belle novelle del mondo'" (VI 1,7). The *novellare,* here figuratively rendered in equestrian terms, is seen as the best way to entertain the group. It therefore links the protagonists of the story and the *brigata,* who, when they reorganized themselves in the country before Day I, had also unanimously decided to divert each other with tales. Similar instances appear in other stories of the same day; one of Giotto's most valuable traits is that he is a "bellissimo favellatore" (VI 5,13), while Michele Scalza owes his popularity in Florence to the fact that he tells "le più nuove novelle . . . per la qual cosa i giovani fiorentini avevan molto caro, quando in brigata si trovavano, di potere aver lui" (VI 6,4). In the novella of madonna Filippa, the importance of "saper ben parlare . . . dove la necessità il richiede" (VI 7,3) is strongly emphasized, and Dioneo himself, the individualist of the *brigata,* also mentions the importance of the art of storytelling in his introduction to the concluding *novella* of the day: "'Né vi dovrà esser grave, perché io, per *ben dir la novella compiuta*, alquanto in parlar mi distenda'" (VI 10,4). It is no wonder that Frate Cipolla, the protagonist of Dioneo's *novella*, is the grand master of the art of speaking second to none — not even to the great master of prevarication, Ser Ciappelletto, who opens Day I. In addition to advocating the art of speaking and of telling tales, the Sixth Day also places strong emphasis on the power of the word. The word as motto or punchline is the essential ingredient of each *novella* in this day, as it was to a lesser degree in the *novelle* of Day I. As such it brings dramatic action to a humorous culmination; as a supple instrument in the hands of the *novellatori*, it is the device through which Florentine characters of all classes and backgrounds are perfectly limned. The protagonists of the *novelle* do, in fact, represent a wide range of social classes; there are noblemen, such as Geri Spina (VI 2), Currado Gianfigliazi (VI 4), and Guido Cavalcanti (VI 9); professionals and artists such as messer Forese and maestro Giotto (VI 5); commoners, such as Cisti (VI 2), Michele Scalza (VI 6), and Fresco da Celatico (VI 8); and witty women, such as madonna Oretta (VI 1) or madonna Filippa (VI 7), a champion of women's rights whom any "Woman's Lib" group would be proud to claim as an ancestress.

Structurally, each *novella* of this day develops in three basic steps: 1) the initial situation presents a potential difficulty for the protagonist which involves him in a confrontation with society; 2) the protagonist reverses his disadvantaged situation through witty manipulation of the verbal instruments at his disposal; and finally 3) he/she is reintegrated into society in the final vision of comic harmony.

The first novella of the Day, concerning madonna Oretta and the knight who is a poor teller of tales, follows this basic pattern with a few deviations which seem intended to create a connection with the previous stories of Day V. Its setting, for instance, is the countryside around Florence, reminiscent of the natural background of Day V *novelle* and of its positive influence on the outcome of the main characters' adventures. Furthermore, while madonna Oretta is never set in confrontation with her society, she is the means by which the bad storyteller of her circle is reaccepted into their group after his inadequate performance. In this way madonna Oretta displays a harmonizing influence on her society and especially vis-à-vis a male character: this function is very close to the similar roles played by most Day V characters, and particularly by the women characters of V 8 and 9. In fact, when the knight's storytelling becomes unbearable, madonna Oretta must correct the unpleasant situation through her own verbal facility. She suggests "piacevolmente": "'Messer, questo vostro cavallo ha troppo duro trotto, per che io vi priego che vi piaccia di pormi a piè'" (VI 1,11). She thus eases the discomfort of her entire *brigata* and restores their good humor with her witty *motto*. The atmosphere of open-mindedness and affability is conveyed through the lady's wit and the good-natured reaction of the *cavaliere*, who takes the jibe "in festa e in gabbo" (VI,1,12).

At the same time, because of its concern for *novellare* and because of madonna Oretta's clever response, this first *novella* provides an ideal introduction to the themes and tone of the entire day. Moreover, the connection between the *brigata* and the fictional realm of the *novelle* is heightened by the common mood of conviviality linking the storytellers' world and this initial *novella's*.

The following story stresses the same lightheartedness as did the tale of madonna Oretta, but occurs in Florence itself rather than in the *contado*. Here, however, Cisti's petit-bourgeois world attracts other characters from higher social levels such as Geri Spina and the Pope's ambassadors:

> E avendo un farsetto bianchissimo indosso e un grembiule di bucato innanzi sempre . . . ogni mattina in su l'ora che egli avvisava che messer Geri con gli ambasciadori dover passare si faceva davanti all'uscio suo recare una secchia nuova e stagnata d'acqua fresca e un picciolo orcioletto bolognese nuovo del suo buon vin bianco e due bicchieri che parevano d'ariento, sì eran chiari: e a seder postosi, come essi passavano . . . cominciava a ber sì saporitamente questo suo vino, che egli n'avrebbe fatta venir voglia a'morti.
>
> La qual cosa avendo messer Geri una e due mattine veduta, disse la terza: 'Chente è, Cisti? è buono?'
>
> (VI 2,11-13)

The careful presentation of the minutiae of Cisti's meticulous attire and actions, create a microcosm of limited dimensions and modest social class, which is nevertheless endowed with remarkable aesthetic and intellectual sophistication. Such a world attracts into its orbit the other characters in the *novella:*" . . . mentre gli ambasciador vi stettero, quasi ogni mattina con loro insieme n'andò a ber messer Geri" (VI 2,17). The narrative proceeds to illustrate its pivotal points of aesthetic consciousness, conviviality and *ingegno*, through Cisti's *motto* to the servant and its results: "'Figliuolo, messer Geri non ti manda a me . . . (ti manda) A Arno'" (VI 2,20-25). In this *novella* the structural pattern typical of the day is repeated twice, with Cisti successfully manipulating the situation in both cases: first, in his circumvention of the social prohibitions restraining him from inviting members of the aristocracy into his establishment, and then in his clever outwitting of messer Geri's greedy servant. In both cases, Cisti avoids a touchy situation through his verbal cleverness and, as other characters of Day I, (Melchisedec in I 3 and Bergamino in I 7, among them), had successfully done and achieves personal satisfaction as well as harmony with others in society.

The *novella* of monna Nonna de'Pulci (VI 3) presents a vision of convivial Florentine street life on "il dì di san Giovanni" as Dego della Ratta and the bishop ride side by side "veggendo le donne per la via onde il palio si corre" (VI

3,8). Brief as it is, this *novella* unfolds in a pattern typical of this day: 1) monna Nonna encounters unpleasantness with the bishop's presumptuous remark, 2) she turns the unpleasantness into a verbal victory of her own through her witticism, and 3) she leaves the bishop and the general abashed and ashamed of their present and past indiscretions. The bishop's offensive question about Dego, "'Nonna, che ti par di costui? crederestil vincere?" (VI 3,9) earns Nonna's sharp response: "'Messere, e forse non vincerebbe me; ma vorrei buona moneta'" (VI 3,10). She refers to Dego's infamous bargain with the bishop's relative through which he managed to sleep with the man's wife and to pay him for the pleasure with false florins. Because the bargain is widely-known in Florence, and because she is surrounded on the busy street by the Florentines "che molti v'erano, che l'udirono" (VI 3,10), Nonna's retort not only saves her own reputation, but brings public censure to bear on the guileful Dego and on the bishop who had tacitly born Dego's insult to his family. As the bishop and Dego ride away, stung by Nonna's remark, a sense of shame is clearly awakened in them both: "La qual parola udita il maliscalco e 'l vescovo, sentendosi parimente trafitti . . . senza guardar l'un l'altro vergognosi e taciti se n'andarono . . ." (VI 3,11). The power of the word thus enables monna Nonna to arouse the dormant social consciences of powerful representatives of the ruling class.

The *novella* of Chichibio and Currado Gianfigliazzi (VI 4), which unfolds alternately in Florence and the *contado*, adapts the usual pattern of the Sixth Day to place special emphasis on the initial confrontation between the two protagonists. This first stage of the narrative, given by far the largest portion of narrative space, pits servant and master against each other. As in the *novella* of messer Geri and Cisti (VI 2), there is a wide gap in their social status. In this case, this gap heightens the intensity of the conflict between them. The splendor and nobility of Currado's aristocratic Florentine life are significant in this light:

> sempre della nostra città è stato notabile cittadino liberale e magnifico, e vita cavalleresca tenendo continuamente in cani e in uccelli s' è dilettato . . .
> (VI 4,4,)

As Chichibio prepares his master's banquet, the rich, almost Flemish atmosphere of the kitchen adds to the vision of gaiety and warmth surrounding Currado.

The linguistic texture of the *novella* dramatizes the lively movement of the narrative.[5] Throughout the tale, word arrangements produce broken rhythm suggestive of hopping, which effectively recalls the story's central motif, a crane with only one leg. This hopping rhythm is often produced by short words — frequently oxytones — such as *mai più, gru, avrì, in fé, piè, colà, ho ho*, etc. It is also conveyed through the syntactical construction of the *novella*, made up of short clauses which, in addition to oxytones, consist of fast-moving finite verb forms. At times the brevity of the clauses and the repetition of similar words and rhythms impart a sing-song cadence to the language of the *novella*, particularly to Chichibio's speech rejecting donna Brunetta's request for one of the crane's legs: "Voi non l'avrì da mi, donna Brunetta, voi non l'avrì da mi'" (VI 4,8). Eventually Chichibio, the "nuovo bergolo" (VI 4,6), the "vinizian bugiardo" (VI 4,10), cannot resist his lady's provocations: "'tu non avrai mai da me cosa che ti piaccia'" (VI 4,9) and dutifully sacrifices one of the crane's legs to her. Chichibio then switches from action to words by covering up his misdeed with a *motto:* "'le gru non hanno se non una coscia e una gamba.'" The humorous bickering with his master over the crane's missing leg thus begins:

> Currado allora turbato disse: 'Come diavol non hanno che una coscia e una gamba? non vid'io mai più gru che questa?'
> Chichibio seguitò: 'Egli è, messer, com'io vi dico; e quando vi piaccia, io il vi farò veder ne' vivi.'
> (VI 4,10-12)

Chichibio's lie then provokes a counteraction — the trip to the *contado* to see live cranes — which in turn elicits Chichibio's final *motto:* "'Messer sì, ma voi non gridaste 'ho ho!' a quella d'iersera'" (VI 4,18). With his final witticism, Chichibio converts the atmosphere of the tale to one of festivity and conviviality. Word finally triumphs over deed to restore Currado's good spirits — and to save Chichibio's neck!

The *contado* — more precisely the road from Mugello to Florence — serves as backdrop for messer Forese and Giotto's encounter in VI 5. The rain and mud along the road accentuate the disreputable appearance of the travelers, neither of whom is especially good looking to begin with. When they borrow old clothes from a laborer to protect themselves from the inclement weather, things go from bad to worse:

> . . . presi dal lavoratore in prestanza due mantellacci vecchi di romagnuolo e due cappelli tutti rosi dalla vecchiezza, per ciò che migliori non v'erano, cominciarono a camminare.
> Ora, essendo essi alquanto andati e tutti molli veggendosi e per gli schizzi che i ronzini fanno co' piedi in quantità zaccherosi . . .
> (VI 5,11-12)

Their external ugliness, emphasized by the bemired country road, conceals the great inner beauty of the two men. When they speak, their exchange of witticisms reveals the humor and perception within their malformed bodies:

> 'Giotto, a che ora venendo di qua allo 'ncontro di noi un

> forestiere che mai veduto non t'avesse, credi tu che egli
> credesse che tu fossi il migliore dipintore del mondo,
> come tu se'?'
>
> A cui Giotto prestamente rispose: 'Messere, credo che
> egli il crederebbe allora che, guardando voi, egli
> crederebbe che voi sapeste l'abicì.'
>
> (VI 5,14-15)

Here appearance and essence play off each other to emphasize the contrast between the protagonists' rustic appearance and subtle intellects. And once again, characters triumph over an unpleasant situation and restore each other's joviality through the all-powerful word.

The situation which unfolds in the *novella* of Michele Scalza, "il più piacevole e il più sollazzevole uom del mondo" (VI 6,4), is very similar to that of the *onesta brigata:* a group of young people has assembled in a fine house on Montughi, a hill near Florence covered by the villas of wealthy Florentines,[6] in order to amuse each other with verbal play. Not only is the physical atmosphere similar, but storytellers and the *novella's* protagonists are also linked by their common air of festivity and joviality.

The structural outline of the *novella* follows the prescribed pattern for the day. It begins with a moment of confrontation when Michele sets himself a seemingly impossible task: to prove to his companions that the Baronci are the oldest — and therefore most noble — family in the world. Scalza resolves the conflict with his clever interpretation of Genesis. He thus wins his bet, amuses his friends, and convinces them that he is as witty as he is "sollazzevole." The story concludes with a final vision of comic harmony: "tutti cominciarono a ridere e a affermare che lo Scalza aveva la ragione . . . e che per certo i Baronci erano i più gentili uomini e i più antichi che fossero . . ." (VI 6,16).

In these last two *novelle* lighthearted and witty interplay between characters takes place in an ideal natural setting reminiscent of the gardens where the narrators tell their stories. The next three novelle, instead, are set in the city and they, at least VI 7 and 9, more dramatically render the conflict between individual and society which must be solved through verbal skill. The seventh *novella* concerns madonna Filippa, one of the first and most outstanding representatives of the free-thinking woman in the modern narrative.[7] Love's natural law plays an important role in madonna Filippa's life, as it does for the "donne innamorate" of the Fourth and Fifth Days:

> . . . una gentil donna e bella e oltre a ogni altra
> innamorata, il cui nome fu madonna Filippa, fu trovata
> nella sua propria camera una notte da Rinaldo de'
> Pugliesi suo marito nelle braccia di Lazzarino de' Guaz-
> zagliotri, nobile giovane e bello di quella terra, il quale

> ella quanto se medesima amava.
> (VI 7,5)[8]

It is not madonna Filippa's love affair, however, which is the pivotal point of the narrative, but rather her struggle for survival in the face of

> uno statuto, nel vero non men biasimevole che aspro, il quale senza alcuna distinzion far comandava che così fosse arsa quella donna che dal marito fosse con alcun suo amante trovata in adulterio, come quella che per denari con qualunque altro uomo stata trovata fosse.
> (VI 7,4)

Madonna Filippa's objections to this law, while clearly suggesting her creator's training in medieval law and rhetoric[9], endow her fight for survival with a surprisingly modern outlook on women's rights. In fact, madonna Filippa enters into open debate with the *podestà* on the very legality of the statute, by introducing the argument of "Quod omnes tangit ab omnibus approbari debet" which, as Pennington aptly puts it, "is a common staple of medieval thought . . . which . . . established itself as an important theoretical concept for many different medieval assemblies . . . but its logic was never extended to women in the Middle Ages."[10] Boccaccio's heroine, instead, uses it in a similar "medieval assembly", in the presence of the mayor and "quasi tutti i pratesi", that is, in the most public manner possible:

> . . . le leggi deono esser comuni e fatte con consentimento di coloro a cui toccano. Le quali cose di questa (legge) non avvengono, ché essa solamente le donne tapinelle costrigne . . . e oltre a questo, non che alcuna donna, quando fatta fu, ci prestasse consentimento, ma niuna ce ne fu mai chiamata: per le quali cose meritamente malvagia si può chiamare.
> (VI 7, 13-14)

Was Boccaccio ironically ridiculing the legislative system of a long-time enemy city which only recently had been reduced to a Florentine territory?[11] Or was he simply trying to amuse his readers (especially through the sexual innuendos) by inventing a story with characters taken from real Prato families, which could never have happened at that particular time.[12] The insertion of this story in the Sixth Day seems to point in another direction as well, for here the individual — an outstanding woman endowed with superior intellectual powers — confronts her conventional and antipathetic society. With her life at stake, madonna Filippa uses her charm, self-assurance, and artistry with words to draw this antagonistic society to her side. Wholly reconciled to her indiscretion, they become a happy and harmonious congregation: "dopo molte risa, quasi ad una voce tutti gridarono la donna aver ragione e dir bene . . ." (VI

7,18). Resolution of the conflict brings about not only Filippa's triumphant acquittal, but the more complex social process of changing the unjust statute as well:

> . . . quasi tutti i pratesi . . . prima che di quivi si partissono, a ciò confortandogli il podestà, modificarono il crudele statuto e lasciarono che egli s'intendesse solamente per quelle donne le quali per denari a' lor mariti facesser fallo.
>
> (VI 7,18)

A passive and conventional society that was previously ready to condemn madonna Filippa to the flames eventually becomes willing to accept her unconventional outlook on life and legal matters. Public reconciliation reaches its climax with Filippa's triumphal return to her home: "la donna lieta e libera, quasi dal fuoco risuscitata, alla sua casa se ne tornò gloriosa" (VI 7,19). This glorification of woman's freedom of mind and body is achieved through madonna Filippa's manipulation of words, as we see when she defends her unlimited physical capacity for love:

> 'Adunque,' seguì prestamente la donna, 'domando io voi, messer podestà, se egli ha sempre di me preso quello che gli è bisognato e piaciuto, io che doveva fare o debbo di quel che gli avanza? debbolo io gittare a' cani? non è egli meglio servirne un gentile uomo che più che sé m'ama, che lasciarlo perdere o guastare?'
>
> (VI 7,17)

In format this *novella* most fully articulates the pattern prescribed for the *novelle* of the Sixth Day. It presents a precise first moment of confrontation in which madonna Filippa is challenged by a hostile society; there follows a sequence in which, through her clever use of words, she not only saves her own life, but changes an unjust social attitude: and finally, public and private worlds are reconciled in comic harmony.

The following *novella*, narrated by Elissa, presents a contrasting picture of womanhood in the "spiacevole, sazievole e stizzosa" (VI 8,5) niece of Fresco da Celatico. Here, instead of a reconciliation with society, the girl is completely alienated from it: "'io non credo,'" she says,

> 'che mai in questa terra fossero e uomini e femine tanto spiacevoli e rincrescevoli quanto sono oggi, e non ne passa per via uno che non mi spiaccia come la mala ventura; e io non credo che sia al mondo femina a cui più sia noioso il vedere gli spiacevoli che è a me, e per

> non vedergli così tosto me ne son venuta.'
> (VI 8,8)

Her egocentrism and foolishness become the target of her uncle's witty barb: "'Figliuola, se così ti dispiaccion gli spiacevoli, come tu di', se tu vuoi viver lieta non ti specchiar giammai" (VI 8,9). Fresco's *motto* — which falls on the deaf ear of his niece — suggests through its ironic overtones the conflict between his own intellectual awareness and social involvement and his niece's dullness and misanthropy. The bustling city background described in terms analogous to that in the *novella* of monna Nonna (VI 2) suggests the potential for conflict between individual and society. But where that conflict was in large measure overcome by Nonna's intelligence, here it remains unresolved because of the girl's utter obtuseness: "e così nella sua grossezza si rimase e ancor vi si sta" (VI 8,10).

To complete the panorama of exceptional Tuscan personalities in this Sixth Day, the figure of Guido Cavalcanti is introduced in VI 9. His wit and elegance enable him to escape an unpleasant encounter with the members of a boisterous *brigata* and to shame them at the same time. Once again, a portrait of traditional Florentine customs opens the *novella*:

> ... in diversi luoghi per Firenze si ragunavano insieme i gentil uomini delle contrade e facevano lor brigate di certo numero ... spesse volte onoravano e gentili uomini forestieri ... e ancora de' cittadini ... e insieme i dì più notabili cavalcavano per la città e talora armeggiavano, e massimamente per le feste principali o quando alcuna lieta novella di vittoria o d'altro fosse venuta nella città.
> (VI 9,5-6)

The solitary personality of Guido detaches itself with statuesque grandeur from this bustling city background of armed *brigate*. He stands apart, amidst artistic monuments and the vestiges of civic greatness:

> ... essendo Guido partito d'Orto San Michele e venutosene per lo Corso degli Adimari infino a San Giovanni, il quale spesse volte era suo cammino, essendo arche grandi di marmo, che oggi sono in Santa Reparata, e molte altre dintorno a San Giovanni, e egli essendo tralle colonne del porfido che vi sono e quelle arche e la porta di San Giovanni, che serrata era, messer Betto con sua brigata a caval venendo su per la piazza di Santa Reparata, vedendo Guido là tra quelle sepolture, dissero: 'Andiamo a dargli briga' ...
> (VI 9,10)

The Florentine environment in all its vitality is captured in this *novella:* social atmosphere, culture, and art are carefully portrayed to underscore the contrast between the gregarious messer Betto and the reclusive Guido. Cavalcanti's love of solitude is suggested by his lonely walks amidst the *sepolture* — images of his silent and contemplative approach to life and death. When messer Betto and his *brigata* ride up to Guido and challenge him, his elegant and witty retort demonstrates not only his physical and mental agility, but his unique outlook on existence as well:

> 'Signori, voi mi potete dire a casa vostra ciò che vi piace'; e posta la mano sopra una di quelle arche, che grandi erano, sì come colui che leggerissimo era, prese un salto e fusi gittato dall'altra parte, e sviluppatosi da loro se n'andò.
>
> (VI 9,12)

Guido is committed to his own idea of how life should be led and to the remnants of his tradition and culture. He is unwilling to compromise his standards by exposing them to his intellectual inferiors. Perhaps the most striking feature of the *novella* is not the extraordinary character of Guido, but his effect on messer Betto and his men and their response to his refusal to conform to social customs. Messer Betto's apt interpretation of Guido's *motto* sends tremors of awe and admiration for the poet through the members of the *brigata:*

> '. . . noi e gli altri uomini idioti e non letterati siamo, a comparazion di lui e degli altri uomini scienziati, peggio che uomini morti, e per ciò, qui essendo (amidst the tombs), noi siamo a casa nostra.'
> Allora ciascuno intese quello che Guido aveva voluto dire e vergognossi, né mai più gli diedero briga . . .
>
> (VI 9, 14-15)

The three most fully elaborated city *novelle* of this day — VI 2,7, and 9 — establish a progressive pattern in the relationship between individual and society: 1) in VI 2, the individual (Cisti) realizes that, as a social inferior, he must keep himself well apart from the aristocratic society with which he must deal; 2) in VI 7, the individual (madonna Filippa), although ostracized from and menaced by society publicly reverses her circumstances through self-confidence, charm, and deft oratory, and is triumphantly restored to her former state; and finally, 3) in VI 9 the individual (Guido Cavalcanti) is so far superior to society at large that he refuses to be absorbed into it and is universally regarded to be beyond its dictates. Thus by the end of the ninth tale, the individual is projected as a highly resourceful, healthy, and unique element of a society in the process of being remolded and improved by his scrutiny and emandation.

The last *novella* of the Sixth Day, like VI 9, presents an individual, Frate Cipolla, whose mental agility and wordly experience make him vastly superior to his rustic and unsophisticated society. The friar preaches in Certaldo—a Tuscan village dear to Boccaccio's heart—whose social functions occur in one of two major settings: either in the church—*Certaldo alto*—where Frate Cipolla holds forth to his congregation, beseeching their alms, or the tavern—*Certaldo basso*—where his servant, Guccio Imbratta, holds forth to Nuta, "fante . . . grassa e grossa e piccola e mal fatta . . ." (VI 10,21), beseeching her charms. The narrative swiftly moves back and forth between *Certaldo alto* and *Certaldo basso* through the machinations of two young men who wish to put Frate Cipolla's verbal skills to their ultimate test. By secretly exchanging the friar's supposed relic, "una delle penne dell'agnol Gabriello" (VI 10,11), for some lumps of coal, they hope to trip his silver tongue:

> . . . all'albergo dove il frate era smontato se n'andarono
> con questo proponimento, che Biagio dovesse tenere a
> parole il fante di frate Cipolla e Giovanni dovesse tralle
> cose del frate cercare di questa penna, chente che ella si
> fosse, e torgliele, *per vedere come egli di questo fatto
> poi dovesse al popol dire.*
> (VI 10,14)

Cipolla, having discovered his loss, "senza mutar colore" (VI 10,36) prevaricates and procrastinates to divert the throng of *certaldesi* gathered to see Gabriel's feather. Never at a loss for words, he takes the congregants on a verbal voyage to places common enough to sophisticated Florentines, but to the *certaldesi's* rustic ears, exotic and fantastic: "i privilegi del Porcellana . . . lo Borgo de' Greci . . . lo reame del Garbo . . . il Braccio di San Giorgio, in Truffia e in Buffia . . . terra di Manzogna . . . India Pastinaca . . ." (VI 10,37-42). His interminable travels are described in words which mean nothing or even mean the opposite of what they seem to: "io fui mandato dal mio superiore in quelle parti dove apparisce il sole" (VI 10,37); or "dove molti de'nostri frati e d'altre religioni trovai assai, li quali tutti il disagio andavan per l'amor di Dio schifando" (VI 10,39); or "là . . . io vidi volare i pennati, cosa incredibile a chi non gli avesse veduti" (VI 10,42); or yet "Maso del Saggio . . . gran mercatante io trovai là, che schiacciava noci e vendeva gusci a ritaglio" (VI 10,42). This masterful double-talk-—and *double-entendre*—reaches its climax with Cipolla's description of the relics he has seen during his mythical travels. He creates a delightfully comic discrepancy between the spiritual essence anticipated in such holy objects and their crude, palpable physicality:

> '. . . mi mostrò il *dito* dello Spirito Santo così *intero e
> saldo* come fu mai, e il *ciuffetto* del serafino che apparve
> a san Francesco, e una dell' *unghie* de'gherubini, e una
> delle *coste* del *Verbum-caro-fatti-alle-finestre* e de'

> *vestimenti* della santa Fé catolica . . . e una *ampolla del sudore* di san Michele quando combatté col diavolo, e la *mascella* della Morte di san Lazzero . . .
>
> (VI 10,45)

This vertiginous spiral of comic reveries and fabulous *double-entendres*—poured forth, we must assume, with the urgency and breathlessness befitting such a great *rhétoriqueur*—a second "Tullio . . . o forse Quintiliano" (VI 10,7)—thoroughly dumbfounds the mass of *certaldesi*. Cipolla then deftly sidesteps "la penna dello agnolo Gabriello" and presents "i carboni co' quali fu arrostito san Lorenzo" (VI 10,49) as the *pièce de résistance* of his long speech:

> E . . . aperse la cassetta e mostrò i carboni; li quali poi che alquanto la stolta moltitudine ebbe con ammirazione reverentemente guardati, con grandissima calca tutti s'appressarono a frate Cipolla . . .
>
> (VI 10,53)

The friar collects tremendous sums in alms and, through his unparalleled oratorical skill, brings the townspeople to a final vision of festivity and harmony—even the *schernatori* themselves, who "poi che partito si fu il vulgo, a lui andatisene, con la maggior festa del mondo ciò che fatto avevan gli discoprirono . . ." (VI 10,56). Thus the last *novella* closes with an aura of great joviality, lending a joyous touch to the end of this day's *novellare*.

If compared with that other great *rhétoriqueur*, Ser Ciappelletto, Frate Cipolla's exploits are significant. In I 1, the laymen Ser Ciappelletto, in order to help his business associates and himself out of a dangerous situation in foreign, unfriendly territory, adroitly uses verbal mastery to exploit a holy friar, his co-friars, and a whole congregation. He himself becomes a relic to be devoutly venerated by them all. The outcome of the story is ambiguously harmonious, offering the view of a corrupt and unfriendly society turned to bigotry for obviously utilitarian reasons and being tricked on those premises. In VI 10, Cipolla, himself a friar, uses his verbal skills to extricate himself from a benign trick played on him by friends, and in turn to trick his gullible congregation into venerating a false relic. He further succeeds in producing abundant alms for himself and his convent. Although they present fictional characters with similar traits, the two *novelle*—the one opening the First Day, the other closing the Sixth—differ in narrative tone and social effect. Compared to Day I, in fact, Frate Cipolla's *novella* shows a pleasant, friendly rustic world where the comedy develops out of the playful and joyous interchange of an obviously sympathetic and open society.

The individuals peopling the tales of the Sixth Day balance action with words—and master both. At the end of each tale, protagonists have created a wholly positive relationship with their society and frequently have wrought changes for its improvement. In this Day society is openly democratic; it prospers not from the fragmentation of its members into discreet social classes, but rather from healthy communication between them. Ingenuity, high spirits, and quick wits, prevalent throughout the *novelle*, combine with society's greatest gifts, verbal facility and good will, to create a pleasant and coherent human world. Moreover, the day's tales seem to have been conceived as *exempla* and as such they strengthen the overall structural configuration of the work with its interconnected *cornice* and *novelle:* should the members of the *brigata* emulate the Sixth Day's resourceful and witty *novelle* characters with whom they have identified themselves, they might better revive and reorganize the plague-stricken Florence of Day I to which they will return after the Tenth Day.

While the *novelle* of the Sixth Day present an idealized urban world concentrated largely in the city of Florence, the concluding *cornice* sequence in the *Valle delle Donne* presents idealized nature:

> Le donne . . . né guari più d'un miglio furono andate, che alla Valle delle Donne pervennero. Dentro dalla quale per una via assai stretta, dall'una delle parti della qual è un chiarissimo fiumicello, entrarono, e viderla tanto bella e tanto dilettevole . . . E secondo che alcuna di loro poi mi ridisse, il piano . . . era di giro poco più che un mezzo miglio, intorniato di sei montagnette di non troppa altezza, e in su la sommità di ciascuna si vedeva un palagio quasi in forma fatto d'un bel castelletto.
> Le piagge delle quali montagnette così digradando giuso verso il pian discendevano, come ne' teatri . . . E erano . . . tutte di vigne, d'ulivi, di mandorli, di ciriegi, di fichi, e d'altre maniere assai d'alberi fruttiferi piene . . .
> (VI, Conclusione, 19-22)

The passage sets forth a careful combination of natural elements—the "chiarissimo fiumicello," "piano," and "montagnette"—with those which are either man-made—the "palagio" and "bel castelletto"—or which require human skill applied to nature—the vines and fruit trees. The general Narrator's reference to his own personal connection with the female storytellers in the midst of his description ("secondo che alcuna di loro poi mi ridisse") once again unites all members of the Decameronian world—the Narrator, storytellers, and *novelle* characters—with perfected nature. The passage draws the Sixth Day to a close by suggesting that the *brigata's* oasis of civic splendor may exist only within a setting created by nature and perfected by man.

2. Day VII: The Hazards of Marriage: Individual Solutions

At the end of Day VI, King Dioneo decides to move the next day's storytelling to the idyllic location of the *Valle delle Donne*, where the slopes descend "come ne' teatri." In this way, he seems to aim at stressing the storytellers' aesthetic distance from the risqué themes of the Seventh Day's ribald tales. As they bathe in preparation for the next day's *novellare*, their immersion in the waters of the *Valle's* lake takes on an almost ritualistic dimension, suggesting their desire to purify their minds as well as to cleanse their bodies. After their immersion in the lake's waters, the women are ready to face the unusual topic of women's "amorosi inganni."

Unlike any other day of the *Decameron*, marital relationships provide the narrative focus of each *novella* of this day (with the usual exception of the tenth and last tale). And, in another Decameronian innovation, women and not men are the prime movers of all the complicated exploits recounted; the comic mood infusing the tales derives from the "beffe" performed by women on their less intelligent husbands. Play between appearance and reality recalls the atmosphere of the Third Day's *novelle*, but here women with quick tongues and sharp minds predominate exclusively. Such is the case of the "savia e avveduta molto" monna Tessa in VII 1, of the "bella e vaga" Peronella in VII 2, of the "bellissima" monna Ghita in VII 4, of the deft madonna Isabella in VII 5, and of the other female protagonists who control relationships between characters with their wit, verbal dexterity, and foresightedness. The husbands, on the other hand, are either smallminded and myopic tyrants (VII 4,5, and 8) or are so simpleminded (VII 1,2, and 3) or senile (VII 7 and 9) that they are unable to cope with their wives.

Conflicts between characters frequently arise from imbalances in social status, particularly where refined, aristocratic women are married to rich but uncouth husbands, who often belong to a lower social class. Such is the case of Gianni Lotteringhi in VII 1, of Tofano in VII 4, of the "mercatante ricco e di possessioni e di denari assai" in VII 5, and of Arriguccio Berlinghieri in VII 8. In three of these four cases, lack of social grace goes hand in hand with unreasonable jealousy. The wives armed with superior reasoning power and the ability to express it, succeed not only in improving their own situations, but in convincing their communities to accept their unconventional views on love and marriage. Individual and society are thus once again projected in conflict, this time over the issue of marriage, with errant women triumphing over conventional mores to produce a harmonious outcome. With such a topical matter at issue, it is no surprise that most of the *novelle* are set in times contemporary to the *Decameron*, with the exception of Lidia and Pirro's tale (VII 9), set in ancient Greece, and of the story of Ludovico, Egano, and Beatrice (VII 7), where the courtly references suggest the late thirteenth century.

A basic four-step structure develops in each *novella*: 1) a rendez-vous between a married woman and her lover occurs or is planned; 2) an intrusion, usually by the husband, brings the action to a danger point; 3) the woman reacts — usually by playing on appearance vs. reality — to neutralize the danger; and 4) final harmony results. The third narrative step occupies the greatest time and interest in each tale. Although most of the tales unfold in urban settings, the natural world appears in VII 1,6,7, and 9 and, with its implied city-country contrast, adds complexity to the basic narrative conflict between appearance and reality.

In the first *novella* of the day, monna Tessa is the "bellissima e vaga . . . moglie" of the "sofficiente lavaceci," Gianni Lotteringhi, and the mistress of the "giovane e fresco" Federigo de' Neri Pegolotti. The action occurs in the *contado* near Florence (close to the storytellers' present location) "in un luogo molto bello . . . in Camerata" (VII 1,6), and is triggered by the alternating visits of lover and husband who travel from Florence to Camerata to enjoy monna Tessa's embraces. Monna Tessa signals to Federigo with the skull of an ass mounted in her vineyard; when the jawbone points toward Florence, Gianni is away and Federigo may come to her; when, on the other hand, it points to the *contado* village of Fiesole, her husband is present and her lover must stay away.[13] The system functions smoothly until Gianni unexpectedly returns from Florence on an evening when Federigo is due. Monna Tessa tries to remedy the situation by sending her maid into the garden to set out a good dinner for Federigo so that, at the very least, he will not go hungry. But in her haste she neglects to have the skull turned around to warn him that her husband has returned. When the unsuspecting Federigo knocks at her chamber door while she is with Gianni, the situation becomes critical. Monna Tessa deftly avoids a crisis by playing upon Gianni's superstitious nature; she introduces a *fantasima* into the nocturnal scene and overturns illusion and reality: "'Oimè,'" she cries, "'Gianni mio, or non sai tu quello ch'egli è? Egli è la fantasima, della quale io ho avuta a queste notti la maggior paura che mai s'avesse . . .'" (VII 1,19). Gianni's response reveals that weakness which his clever wife is eager to exploit:

> 'Va, donna, non aver paura se ciò è, ché io dissi dianzi il
> *Te lucis* e la'*ntemerata* e tante altre buone orazioni . . . e
> anche segnai il letto di canto in canto al nome del Patre
> e del Filio e dello Spirito Sancto, che temere non ci
> bisogna . . .'
>
> (VII 1,20)

The conflict between appearance and reality is evident in this last interchange where Gianni accepts monna Tessa's fantastic ghost story as fact. Gianni compounds his stupidity not only by confusing superstition and religion, but by unwittingly inserting sexual imagery into his "religious" practices. When he chants and makes the sign of the cross around his and monna Tessa's bed, he is clearly unaware of his absurd collocation of the religious and the sexual. Monna Tessa, on the other hand, intentionally joins religious and sexual allusions in her mock incantation to the *fantasima* / lover. She thus averts a potential danger by transforming reality into a moment of high farce. She delivers her instructions to her lover as if performing a religious exorcism, her words resonant with sexual nuance:

> 'Fantasima, fantasima che di notte vai, a coda ritta ci venisti, a coda ritta te n'andrai: va nell'orto, a piè del pesco grosso troverai unto bisunto e cento cacherelli della gallina mia: pon bocca al fiasco e vatti via, e non far male né a me né a Gianni mio.'
>
> (VII 1,27)

The supposedly incorporeal *fantasima* is given physical form with monna Tessa's suggestive reference to its *coda ritta*. The list of instructions she sets forth for it are grounded in comic physical detail: she sends it to a precise location in her garden, "*a piè del pesco grosso*," offers it food with "*unto bisunto*" and the semi-scatological "*cento cacherelli della gallina mia*," and orders it to drink with "*pon bocca al fiasco.*" She culminates her speech with a last command to Gianni which is the epitome of crude physicality: "'Sputa, Gianni' e Gianni sputò " (VI 1,27).[14] A striking contrast emerges in the instructions given to lover and husband: one is ordered "pon bocca al fiasco," the other "Sputa." Monna Tessa thus suggests her lover's conviviality and pleasure in social intercourse with the metaphor of drinking while summoning a contrasting image of her husband violently expelling, an act with asocial connotations. At the end of the *novella* the incantation is explained: the lover has been directed to the orchard where he may enjoy the pleasures of food and drink, if not those of sex.

The action of this *novella* develops through the four basic steps characteristic of this day, the third and most crucial of which is the suspenseful and potentially dangerous encounter between husband and lover. The resourceful woman, however, defuses the dangerous situation and transforms it into a humorous one. Through her eloquence and enterprise she creates a satisfactory situation for both husband and lover and maintains her marital relationship as well as her extra-conjugal affair on a good working level.

The following *novella* (VII 2) presents a love triangle in a Neapolitan setting and it develops through the usual four steps: 1) the woman, Peronella, entertains her lover Giannello in her room, when 2) her husband (who does not have a name in the story) returns unexpectedly. Peronella's reaction enables her to 3) resolve the situation by hiding her lover in a tub and convincing her husband that she has sold it to Giannello. Complete satisfaction results at the end when 4) the husband happily scrubs the tub for seven *denari* while the lover satisfies his sexual urges with a strategically positioned Peronella. The action of entering and emerging from the tub by both lover and husband lends the *novella* a pattern suggestive of the love-making at its heart. The bawdy imagery is underlined at the end of the passage:

> . . . e in quella guisa che negli ampi campi gli sfrenati cavalli e d'amor caldi le cavalle di Partia assaliscono, a effetto recò il giovanil desiderio . . .
>
> (VII 2,34)

The phrase "ampi campi" not only works well rhythmically next to "sfrenati cavalli e d'amore caldi," through alliteration, assonance, and rhyme, but stands also in ironic contrast to the actual narrow and enclosed position in which Peronella finds herself. The contrasting image of the horses in *ampi campi* heightens the visual impact of the scene in which Peronella is balanced over the small opening of the tub. Moreover, the use of such adjectives as *sfrenati* and *d'amor caldi* stresses the sexual urges common to both *cavalli* and Giannello. The implicit equation of man and animal (which is not present in Boccaccio's principal source for this tale)[15] captures the general spirit of the novella: even in a man-made, circumscribed urban environment, natural instincts lie at the base of man's behavior. And it is Peronella's quick-wittedness which gives her natural instincts free reign and enables her to avert marital disaster. The tale ends with lover, husband, and wife all satisfied and in harmony.

In the following *novella* of Friar Rinaldo and his *comare* (VII 3), many elements of the previous *novelle* are reintroduced with interesting repetitions and variations. For instance, the love affair between the friar and the *comare* is paired with the one between his companion and the woman's maid. The narrative function of the companion emerges especially at the end of the tale when he contributes his "quattro orazioni" to Friar Rinaldo's incantation.[16] Furthermore, the main characters alternate in the leading role: in the first two moments of the narrative Friar Rinaldo manoeuvres the events to suit his will; in the third and most crucial moment, however, the woman takes over and independently directs the action to a satisfactory outcome:

> La donna, da subito consiglio aiutata, disse: 'Or vi vestite; e vestito che voi siete, recatevi in braccio vostro figlioccio e ascolterete bene ciò che io gli dirò, sì che le vostre parole poi s'accordino colle mie, e lasciate fare a me.'
>
> (VII 3,27)

When the husband intrudes on the amorous couple, the child, who has been present throughout, becomes an essential ingredient in his mother's plot to extricate herself from a dangerous situation. In seconds she formulates the ingenious pretense of her child's *vermini*, thus the friar's presence in her bedroom in the role of religious healer is unquestioned by the doting father. As in the *novella* of monna Tessa and Gianni, the wife manipulates reality by fabricating an incantation to play upon her husband's superstitious nature. And again, the tale's action develops in up-and-down, in-and-out patterns which suggest obvious sexual parallels. We follow the friar and his companion as they enter the *comare's* house and proceed to their respective assignations, one in the *comare's* bedroom, the other upstairs with the maid. The returned husband is kept symbolically outside his wife's chamber while the friar supposedly exorcizes the *vermini* inside. Finally, the companion "se ne venne giuso e entrato nella camera" (VII 3,39), as does the husband, completing the last up-down and in-out cycle.

A similar rhythmic narrative movement returns with a wider range of motifs in the *novella* of Tofano and Ghita (VII 4). Here again we find an in-and-out pattern which describes the relative positions of the two main characters. This pattern is combined with an up-and-down movement which involves not only the jealous Tofano and the witty Ghita, but the neighbors, who provide a choral backdrop for the story. The first two moments of the narrative action are handled differently here than in the previous *novelle*, where the lovers' rendezvous took place in the woman's home and the husband's unexpected return precipitated the danger. Here, instead, the woman leaves her house and joins her lover at his home while the husband is fast asleep in his bed, pretending to be in his usual drunken stupor. The most crucial sequences thus take place outside the woman's house, and the lover never comes into sight. The crisis is touched off when Tofano, suspecting Ghita's infidelity, locks her out of the house: "andatosene alla sua porta quella serrò dentro e posesi alle finestre" (VII 4,11). The in-out and up-down patterns of the story are established: the husband is inside, at the window, looking down on the street outside. The situation reaches its danger point when the woman returns and finds herself "serrata di fuori" (VII 4,11). A complete reversal, however, takes place in the third moment, when the wife conceives a way out of her predicaments by substituting "una grandissima pietra" for herself:

> 'Or ecco, io non posso più sofferire questo tuo fastidio: Dio il ti perdoni! farai riporre questa mia rocca che io lascio qui'; e questo detto, essendo la notte tanto obscura, che appena si sarebbe potuto veder l'un l'altro per la via, se n'andò la donna verso il pozzo, e presa una grandissim pietra che a piè del pozzo era, gridando 'Idio, perdonami!' la lasciò cadere entro nel pozzo.
>
> (VII 4, 17-18)

The stone that Ghita throws into the well transforms the entire situation: Tofano, believing the stone to be his wife, panics and "presa la secchia colla fune, subitamente si gittò di casa . . . e corse al pozzo" (VII 4,19), ending up literally and figuratively down and out. Ghita, "come vide (Tofano) correre al pozzo, così ricoverò in casa e serrossi dentro e andossene alle finestre" (VII 4,20), thus describing the opposite in-up movement. She now commands the strong hold of security and accordingly initiates a loud conversation through which to manipulate reality, this time verbally. She makes her husband the target of her half-truths and her neighbors her unwitting accomplices. In the new "reality" Tofano is the culprit and he is loudly accused of drunkenness by his enraged, wounded wife:

> Ella, lasciato stare il parlar piano come infino allora aveva fatto, quasi gridando cominciò a dire: 'Alla croce di Dio, ubriaco fastidioso, tu non c'enterai stanotte . . . egli convien che io faccia vedere a ogn'uomo chi tu se' e a che ora tu torni la notte a casa.'
>
> (VII 4,22)

The scene becomes more animated with the intervention of the neighbors, who introduce another innovation to the structure of this *novella*: "i vicini sentendo il romore si levarono, e uomini e donne, e fecersi alle finestre e domandarono che ciò fosse" (VII 4,23). They provide an audience for Ghita's oratorical display when she addresses them directly:

> Che direste voi se io fossi nella via come è egli, e egli fosse in casa come sono io? In fè di Dio che io dubito che voi non credeste che egli dicesse il vero . . . Egli dice a punto che io ho fatto ciò che io credo che egli abbia fatto egli.
>
> (VII 4, 26-27)

The passage plays on contrasting parallel constructions of verbs and pronouns: "fossi" versus "è," "fosse" versus "sono," and "io" versus "egli" appear at the beginning and end of the first "if" clause with their positions reversed in the second. This antithetical construction emphasizes the underlying opposition of character and situations which is spelled out in the last part of the passage. The irony of the passage develops out of the use of tenses and moods that play upon the inversion of reality and appearance. Ghita's appeal to the neighbors—"che direste voi . . . io dubito che voi non credeste"—actually presents in interrogative and negative-dubitative phrases the "real" situation as it occurred at the outset of her ordeal. From there, she moves on to present her own manipulation of the event in firm indicative statements. She thus leads her audience to believe her apparently sensible, although totally fantastic explanations. With such a powerful rhetorical ability, Ghita convinces her neighbors of Tofano's guilt:

> e gli uomini e le donne, cominciarono a riprendere tututti Tofano e a dar la colpa a lui . . . e in brieve tanto andò il romore di vicino in vicino, che egli pervenne

> infino a' parenti della donna. Li quali venuti là, e udendo la cosa e da un vicino e da altro, presero Tofano e diedergli tante busse, che tutto il ruppono; poi, andati in casa, presero le cose della donna e con lei si ritornarono a casa loro . . .
>
> (VII 4, 28-29)

The narrative function of the neighbors then is to propel the action toward the goal suggested by Ghita in her first loud speech to Tofano: "egli convien che io faccia vedere ad ogn'uomo chi tu se' . . ." (VII 4,22). Ghita puts on a show to convince "tututti" of her righteous anger and transforms the "notte tanto obscura che appena si sarebbe potuto veder l'un l'altro per la via" into a lively comedy of errors where she manipulates both husband and neighbors. The neighbors' presence as Ghita's witnesses differentiates this tale from the previous *novelle* in another significant way. Where previously the husbands were totally unaware of their wives' infidelities, and the wives' manipulations of reality served to maintain the *status quo*, here instead Tofano knows about Ghita's indiscretion and is therefore at her level of awareness. Ghita in turn, recognizes her husband's knowledge and her own dangerous situation if he should succeed in putting his threats into action: "abbi per certo che tu non ci tornerai mai infino a tanto che io di questa cosa in presenza de' parenti tuoi e de' vicini, te n'avrò fatto quello onore che ti si conviene'" (VII 4,12). She therefore promptly provides herself with witnesses on her behalf. (In so doing, she also proves her familiarity—or rather Boccaccio's—with secular laws on adultery.) She thus succeeds in manipulating the facts and disqualifying her husband's accusations. This story thus creates a more complex nexus of human relationships than the usual husband-wife-lover triad. In an ever-widening circle, it encompasses "i vicini . . . e uomini e donne," "i parenti della donna," who side with her, and finally "alcuni amici mezzani" of Tofano's who respond to his requests and arrange matters so that "egli con buona pace riebbe la donna a casa sua" (VII 4,30). As the story ends, harmony is restored within and without the couple's home, and once again the institution of marriage is upheld even after the jealous and foolish husband has acknowledged his wife's indiscretion and witty lies. Ghita's intellectual vivacity and physical promptness mark her as a winner, and her society recognizes her as such.

In VII 5, both the problem of jealousy and the theme of woman's cleverness in eliminating it are raised again. In contrast to the previous *novella* of Tofano and Ghita, where the action takes place almost wholly outside their urban home, here interior city scenes predominate. The concentration of indoor activity stresses the woman's confinement, for she is kept prisoner within her own house by her unreasonably jealous husband: "La donna . . . non osava farsi a alcuna finestra né fuor della casa guardare per alcuna cagione . . ." (VII 5,9). This confinement does not, however, prevent her from finding a way to revenge herself on her husband by searching for a lover. And although her search is restricted to interior settings, she succeeds in her enterprise:

> ... sappiendo che nella casa la quale era allato alla sua aveva alcun giovane e bello e piacevole, si pensò, se pertugio alcun fosse nel muro che la sua casa divideva da quella, di dovere per quello tante volte guatare, che elle vedrebbe il giovane in atto da potergli parlare, e di donargli il suo amore, se egli il volesse ricevere ...
> (VII 5,11)

The confession episode in this novella (which recalls the similar play of reality and illusion in III 3,) also takes place in a confined setting where the woman is supposed to come into contact only with her confessor. Because she is aware of her husband's pathological jealousy, she knows beforehand that he will take the priest's place. She therefore fabricates a confession where she admits to having a priest as a lover and pretends not to know that her husband has donned "una delle robe del prete". The final stage of the *beffa* is enacted with the woman once again inside her house:

> Venuta la notte, il geloso con sue armi tacitamente si nascose *in una camera terrena*. E la donna avendo fatti serrar *tutti gli usci,* e massimamente *quello da mezza scala* ... il giovane per via assai cauta dal suo lato se ne venne; e andaronsi a letto ... e venuto il dì, il giovane se ne tornò in casa sua.
> (VII 5,42)

Even at the story's end, the woman is still inside the house:

> ... senza far venire il suo amante *su per lo tetto* come vanno le gatte, ma pur *per l'uscio,* discretamente operando, poi più volte con lui buon tempo e lieta vita si diede.
> (VII 5,59)

The stress placed on interiors is thus functionally relevant in emphasizing the woman's secluded condition as prisoner in her own house and her lack of interaction with the outside world. In fact, in contrast to the previous *novella*, the outside world is not brought into contact with her at all and she is left to handle her situation within the confines of her home.

This treatment of the confined woman's situation is underscored by changes in the four basic narrative steps typical of the Seventh Day. Unlike most of the other tales, and only partially like the beginning of VII 4, the initial situation in VII 5 does not consist of an actual or planned rendez-vous between wife and lover. Rather, it presents a woman's decision to make her husband's unreasonable jealousy a self-fulfilling prophecy: she will find a lover to spite—and in spite of—him. The tale's second step offers a variation on the husband's customary intrusion. Instead of finding his wife in *flagrante delicto*, he resorts to a *travestissement*, dons a priest's robes, and hears his wife's false confession. The wife is thus able to intensify her husband's jealousy and thereby provides herself with an opportunity to receive her lover. Where an unwitting husband usually catalyzes the errant wife's ingenious machinations by intruding on her liaison, here unwarranted jealousy catalyzes a wife's plot to get her husband out of and her would-be lover into her bedroom. The third narrative stage brings the husband's exit from his wife's chamber and his descent to the bottom of the stairs to keep watch for the hypothetical intruder. Meanwhile, the actual intruder descends to the wife's room from the roof. The final stage of the tale is similar to the fourth step in the other *novelle* of this day: everyone, husband included, ends up happy and satisfied.

In this *novella*, the second step is actually the most interesting; it presents both main characters facing each other under false pretenses — the husband in actions and the wife in words. The husband, in order to maintain total control of his wife's life, tries to change his identity. The woman, instead, simply uses verbal dexterity and wit to manipulate reality. The woman's superiority is reveal be her quick recognition of her husband's *travestissement* and her subsequent resolution to make fun of him: "'Lodato sia Iddio che costui di geloso è divenuto prete; ma pure lascia fare, ché io gli darò quello che egli va cercando'' (VII, 5,22-3). The husband, however, takes everything she says seriously and is deeply hurt: "Quando il geloso udì questo, e' gli parve che gli fosse dato d'un coltello nel cuore . . ." (VII 5, 25). The power of words is heavily underscored in this scene and calls to mind similar scenes in other *novelle;* just as Ser Ciappelletto's confession in I 1 transforms reality to benefit all the people involved with him, so in VII 5 the woman's false confession transforms reality to completely remedy her predicament: and like the other clever woman of III 3 who duped her obtuse confessor into bringing her would-be lover to her bed unknowingly, the clever woman of VII 5 influences her false confessor to unite her with her own would-be lover.

The story closes with the woman's long speech in which she modestly and humorously comments on her own trickery and her husband's undignified stupidity and meanness:

> 'Egli mi giova molto quando un savio uomo è da una donna semplice menato come si mena un montone per le corna in becheria . . . e tanto quanto tu se' più sciocco e più bestiale, cotanto ne diviene la gloria mia minore . . .'
> (VII 5,52)

Here contrary to III 3, the woman forces her husband to recognize the resourcefulness and verbal dexterity she has demonstrated throughout the whole affair. She convinces him of her superiority and succeeds in making him renounce his jealousy: "e quando la gelosia gli bisognava del tutto se la spogliò, così come, quando bisogno non gli era, se l'aveva vestita" (VII 5,59).

Ghita, in VII 4, uses her verbal ability to indict her husband on grounds that are only half true and to convince the society around her to aid her in her feud. Here, instead, the woman uses her verbal powers to create an imaginary lover. She thus forces her husband to participate in her manipulation of reality without allowing him to perceive his role until she reveals it. She wins her sexual freedom and convinces her husband of her superior intelligence.

An interesting pattern which we have noted in previous *novelle*, particularly in VII 4, appears once again in the fifth *novella*: we see the conspicuous up-and-down movement of wife, husband, and lover. In church, for instance, the wife "si pose a' piedi" of her husband; later, the husband stands "a guardia dell'uscio" while the woman is three flights above. The wife has her lover come to her "su per lo tetto," while her husband stands watch below. These vertical interactions suggest the disharmonious relationship between husband and wife, as well as the potentially explosive situation created by the husband-wife-lover triangle. At the same time, the interaction between the woman and her lover takes place on the same level, thus implying a harmonious relationship. They begin by touching hands through a hole in the wall and end by "andaronsi a letto, dandosi l'un dell'altro piacere e buon tempo" (VII 5,42). These spatial configurations thus underscore the relationships among the three main characters of the story.[17] On the whole, this *novella* builds the theme of feminine intellectual superiority to an even greater extent than the other tales of this day. Woman's coolness and poise emerge unscathed from the attacks on her personal freedom by a husband's irrationality and jealousy.

Novella VII 8 further investigates the role of jealousy in married life and presents both innovations on and similarities to the *novelle* just discussed. Like his predecessors, the husband in this story is very rich. The details of his flawed relationship with his wife are presented in greater depth than in previous tales, and with greater historical accuracy. Neifile, the narrator, comments on Arriguccio's flaws both as a specific individual and as a member of the merchant class:

> . . . nella nostra città fu già un ricchissimo mercatante chiamato Arriguccio Berlinghieri, il quale sciocamente, *sì come ancora oggi fanno tutto 'l dì i mercatanti*, pensò di volere ingentilire per moglie . . . per ciò che egli, *sì come i mercatanti fanno*, andava molto da torno e poco con lei dimorava . . .
>
> (VII 8, 4-5)

The wives in *novelle* VII 4 and 8 both take advantage of their husbands' sound sleep in order to find time to enjoy their lovers' company. But while Tofano in VII 4 simply feigns drunkenness and locks his wife out, Arriguccio actually discovers the string tied to his wife's toe and, realizing her lover is outside the window, runs out to confront him. In this narrative we notice yet another play on the in-out movement and the up-down perspective which precipitates the conflict and animates the story. As in the tale of Ghita, the woman's presence of mind enables her to protect herself and her reputation not only from her husband's wrath, but from public and familiar denunciation as well.[18]

Furthermore, while the action follows the usual four-step pattern, each of the steps introduces innovations which differentiate this tale from the previous ones. As is clearly suggested by Neifile's previously cited comments, the husband's profession as "mercatante" and his long absences from home are the direct cause of his wife's increasing interest in her lover Ruberto. Arriguccio's jealousy, unlike that of the previous husbands, arises from his realization that his wife is, indeed, having a love affair:

> . . . o che Arriguccio alcuna cosa ne sentisse o come che s'andasse, egli ne diventò il più geloso uomo del mondo, e lascionne stare l'andar da torno e ogn'altro suo fatto e quasi tutta la sua sollicitudine aveva posta in guardar ben costei . . .
>
> (VII 8,6)

His strict surveillance provokes his wife's ingenuity in finding a way to meet her lover: "divisò di mandare uno spaghetto fuori della finestra della camera . . . e quando essa nel letto fosse, legallosi al dito grosso del piede . . ." (VII 8,8-9). A dangerous situation arises when, at the opening of the second narrative moment, Arriguccio finds the string and goes off to face his rival. The detailed confrontation between lover and husband is yet another innovation and it is immediately followed by Arriguccio's violent attack on the woman he assumes to be his wife. His crescendo of rage reveals Arriguccio's exuberant and emotional character and creates a sharp contrast to his calm and rational wife, madonna Sismonda.

The woman takes over as protagonist as soon as Arriguccio steps out to face his rival—that is, at the peak of danger. Her machinations bring about a total transformation of reality, first through actions, and then through words. Like Ghita in VII 4, who had substituted a large stone for her own body, madonna Sismonda substitutes her maid for herself in bed so that she will not be the victim of Arriguccio's blows. As a result, she makes herself the physical contradiction of the accusations Arriguccio makes against her to her family. Once her brothers see their sister sitting unscathed, calmly sewing, their former complete faith in Arriguccio is shaken. Madonna Sismonda then further reshapes reality by delivering a long speech (reminiscent again of Ghita's to her neighbors) in which she discredits Arriguccio completely and endows herself with the virtues of humility, patience, and modesty: "'Ma tuttavia, che che egli s'abbia di me detto, io non voglio che voi il vi rechiate se non come da uno ubriaco; e poscia che io gli perdono io, gli perdonate voi altressí" (VII 8,44). The woman has by now outsmarted her opponent and has transformed her own dangerous situation into a wholly safe one. And yet, before madonna Sismonda leaves her home in triumph, her mother interjects a long diatribe against "mercatanti" which seems at first unnecessary to plot development and which is completely absent in all the *novella's* sources.[18] The angry speech does, however, echo a theme introduced in Neifile's comments on the tale when she remarks that merchants attempt to "ingentilire per moglie." Madonna Sismonda's mother seizes this theme and gives us a heated commentary on fourteenth-century Florentine class struggles. The older urban aristocracy, by then in financial strictures, deeply resented the new mercantile class which had recently immigrated from the *contado* and had prospered through successful dealings in the woolen industry.[19] The feud between these two classes lies at the heart of the old woman's outburst against her son-in-law:

> . . . mercatantuzzo di feccia d'asino, che venutici di contado e usciti delle troiate vestiti di romagnuolo, con le calze a campanile e colla penna in culo, come egli hanno tre soldi, vogliono le figliuole de' gentili uomini e delle buone donne per moglie . . .
> (VII 8,46)

As Brucker notes, the commune society was based on "the critical importance of wealth." Conflict was bound to arise when the traditional social order, founded on a static, hierarchic base, was challenged by powerful individuals who, notwithstanding their social inferiority, dominated their betters through innovation and economic power. This episode in VII 8 is testimony to such a critical social situation in fourteenth-century Florence. At the same time, this episode is also structurally effective inasmuch as it prepares the groundwork for the *novella's* outcome; the husband-wife roles ultimately conform to the couple's class differences.

In the conclusion to VII 8 the husband's reaction to his wife's quickwittedness is treated extensively, implying his feelings of inferiority to his intellectually and socially superior wife: "Arriguccio, rimaso come uno smemorato, seco stesso non sappiendo se quello che fatto avea era stato vero o se egli aveva sognato, senza più farne parola, lasciò la moglie in pace" (VII 8,50). The woman's words and actions have shattered Arriguccio's confidence in himself. He is reduced from forceful exuberance to silent passivity. The woman, therefore, as representative of the old Florentine aristocracy, obtains complete freedom of action and cows her husband to permanent meekness: "la qual non solamente con la sua sagacità fuggì il pericolo soprastante, ma s'aperse la via a poter fare nel tempo avvenire ogni suo piacere, senza paura alcuna più aver del marito" (VII 8,50). The novella's source, the old French fabliau *Des tresces*, gives way to a contemporary dramatic rendition of lively class conflict. Here Boccaccio endows a woman's intellectual superiority with class superiority as well.

Boccaccio, ever the master of *variatio*, introduces a new dimension to the love triangle by adding an extra angle in the tale of madonna Isabella and her lovers (VII 6). Like monna Tessa in VII 1, Isabella takes advantage of the fine weather to repair to her country estate: ". . . andata, come nostro costume è di state, a stare in una sua bellissima possessione in contado" (VII 6,7). The new dimension in plot structure adds an extra step to the usual Day VII pattern: madonna Isabella entertains not one, but two lovers *in contado*. She is first visited by her favorite lover, Leonetto. They are interrupted, however, not by her husband, but by a less favored suitor, Lambertuccio, only to be interrupted by her husband. At this point, the pattern repeats itself in the normal Day VII manner: 1) madonna Isabella has her *tète-à-tète* with messer Lambertuccio when 2) her husband arrives unexpectedly. 3) She quickly conjures a plan to defuse the situation and orchestrates a drama involving the men in her *ménage-à-quatre* to 4) a successful ending.

Here, as in VII 5 and 9, the woman's maid plays the role of accomplice. She informs madonna Isabella of the arrivals first of messer Lambertuccio and then of her husband, enabling her to formulate her plans with some advance warning. Isabella may then manipulate the scene so that her lovers play their parts in front of her husband, himself a most engaged audience of one. The woman's strategem thus involves every character in the *novella* action. And once again we follow the players in and out of the lady's chamber and palace, as well as up and down the stairs which lead to her room.[20] Thus the narrative clearly emphasizes their exaggerated movements in order to produce a strongly theatrical effect. Such theatricality is enforced by the markedly short interrogative phrases that occur at the tale's most dramatic moments and never receive an adequate answer: "'Che è questo, messere?'" (VII 6,17) asks the husband: "'Al corpo di Dio, io il giugnerò altrove'" (VII 6,18), responds messer Lambertuccio. Again the husband asks, "Che cosa è questa? (VII 6,19), without receiving any logical reply. In madonna Isabella's fabricated tale, messer Lambertuccio is supposed to have demanded, "'Dove se', traditore?'" (VII 6,21). Her husband pursues the line of questioning with "'Ove se' tu? Esci fuori sicuramente'" (VII 6,24): and when Leonetto comes out of hiding, the husband continues the interrogation: "'Che hai tu a fare con messer Lambertuccio?'" (VII 6,26). The tale's outcome brings complete understanding between lovers and mistress, while the husband's confidence in his wife is never shaken: "mai per ciò il cavalier non s'accorse della beffa fattagli dalla moglie" (VII 6,29).

The remote setting in the *contado* here, as well as in VII 1, provides a background in which the lovers can come and go unnoticed from the woman's house without damaging her reputation. The institution of marriage thus goes unchallenged, at least as far as society at large is concerned. In the *novelle* set in the city, instead, specific details are inserted to provide safeguards for the woman's reputation and her matrimonial status. In the *novella* of Peronella, for instance, Filostrato, the narrator, stresses the time of day and the location of Peronella's house in order to emphasize the secrecy she uses to carry on her love affair:

> . . . con ciò fosse cosa che il marito di lei si levasse *ogni mattina per tempo* per andare a lavorare o a trovar lavorio, che il giovane fosse in parte che uscir lo vedesse fuori; ed essendo la contrada, che Avorio si chiama, *molto solitaria* dove stava, uscito lui, egli in casa di lei se n'entrasse: e così molte volte fecero.
>
> (VII 2,9)

In the *novella* of Tofano and Ghita, the woman's wisdom is measured in terms of her care in keeping her affair from becoming public: "*discretamente* con lui s'incominciò ad intendere": "*sicuramente* più volte di ritrovarsi con lui continuò" (VII 4, 6; 87). Ghita's wisdom is clearly contrasted with her husband's stupidity in dealing with the same situation: "*quella bestia* era pur disposto a volere che *tutti gli aretin* sapessero la loro vergogna, là dove *niun la sapeva*" (VII 4,13). In addition, the *novella* takes place in the darkness of night, as in VII 8, the best setting for assuring the privacy of the lovers' relationship. In the story of the jealous husband who keeps his wife prisoner in their house (VII 5), the woman's confinement similarly assures a completely private encounter between the lovers. It seems, therefore, that a special effort is made in each of the tales of the Seventh Day both to protect the ladies' reputations and to safeguard the institution of marriage.

The structure of the *novella* of Lodovico and madonna Beatrice (VII 7) presents still further variations on the basic format of the day's tales. At the moment of the amorous encounter (1), the two in bed together are the husband and wife, and it is the potential lover who, in the second stage (2), intrudes into their bedroom. The woman's reaction (3), seems to be an open accusation of her lover, but she succeeds in sending her husband out into the garden while her lover joins her in bed. The garden, as we have seen, often suggests love and fulfillment of sexual desires in the *Decameron*. But here, in a day in which characters constantly transform and manipulate reality, we find an interesting twist on the *giardino* motif. According to madonna Beatrice, the garden should at the same time be the site of her amorous rendez-vous with Lodovico/Anichino and the testing-ground for his loyalty to her husband. In fact, it becomes the scene of a double travesty: Egano, the husband, disguises himself as his wife to trap Anichino, and Anichino, in the role of moralist, then pretends to take Egano for his wife and beats him in the name of a non-existent loyalty to his lord. Yet the garden scene also enables the lovers to meet without allowing anything to threaten madonna Beatrice, her lover, or her marriage:

> . . . per la qual cosa, come che poi più volte con Anichino e egli e la donna ridesser di questo fatto, Anichino e la donna ebbero assai agio di quello per avventura avuto non avrebbeno a far di quello che loro era diletto e piacere . . .
>
> (VII 7,46)

In its ambiguous role in this *novella*, the garden thus represents the realm of appearance; when Egano accepts its premises, he views "reality" in a new way and accepts as reality the fabrications of his wife and servant:

> (Egano)era in opinione d'avere la più leal donna e il più fedel servidore che mai avesse alcun gentile uomo
>
> (VII 7,46)

An ironic shift in tone breaks this *novella* in two.[21] In the first part of the story, a courtly, chivalric ambience conveys the character of Lodovico-Anichino's ideal love for Beatrice; in the second sequence, farce and vulgarity predominate as Beatrice takes over the role of *"agente"* and initiates a *beffa* against Egano. This second part of the *novella* concentrates on Beatrice's desire for bedroom sport and cruel pranks. It thus stands in ironic contrast to the first sequence, in which Lodovico's search for an idealized woman is based on the lofty canons of courtly love. This conflict between courtly conventions and bawdy practice suggests the multi-faceted reality of the medieval world. It also seems to play upon the medieval canon of "moderatio" which dominates most of the *Decameron's* narrative situations. The obvious irony of madonna Beatrice's bawdy and rough play in contrast to Lodovico's idealized expectations of her seems to warn young men against an unrealistically lofty and abstracted view of women. Such a view is as far from reality as is madonna Beatrice's penchant for violent pranks. The *novella's* irony is further stressed by its theme of class differences: prefatory remarks to VII 7 introduce the issue of class mobility through the description of Lodovico's father and the education he provides for his son: "in Parigi fu già un gentile uomo fiorentino, il quale per povertà divenuto era mercatante, ed eragli sì bene avvenuto della mercatantia, che egli n'era fatto ricchissimo . . ." (VII 7,4). Here we have a glimpse of the economic and social changes produced and allowed by the new wealth of mercantile interests. The merchant profession is not, however, good enough for the son of a *"gentile uomo"*:

> E perché egli alla nobiltà del padre e non alla mercatantia si traesse, non l'aveva il padre voluto mettere ad alcun fondaco, ma l'avea messo a essere con altri gentili uomini al servigio del re di Francia, là dove egli assai di be' costumi e di buone cose aveva apprese.
>
> (VII 7,5-6)

Lodovico's chivalric view of life and love develops in this courtly environment. The *novella's* ironic tone emerges from the suggested opposition between the merchant and noble classes: madonna Beatrice, adored and idealized by the "gentili uomini" who are schooled "di be' costumi e di buone cose," turns out to be a licentious and unscrupulous trickster. And Lodovico-Anichino himself, shielded from the *déclassé fondaco* and raised as a nobleman, not only acquiesces to madonna Beatrice's lewd *beffa*, but takes an active role in the plot by beating her unwitting husband—who is also his feudal lord—senseless. These ironic vibrations deftly undermine the tale's initial opposition between *nobiltà* and *mercatantia*. At the same time, the conflict between *nobiltà* and *mercatantia*, between *servizio del re* and *fondaco*, lays the groundwork for the conflict between the mercatante Arriguccio and the "nobile donna Sismonda" in the following *novella*. There Sismonda's *nobiltà* unquestionably accounts for her intelligence and poise, and Arriguccio's lower-class origins for his uncontrolled emotions and overweaning jealousy. And yet, with Sismonda's aristocratic mother, Boccaccio once again undercuts the pose of polished nobility. The old woman's vulgar and uncouth attack on her merchant son-in-law is hardly what we would expect of a "gentildonna fiorentina." *Novelle* VII 7 and 8 are thus clearly linked in their ironic discussions of the *nobiltà-mercatantia* conflict as it relates to marriage, extra-marital affairs, and feminine resourcefulness.

Resourcefulness and determination are Lidia's outstanding qualities in VII 9. Her desire for Pirro initiates an affair which is complicated by her lover's three stipulations to test her love for him. From a structural point of view, this *novella* is the culmination of all previous ones: it not only twice recapitulates the basic steps of the Day VII *novelle* as does VII 6, but it also combines many narrative sequences which occur in different *novelle* of the day. In the first sequence, Lidia falls in love with Pirro, "un giovinetto leggiadro e addorno e bello della persona" (VII 9,6) who is in the service of her husband, Nicostrato. The consummation of her love is not, however, easily obtained: Pirro, after his initial refusal, imposes three trials upon her as conditions for his favors. Thus in the second moment, we find not a rendez-vous between the lovers, but a threefold ordeal for the woman. The completion of these tasks occupies the third movement. There Lidia verbally redesigns reality in order to make her actions acceptable to her husband and his entourage. She accomplishes each of her three tasks differently. First she kills her husband's prized hawk, and like Ghita in VII 4 she convinces the public of her right to do so. Then, like the women in VII 1 and 5, she skillfully combines word and deed and pulls out a handful of her husband's beard. Finally she pulls out one of his healthy teeth by coercing other characters to become her accomplices. With their help, she creates a false reality, as did the women in VII 3 and 6. The successful completion of all three tasks brings Lidia the fulfillment of her desire: "La donna, preso il dente, tantosto al suo amante il mandò: il quale, già certo del suo amore sé ad ogni suo piacere offerse apparecchiato" (VII 9,56). The second part of the *novella* brings

Lidia's descent from her pedestal. She not only wishes to consummate her relationship with Pirro, but, like madonna Beatrice, desires to humiliate her husband as well. She intentionally complicates her tryst with Pirro by improvising a means to perform sexually in front of her husband, Nicostrato. Her real ingenuity shows in convincing him that he has confused appearance and reality. The pear tree in her garden becomes the central image in the appearance-versus-reality motif; Lidia persuades Nicostrato that the tree causes one to imagine that others are performing sexual acts while one is perched in its branches. Thus Pirro, perched high in the *pero*, exclaims that his lord and lady below should refrain from lewd embraces while he is present. Nicostrato and Lidia proclaim their innocence. When Nicostrato exchanges places with Pirro, he assumes that the tree — not his wife and servant — provides the lusty scene he sees: "Nicostrato . . . cominciò a ragionare della novità del fatto e del miracolo della vista che così si cambiava a chi sù vi montava" (VII 9,76). The ultimate felling of the "lewd" tree reestablishes harmony and preserves Lidia and Nicostrato's marriage.

In the last *novella* of the day, which, as usual, is outside the thematic concerns of the other *novelle*, Dioneo ridicules earthly concerns over the spiritual consequences of an illicit love affair with one's *comare*. He tells the tale of a dead man who comes back to earth to report the state of the other world. In the afterlife, he says, such petty concerns are totally disregarded. Indeed, an inhabitant of the next world cries, "'Va, sciocco, non dubitare, ché di qua non si tiene ragione alcuna delle comari!'" (VII 10,28). This may imply, in Dioneo's characteristically ironic outlook, a healthy deflation of the self-centered concern for social conventions shared by several male characters in this day's *novelle*. He provides a sane reminder of the society-oriented role any individual must play and prepares the reader for the more sober and critical outlook on society offered by the tales of the Eighth Day.

On the whole, then, the Seventh Day presents a world where the social institution of marriage exists and even prospers in a general atmosphere of joviality and playfulness.[22] This becomes particularly clear if the Day's *novelle* are compared with some of the stories of Day II or III, which Day VII corresponds to and amplifies upon in the general structure of the work. In Day II women's lot is not that important in the first eight *novelle* where they are usually placed in secondary roles or are victims either of fate (madonna Beritola of II 6), or of fate and man's lust (Alatiel in II,7). The last two stories of the day, on the other hand, introduce women characters who are the true precursors of our Day VII protagonists: the Genoese madonna Zinevra (II 9) and the Pisan madonna Bartolomea (II 10). Madonna Zinevra shows the same level of intelligence and promptness in escaping her husband's unfounded wrath as Ghita or madonna Sismonda of Day VII, 4 and 8. Yet, Zinevra in spite of her complete innocence, has to leave her society, assume a new identity by passing as a man, and count on the Sultan's power and assistance in order to be able to transforms her lot, convince her husband of her innocence, and reform the marriage bond. Our Day VII heroines, on the other hand, while much less innocent than Zinevra, are able to achieve the same ends by themselves, within their own environments, and with support of a society of which they are an integral part. Madonna Bartolomea's drive for a healthy sexual relationship can be satisfied by her pirate lover, but only outside her Pisan environment. She clearly rejects her family and marriage ties and prefers to live as a sexually satisfied outcast in Monaco rather than as a discontented wife in Pisa. The wives of the Day VII stories do not have to make such a drastic choice: through their resourcefulness they successfully maintain a harmonious balance between the lover-woman-husband triangle and their society.

Extramarital affairs are common topics of Day III's *novelle* (III 2,3,4,5,6,7,8) and yet women are seldom the instigators of their sexual ventures. While the fantastic death and Purgatorial punishments of Ferondo (III 8) might appear to be the fulfillment of his wife's wishes, the whole plot is exclusively the result of the "santo abate's" lust for his beautiful parishioner. Self-gratification is the password: no hint is given of any intention to improve social or matrimonial behaviour, or of any expectation to improve the social situation. Similar *menages-à-trois* are organized in III 5 and 6 by Zima and Ricciardo, two ingenious lovers who are motivated exclusively by their sexual urges. Only the clever woman of III 3 is worthy forerunner of our Day VII heroines. She brilliantly plots to deceive her confessor and uses him as a pandar between herself and the man she has chosen for her lover. Yet, despite class differentiations between her and her husband which compare to the situation of madonna Sismonda in VII 8, the husband never appears in III 3 and no lessons on social or matrimonial behavior are implied. The social institution of marriage is thus of little concern for Day III's characters while, instead, it becomes central in Day VII's *novelle*, where female protagonists are intellectually and socially much more aware than their counterparts in Days II and III.

3. Day VIII: Resourcefulness Extended

At the end of Dioneo's reign, the new queen, Lauretta, introduces the topic of the next day's storytelling: "quelle beffe che tutto il giorno o *donna a uomo o uomo a donna o l'uno uomo all'altro si fanno"* (VII, Conclusion, 4). The topic of Day VIII, then, is still the *beffa*, this time with representatives from both sexes as agents; all the *beffe* take aim at social improprieties or misfits. One can expect that social institutions other than marriage, and characters other than husbands will become the target of the storyteller's ironic rebukes. Greedy and lusty women (VIII 1,2,7,10), oversexed priests (VIII 2 and 4), and inept professionals (VIII 5 and 9) are exposed to punishments and/or ridicule, while serious questions are raised about the integrity of the religious and judicial systems (VIII 2,4, and 5) about the soundness of philosophical (VIII 7), medical (VIII 9) or business (VIII 10) educations, and even about human friendship (VIII 8). Calandrino, the epitome of foolishness, and as such the catalyst of many *beffe* and *risi*, plays his dupe's role in two *novelle* of this day, and will reappear in two others of the next. His social role as victim of ridicule is progressively amplified in these *novelle*.

The structural pattern of most of the day's *novelle* is similar to the Seventh Day's and repeats itself with some variations: in a first stage the intended *beffa* takes shape; it is put into effect in a second stage, and is eventually accomplished in a third, where the *beffa's* results are also presented.

In *novelle* 1 and 2 of this day, the first stage establishes dramatic conflict. In both cases, this conflict takes the form of an opposition between two types of sexual motivation, one emotional, the other purely economic. The *beffa* arises from this conflict, and is intended to punish the greedy party. Such is clearly the case of the *'ngorda melanese* of the first *novella*. She is tricked by her resentful German lover into returning to her husband the two hundred gold florins which she believed she had earned by "il disonesto prezzo della sua cattività" (VIII 1,18). A similar pattern appears in the *novella* of the *prete da Varlungo* and monna Belcolore (VIII 2), in which the action develops in the *contado* setting of Varlungo. Here the clear-cut indictment of feminine greed is greatly toned down and is joined with an initial attack on priests' lechery. The *novella*, however, maintains an amiable mood as it conveys the saga of "uno amorazzo contadino" (VII 2,5) between a priest and one of his best-looking parishoners. Panfilo, the tale's narrator, tells us that Varlungo is a "villa assai vicina di qui" (VIII 2,6). In such a rural environment, the priest is one of the most important social figures, and this one, described as "un valente prete e gagliardo della persona ne' servigi delle donne" (VII 2,6), indeed becomes the activating force of the whole story. It is, in fact, his pursuit of monna Belcolore, "una piacevole e fresca foresozza, brunazza e ben tarchiata e atta a meglio saper macinar che alcuna altra" (VIII 2,8), which produces the characteristic beffa *pattern*. The natural environment of the *contado* also affects the description of the novella's uncouth characters and their actions. Their rusticity reaches its most intensely comic point in the list of gifts sent by the priest to his paramour:

> . . . quando le mandava un mazzuol d'agli freschi, ch'
> egli aveva i più belli della contrada in un suo orto che
> egli lavorava a sue mani, e quando un canestruccio di
> baccelli e talora un mazzuolo di cipolle malige o di
> scalogni . . .
>
> (VIII 2,11)

The first stage of the *novella*, a lengthy preparation for the actual meeting of the main characters, deals with the priest's assiduous and unsuccessful courtship of Belcolore. The woman's greed manifests itself when the priest intends to trick her through some ambiguous dealings over the priest's coat. Comedy emerges with the priest's intentionally confusing words:

> Disse il prete: 'Come, che vale? Io voglio che tu sappi ch'egli è di duagio infino in *treagio*, e hacci di quegli nel popolo nostro che il tengon di *quattragio* . . .'
>
> (VIII 2,35)

After the priest finally convinces Belcolore of what a good bargain she is getting, and makes her "parente di messer Domenedio", the plot to trick her out of his coat materializes:

> . . . pensando che quanti moccoli ricoglieva in tutto l'anno d'offerta non valeva la metà di cinque lire, gli parve aver mal fatto e pentessi d'avere lasciato il tabarro e cominciò a pensare in che modo riaver lo potesse senza costo. E per ciò che alquanto era maliziosetto, s'avisò troppo bene come dovesse fare a riaverlo, e vennegli fatto . . .
>
> (VII 2,39-40)

Thus in this *novella*, unlike VIII 1, the *beffa* is not called forth by indignation over female greed, but rather by the priest's own greed, which manifests itself after his sexual desire has been gratified. The two protagonists share the same frailty, and therefore "deserve" each other. The narrative mood of this *novella* is thus kept on a strictly comic level. Even when Belcolore is obliged to return the priest's *tabarro* and to renounce all hope of payment for her love-making, her unhappiness is short-lived. In fact, at the end of the tale we see both characters together again: Belcolore "col mosto e con le castagne calde si rappatumò con lui, e più volte insieme fecer poi gozzoviglia" (VIII 2,46.)

What seems most to contribute to the comic mood of this *novella* — especially in comparison to the gloomy preceding tale — is its rural setting. The predominantly rustic imagery of this "amorazzo contadino, più da ridere per la conclusione che lungo di parole" (VIII 2,5), creates the jolly, down-to-earth narrative atmosphere of the *novella*. Madonna Belcolore's sexual attractiveness, as we have already seen, is measured strictly by rural terms: "messer lo prete ne 'nvaghì sì forte, che egli ne menava smanie e tutto 'l dì andava aiato per poterla vedere" (VIII 2,10). Furthermore, he is often described with animal imagery:

> . . . quando la domenica mattina la sentiva in chiesa, diceva un *Kyrie* e un *Sanctus* sforzandosi ben di mostrarsi un gran maestro di canto, che *pareva uno asino che ragghiasse* . . . guatatala un poco *in cagnesco*, per amorevolezza la rimorchiava . . .
>
> (VIII 2,10-12)

The priest's favors are proffered to Belcolore entirely in agricultural terms. He offers her such dainties as "agli freschi," "cipolle malige" and "scaglioni." His sexual urge is also described in down-to-earth, rustic metaphors: "noi maciniamo a raccolta . . . ho così ritta la ventura . . . aveva carica la balestra" (VIII 2,23,31,37). The sexual act itself is similarly suggested by bawdy, rustic innuendo; a young messenger carries Belcolore's words to the priest:

> . . . dice che fa prego a Dio che voi non pesterete mai più salsa in suo mortaio . . .
> . . . a cui il prete ridendo disse: 'Dira'le, quando tu la vedrai, che s'ella non ci presterà il mortaio, io non presterò a lei il pestello; vada l'un per l'altro.'
> (VIII 2,44-45)

Finally the priest makes peace with Belcolore "col mosto e con le castagne calde," thus concluding the *novella* on the same rustic note with which it began. This general aura of spirited buoyancy created through the *novella's* rural setting thus seems to reduce the conflict between the two protagonists to a purely physical level.

The following *novella*, VIII 3, combines urban and rural backgrounds in staging the adventures of Calandrino, one of the most famous comic characters of the *Decameron*. Here all trickery develops out of the character of Calandrino himself, and not, as in the two preceding *novelle*, from any conflict of love interests. Calandrino's *novella* contains two distinct *beffe*: one is accomplished simply through words, the other through actions. First Maso del Saggio devises a game by which to test Calandrino's gullibility and to determine how many incredible things he can be made to believe:

> . . . Maso del Saggio . . . udendo alcune cose della semplicità di Calandrino, propose di voler prender diletto de' fatti suoi col fargli alcuna beffa, or fargli credere alcuna nuova cosa.
> (VIII 3,5)

Maso then chooses the second possibility—"fargli credere alcuna nuova cosa"—and begins by describing the imaginary Bengodi country with its "montagna tutta di formaggio parmigiano grattugiato, sopra la quale stavan genti che niuna altra cosa facevano che far maccheroni e raviuoli e cuocergli in brodo di capponi" (VIII 3,9). This vision of culinary opulence fascinates Calandrino, who then becomes even more pliable material in Maso's hands. The ingenious Calandrino in fact, eagerly swallows Maso's story of the miraculous heliotrope. According to Maso,

> noi altri lapidarii appelliamo elitropia, pietra di troppo gran vertù, per ciò che qualunque persona la porta sopra di sé, mentre la tiene, non è da alcuna altra per-

sona veduto *dove non è.*

(VIII 3,20)

Maso's attempt to create a new reality for the foolish Calandrino succeeds completely. Calandrino does not register the last three words of Maso's speech "dove non è" and plunges into a world of unreality which only someone as gullible as he could accept. From Maso's initial *beffa,* Bruno and Buffalmacco then develop another. They take up where Maso leaves off, and they lead Calandrino to the deserted banks of the Mugnone in search of heliotrope stones. The contrast between their attitudes and that of their gull defines the comic conflict of the *novella:* where Calandrino eagerly attempts to fill up his "seno . . . i gheroni della gonnella . . . e mantello" with black stones (VIII 3,40), Bruno and Buffalmacco carelessly "quando una e quando un'altra ne ricoglievano" (VIII 3,40). But the humor turns darker when, to convince Calandrino they cannot see him, Bruno and Buffalmacco pelt him with stones. Later, in Calandrino's house, the stones once again figure in an unjust beating: Caladrino vents his anger on his wife, monna Tessa, because he thinks she has broken the heliotrope's spell when she sees him come home:

> . . . scaricate le molte pietre che recate aveva, niquitoso corso verso la moglie, e presala per le treccie la si gittò a' piedi, e quivi . . . pugna e calci, senza lasciarle in capo capello o osso adosso che macero non fosse le diede . . .
>
> (VIII 3,52)

In the final scene of the *novella* the two moments of dramatic action come together. All the participants of the second *beffa* regroup in Calandrino's house, where the image of the stones and the connotations of violence, pain and despair reappear:

> Buffalmacco e Bruno . . . andaron suso e videro la sala piena di pietre e nell'un de' canti la donna scapigliata, stracciata, tutta livida e rotta nel viso, dolorosamente piagnere; e d'altra parte Calandrino scinto e ansando a guisa d'uom lasso, sedersi.
>
> (VIII 3, 53-54)

Violence and pain, essential elements of unsophisticated *beffe,* are suggested by the natural image of the stones. Throughout the story each character, except monna Tessa, is concerned exclusively with his own personal gratification, and is thus willing to perform violent acts to attain his goals.

Calandrino reappears in another *novella* of this same day, VIII 6. This tale takes place almost entirely in the *contado* near Florence, in Calandrino's "poderetto non guari lontan da Firenze che in dote aveva avuto dalla moglie" (VIII 6,4). Here again the *beffa* occurs at Calandrino's expense and is perpetrated by Bruno and Buffalmacco, the same astute characters as in VIII 3. In this story, a first moment delays the development of the *beffa*. Bruno and Buffalmacco try to convince Calandrino to do what they will actually do later: take his hog and pretend it has been stolen. They seem to foreshadow their own plan for Calandrino but he never catches on. Because Calandrino's gullibility is even more evident here than in the previous tale, the ultimate theft of the hog becomes even more comical. Calandrino, largely out of fear of monna Tessa, refuses Bruno and Buffalmacco's suggestion. The two pranksters set the *beffa* in motion in a second moment. They steal the hog, and by means of a false incantation, "prove" Calandrino to be the thief. At the end of the story, Calandrino is alone, embittered by the loss of his hog and of the "due paia di capponi" with which he bought Bruno and Buffalmacco's silence about his alleged affair with a village girl. Although in this *novella* there is no physical aggression against Calandrino, the treatment he receives from his friends is far from amicable. In effect it involves physical as well as moral humiliation: Calandrino is branded as a thief in the presence of the men of his village, who congregate "dinanzi alla chiesa intorno all'olmo," (VIII 6,41), in a scene reminiscent of a public trial. Such a scene is typical of a society which performs most of its important functions either inside the church or in the square in front of it. Yet it is ironic that the ritual performed in the church courtyard has little to do with religion. Rather, it reveals society's easy acceptance of magic formulae to solve real problems. Calandrino is branded a thief not because of a charge based on specific proof, but because his accusers believe that the thief "non potrà mandar giù la galla, anzi gli parrà più amara che veleno, e sputeralla" (VIII 6,43). Bruno and Buffalmacco frame Calandrino by playing on this old superstition, in a ritual testing of innocence through communal eating, "questi che non lo potrà mangiare, a colui s'apponga (la colpa)."[23] When the tricksters feed Calandrino *aloè*, he cannot swallow it:

> Calandrino prestamente là si gittò in bocca e cominciò a masticare, ma sì tosto come la lingua sentì l'aloè, così Calandrino, non potendo l'amaritudine sostenere, la sputò fuori.
>
> (VIII 6,45)

For further proof, the same process is repeated with even more devastating results:

> Calandrino, se la prima gli era paruta amara, questa gli parve amarissima: ma pur vergognandosi di sputarla, alquanto masticandola la tenne in bocca, e tenendola cominciò a gittar le lagrime che parevan nocciuole sì eran grosse; e ultimamente, non potendo più, la gittò fuori come la prima aveva fatto.
>
> (VIII 6,48)

Calandrino's inability to swallow his morsel condemns him in the eyes of his superstitious society. In conformity with their beliefs, without even asking for further evidence, his peers judge him guilty.

The instances of magic in this *novella*—as in VIII 7 and 9—enrich the complexity of the narrative by suggesting a class conflict. The *beffa*, centered on magic ritual, develops from the interplay between the two groups of characters whose motivations are in conflict: on the one hand, we see the village society and Calandrino, who represent the superstitions of a primitive, naive, and often gullible social group. Not coincidentally, they are equated with rural life. Their role is a totally passive one, and therefore they are incapable of becoming a reliable force in society. On the other hand, we see the village priest and the two city tricksters, Bruno and Buffalmacco, who, by taking advantage of the former group's naiveté, present a more aggressive and intellectually superior approach to life. Their more advanced social behavior suggests an urban background. The *novella's* ironic tone develops from this conflict of characters and behaviors. Paradoxically, it is actually the unsuperstitious group which imposes superstitious practices on the others. By doing so, and by tampering with the ritual, Bruno and Buffalmacco successfully orchestrate the whole situation. A comic paradox emerges: those who passively accept overwhelming superhuman forces are made victims of human manipulation. Superstition and magic become synonymous with naiveté, weakness, and ultimately with selfishness and asociality.[24] This equation will become even more apparent in the other two *novelle* of this day in which these elements appear, VIII 7 and 9.

In VIII 6, as in VIII 3, Calandrino suffers two *beffe:* in the first instance—the "action beffa"—his hog is stolen; in the second, a subtle verbal *beffa* involves Bruno and Buffalmacco's manipulation of reality. We have a reversal of the sequence which occurred in VIII 3, where Maso del Saggio's verbal *beffa* led to Bruno and Buffalmacco's physical ruse. In VIII 6 the verbal prank involves not only Calandrino, but the society of superstitious gulls in which he lives. This *beffa* is thus more sophisticated than was Maso's, for it exploits mass superstition rather than individual folly. Calandrino, never able to learn from his misadventures, is the country gull *par excellence.* At the end of the *novella*, he is completely isolated, "col danno e con le beffe" (VIII 6,56).

A similar condition befalls the presumptuous "proposto di Fiesole" in VIII 4 after his night with the hideous Ciutazza. Her portrait is a masterpiece of descriptive grotesquerie:

> . . . il più brutto viso e il più contraffatto che si vedesse
> mai: ché ella aveva il naso schiacciato forte e la bocca
> torta e le labbra grosse e i denti mal composti e grandi, e
> sentiva del guercio, né mai era senza mal d'occhi, con
> un color verde e giallo che pareva che non a Fiesole ma
> a Sinagaglia avesse fatta la state, e oltre a tutto questo

> era sciancata e un poco monca dal lato destro; e il suo nome era Ciuta, e perché così cagnazzo viso aveva, da ogni uomo era chiamata Ciutazza; e benché ella fosse contraffatta della persona, ella era pure alquanto maliziosetta.
>
> (VIII 4, 21-22)

Through the series of adjectives emphasizing Ciutazza's ugliness, deformity, and ill health a picture of a woman is created which contrasts completely with the traditional white and rosy beauty of Boccaccio's time. The grotesque portrait culminates with an interesting psychological nuance: the *contrafatta* servant is *maliziosetta* as well. She is thus the perfect choice to cooperate with her mistress's plan to trick the *proposto* into sleeping with her in her mistress's stead. Here the maid takes place of her mistress as did the servant in VII 8, but she exchanges a sexual diversion for a "camicia" while the other maid suffered a severe beating in exchange for nothing. This lighter, comic mood is strengthened by the portrait of the *impronto proposto*, whose arrogance sets him up for his downfall:

> Era questo proposto d'anni già vecchio ma di senno giovanissimo, baldanzoso e altiero, e di sé gran cosa presummeva con suoi modi e costumi pien di scede e di spiacevolezze, e tanto sazievole e rincrescevole . . .
>
> (VIII 4,7)

The irony of the *novella* reaches its climax when the provost, who considers himself a lady-killer, unwittingly makes love to Ciutazza, imagining her to be the lady of his desires. Ciuta, in return, desires only "una camiscia."

As the *novella* proceeds, its action seems to evolve in three stages: first the priest and Ciutazza make love in the darkness and secrecy of the *donna's* bedroom. Then the *cittadini* and the bishop enter the bedroom to observe and judge the *proposto*. Finally, in a third moment, the priest leaves the room and attempts to rejoin society. The bishop passes judgment on him and everyone else speaks of the shameful affair: "da' fanciulli mostrato a dito, li quali dicevano: 'Vedi colui che giacque con la Ciutazza'" (VIII 4,37). The *proposto*'s role shifts according to these stages as well. While at first he is the agent who woes Ciutazza "in braccio," he later becomes the object of clerical scorn and public ridicule. His response to the *beffa* similarly develops in three stages. When he first realized the "'nganno della donna . . . subito divenne il più doloroso uomo che fosse mai" (VIII 4,35). His sorrow is intensified by the bishop's punishment and his own shame: "Questo peccato gli fece il vescovo piagnere quaranta dì ma amore e isdegno gliele fecero piagnere più di quarantanove" (VIII 4,37). Despite the delightful detail "la Ciutazza guadagnò la camiscia," which appears in the tale's last lines, the *novella* concludes on a caustic note. The priest is universally censured and we are left with a rather sober view of the chastened cleric.

While other priests in the *Decameron* happily fulfill their sexual desires without social censure (cf. I 4, III 4 and 8, and VIII 2), this *proposto's* affair seems to come under attack more because of his advanced age and inflated self-esteem than because of his profession. It seems that the widow of VIII 4 shares the view of the clergy voiced in the fourth *novella* of the Third Day and has acted accordingly. In III 4 Tebaldo delivers a lengthy and violent diatribe against the clergy and strongly urges his former lover, madonna Ermellina, not to listen to their hypocritical and malignant suggestions. In VIII 4, monna Piccarda accepts the admonishment and brings about the downfall of the "impronto proposto." Debased sex, or sex used solely for self-gratification is ridiculed in the person of the pompous provost. His conceit and gullibility make him as poor a holy man as he is a lover, and add his portrait to the gallery of social misfits.

Other professional misfits appear in several *novelle* of the Eighth Day. Our unworthy provost is joined by an incompetent judge in VIII 5, by a scholar who abandons wisdom for love in VIII 7, and by an inept doctor in VIII 9. In each case, a *beffa* punishes the incompetent severely—and often painfully—for his shortcomings.

Maso del Saggio reappears in VIII 5 to ridicule a *giudice marchegiano*. The *beffa* which Maso and his companions devise to shame the judge at once makes the latter the object of scorn and sheds light on some Florentine social problems of Boccaccio's time. Both agent and object are amplified in this *novella*; not only does Maso enlist Ribi and Matteuzzo as his accomplices but the impact of their joke hits Judge Niccola da San Lepidio and the broad class of *marchigiani* to which he belongs as well. In his introduction to the tale, Filostrato refers to the

> 'rettori marchigiani . . . uomini di povero cuore e di vita
> tanto strema e tanto misera . . . e per questa loro innata
> miseria e avarizia menan seco e giudici e notari che
> paiono uomini levati più tosto dall'aratro o tratti dalla
> calzoleria, che delle scuole delle leggi.'

(VIII 5,4)

Filostrato's words reveal the Florentines' resentment of political outsiders from the countryside who fill positions in the city for which they are not qualified. Their unfitness is epitomized by messer Niccola's inappropriate dress, which Maso keenly observes:

> Maso del Saggio . . . venutogli guardato là dove questo
> messer Niccola sedeva, parendogli che fosse un nuovo
> uccellone, tutto il venne considerando. E come che egli
> gli vedesse il vaio tutto affummicato in capo e un pen-

> naiuolo a cintola e più lunga la gonnella che la guarnacca e assai altre cose tutte strane da ordinato e costumato uomo, tra queste una . . . ne gli vide, e ciò fu un paio di brache, le quali, sedendo egli e i panni per istrettezza standogli aperti dinanzi, vide che il fondo loro infino a mezza gamba gli agiugnea.
>
> (VIII 5,6-7)

Maso formulates his *beffa* when he sees the *marchegiano's* breeches. He seizes upon them—literally and figuratively—as a symbol of the judge's lack of culture and education. Stripped of his pants,[25] messer Niccola's weaknesses are apparent:

> Matteuzzo . . . pigliò il fondo delle brache del giudice, e tirò giù forte: le brache ne venner giuso incontanente, per ciò che il giudice era magro e sgroppato . . . e . . . quanti nella corte n'erano s'accorsero essergli state tratte le brache.
>
> (VIII 5, 14-16)

Although the mayor and judge are angered by Maso's *beffa*, there is little they can do; public sentiment against them runs too high because "i fiorentin conoscevano che, dove egli (il podestà) doveva aver menati giudici, egli aveva menati becconi per averne miglior mercato" (VIII 5,20). This concluding equation of *podestà* with animal dealer and judge with animal confirms the sharpness of the Florentine citizens' humor and clear-sightedness. The disdain for deficient public officials pointedly recognized in this novella reveals their desire to revitalize and preserve their society.

Florentine wit and shrewdness, embodied once again in Calandrino's comrades Bruno and Buffalmacco, get the best of another inept professional, a medical doctor from Bologna (VIII 9). Maestro Simone da Villa is characterized throughout the *novella* by such phrases as "una pecora" (VIII 9,3), "uno animale" (VIII 9,10), "pecoraggine,"[26] (VIII 9,15), "la cui scienza non si stendeva forse più oltre che il medicare i fanciulli del lattime" (VIII 9,31), "lavaceci" (VIII 9,52), "medico che s'intenda d'orina d'asino" (VIII 9,70), and "gli facean cavalcar la capra delle maggiori sciocchezze del mondo" (VIII 9,73). As if references to sheep, asses, and goats were not sufficient to convey maestro Simone's limited intellectual gifts, he is also linked with the vegetable world. Bruno and Buffalmacco apostrophize him as "vostra qualitativa mellonaggine," "zucca mia da sale" (VIII 9,15; 22), and "pinca mia da seme' (VIII 9,74). All these images strengthen the comic link between rusticity and stupidity.[27] We are therefore not suprised to learn that maestro Simone's favorite painting is Bruno's "battaglia de' topi e delle gatte" (VIII 9,34). He meets a fitting reward for his stupidity and animality when, after a wild ride on "una bestia nera e cornuta" (VIII 9,82), he finds himself head first in "una . . . (di quelle) fosse, nelle quali i lavoratori di quei campi facevan votare la contessa a Civillari per ingrassare i campi loro" (VIII 9,98). This scatological and animal imagery constantly linked with the doctor makes his final destination in the ditch full of excrement most appropriate.

An implicit contrast between the clever Florentine wits, Bruno and Buffalmacco, and the incompetent foreign-trained doctor, runs throughout the tale. Bruno's comically inappropriate paintings for the wealthy "medico . . . pecora" underscore the artist's desire to mock the foolish doctor:

> Bruno . . . gli aveva dipinta nella sala sua la Quaresima e uno *agnusdei* all'entrar della camera e sopra l'uscio della via uno orinale . . . e in una sua loggetta . . . la battaglia de' topi e delle gatte, la quale troppo bella cosa pareva al medico . . .
>
> (VIII 9,34)

Bruno subtly attacks all of the doctor's weaknesses in these paintings; the *Quaresima* in his living room mocks maestro Simone's flurry of "le più belle cene e i più belli desinari del mondo" (VIII 9,61) to woo acceptance into an exclusive club; the *agnusdei* over the entrance to his bedchamber undermines his fervently areligious desire to bed "la contessa di Civillari"; and the *orinale* is an appropriate although unaesthetic symbol of the "medico che s'intenda d'orina d'asino." The battle of the cats and mice, itself a curious choice for a dining room, may suggest the game that Bruno and Buffalmacco play with their weak-minded prey. Bruno's wit is as keen verbally as it is pictorially; his creative ability reaches its peak when he describes his "club's activities" to the gullible doctor:

> ". . . è maravigliosa cosa a vedere i capoletti intorno alla sala dove mangiamo e le tavole messe alla reale e la quantità de' nobili e belli servidori, così femine come maschi, al piacer di ciascuno che è di tal compagnia, e i bacini, gli orciuoli, i fiaschi e le coppe e l'altro vasellamento d'oro e d'argento . . . e oltre a questo le molte e varie vivande . . . i dolci suoni d'infiniti strumenti, e i canti pieni di melodia . . . né vi potrei dire quanta sia la cera che vi s'arde . . . né quanti sieno i confetti che vi si consumano e come sieno preziosi i vini che vi si beono . . . egli non ve ne è niuno sì cattivo che non vi paresse uno imperadore, sì siamo di cari vestimenti e di belle cose ornati."
>
> (VIII 9, 20-22)

Bruno's description recreates a convivial scene befitting Florentine culture at its best. In keeping with the new society's values, admission to Michele Scotto's group is based upon native culture and intellect, not upon nobility of blood:

> . . . piacendo loro la città e i costumi degli uomini, ci si disposero a voler sempre stare e preserci di grandi e di strette amistà con alcuni, senza guardare chi essi fossero, più gentili che non gentili o più ricchi che poveri, *solamente che uomini fossero conformi a' lor costumi.*
>
> (VIII 9,18)

With their high spirits, wit, and creativity, Bruno and Buffalmacco represent an elite group of Florentines who are as successful in their professions as they are in their diversions. They stand in sharp contrast to the mass of inept outsiders who are forbidden the pleasures of verbal play. This contrast is further sharpened by their choice of mates: Bruno and Buffalmacco choose "la reina di Francia . . . e quella d'Inghilterra" (VIII 9,27), that is, mistresses who, even in a humorous context, suggest a well-defined historical connotation, while maestro Simone's promised lover is described in contradictory terms which confuse the levels of reality and fantasy. The first sentence of the description, for instance, works relatively clearly to stress social power and popularity, thus creating a connection with Bruno and Buffalmacco's mates: "'ella è una troppo gran donna, e poche case ha per lo mondo nelle quali ella non abbia alcuna giurisdizione . . .'" (VIII 9,74). The second sentence, however, "'i frati minori a suon di nacchere le rendon tributo'" (VIII 9,74), introduces verbal signs which work on two different levels: "frati minori . . . le rendon tributo" continues the first sentence's referential level of social reality, while "a suon di nacchere" introduces, on the level of fantasy, excremental imagery. The following long paragraph moves from one referential level to the other to produce an atmosphere of comic suspense. Comically juxtaposed views of the contessa di Civillari present her first as a normal woman engaged in mundane activities ("'quend'ella va da torno, ella si fa ben sentire, benché ella stea il più rinchiusa . . . ella vi passò innanzi all'uscio una notte che andava ad Arno a lavarsi i piedi e per pigliare un poco d'aria'" (VIII 9,75) and then as a purely metaphorical character described in heavily scatological language. Maestro Simone, of course, completely misses the discrepancy. The metaphorical level plays on the comic description of the contessa's "sergenti," who "tutti a dimostrazion della maggioranza di lei portano la verga e il piombo" (tools of the *nettacessi*). Their suggestive names are "Tamagnin dalla Porta, don Meta, Manico di Scopa, lo Squacchera" (VIII 9,76).[28] Bruno's description of the contessa concludes with the all-too-clear comparison of that lady to the "gran donna . . . da Cacavincigli" (VIII 9,77). The *beffa* then changes from purely verbal description to action, which culminates with maestro Simone's actual head-first dive into excrement.[29] The action *beffa* thus actualizes the metaphorical innuendoes of the verbal *beffa* and physically drags the *lattime* doctor from his world of fantasy into the reality of stinking excrement. His social condition, however, does not change, nor is he alienated from his supposed friends: "se da indi a dietro onorati gli avea, molto più gli onorò e careggiò con conviti e altre cose da indi innanzi" (VIII 9,112). The end of the *novella* confirms the lesson derived from the *beffa* played an incompetent professional man: "Così adunque, come udito avete, senno s'insegna a chi tanto non apparò a Bologna" (VIII 9,112).

Neither physical violence nor aggression occurs in the *ménage-à-quatre* which results when the Sienese Zeppa discovers his wife's affair with his best friend Spinello (VIII 8). Zeppa wisely transforms the liaison into a peaceful and mutually satisfactory settlement by which "ciascuna di quelle donne ebbe due mariti e ciascun di loro ebbe due mogli, senza alcuna quistione o zuffa mai per quello insieme averne" (VIII 8,35).

The same lack of physical aggression is evident in VIII 10. This *novella*, not only deals with the prescribed topic of the Day (contrary to most of the tenth *novelle* of the other *Giornate*) but clearly works as the counterpart of VIII 1; both stories deal with *beffe* played on greedy women (one from the North, in VIII 1 and one from the South, in VIII 10) who prostitute themselves for money. VIII 10 increases its impact by doubling the *beffa* pattern. In a first *beffa* played by the Sicilian prostitute Jancofiore on Salabaetto, a Tuscan merchant, she swindles him out of five hundred florins. At this point the *beffa* pattern repeats itself with a reversal of the protagonists: Salabaetto becomes the agent of another *beffa* through which he in turn swindles Jancofiore out of twice the amount of money which he had previously lost. This *novella* offers us a replay, on a lower social plane, and in purely economic terms, of VIII 7, the tale of the scholar and widow, which is also built on a *beffa*-counter-*beffa* pattern. Pampinea, the narrator of the tale, states from the outset the novelty of her story—its theme and structure of retribution: "una giusta retribuzione a una nostra cittadina renduta, alla quale la sua beffa presso che con morte, essendo beffata, ritornò sopra il capo" (VIII 7,3). The reversal pattern is underscored by the antithetical imagery corresponding to the two stages of *beffa* and counter-*beffa*. We might render this graphically:

	LOCATION	CLIMATE	SEASON	TIME of DAY	ATMOSPHERIC IMAGES	RESULTS
BEFFA CITY	Courtyard enclosure	Extreme cold	Winter	Night	Snow	Almost frozen to death
COUNTER-BEFFA COUNTRY	Upper terrace on tower	Extreme heat	Summer	Day	Sunshine	Almost scorched to death

The initial *beffa* develops through the normal three-step pattern of intention, actualization, and result. Madonna Elena, a beautiful widow, acts as agent and the *savio scolare*, messer Rinieri, as the object-victim. The fulfillment of the widow's *beffa*, however, produces a second stage in which she becomes the victim and her victim in turn becomes the agent of a counter-*beffa*. In all the stages of this double *beffa* structure, both words and actions are equally important. Madonna Elena begins her deception by simulating her feelings with actions "artificiosamente movendogli (occhi) . . . s'ingegnava di dimostrargli che di lui gli calesse . . . *mostrava* di vederlo assai volentieri . . . il tenne gran tempo in pastura . . ." (VIII 7,8-14). She continues "'Dira'gli,'" she tells her servant, "'qualora egli ti parla più, che io amo molto più lui che egli non ama me; ma che a me si convien di guardar l'onestà mia . . .'" (VIII 7,12). She then arranges a meeting with the scholar again through her servant: "la sua fante gli mandò, la quale da sua parte gli disse . . . che per le feste del Natale che s' apressava, ella sperava di potere esser con lui" (VIII 7,15).

The same pattern of alternating actions and words emerges in the beffa's actualization: at first, the scholar is locked in the courtyard: "andò alla casa della donna: e messo dalla fante in una corte e dentro serratovi quivi la donna cominciò a aspettare" (VIII 7,17). The widow's comments to her lover reveal her previous dissimulations, "'potrai vedere quanto e quale sia l'amore il quale io ho portato e porto a colui del quale scioccamente hai gelosia presa'" (VIII 7,18). This alternating pattern of action and commentary continues: Rinieri waits patiently below despite the bitter cold: "ogni cosa di neve era coperta; per la qual cosa lo scolare fu poco nella corte dimorato, che egli cominciò a sentir più freddo che voluto non avrebbe . . ." (VIII 7,19); meanwhile Elena, above with her lover, gloats over Rinieri's humiliation: "'guardiamo ciò che colui, di cui se' divenuto geloso, fa, e quello che egli risponderà alla fante, la quale io gli ho mandata a favellare.'" (VIII 7,20). The servant assists in the *beffa* by informing the scholar that: "'egli ci è stasera venuto un de' suoi fratelli e . . . ancora non se n'è andato . . . e per questo non è ella potuto venire a te ma tosto verrà oggimai . . .'" (VIII 7,21).

The *beffa* reaches its climax in the direct confrontation between the widow inside and the scholar outside, with the lover hidden nearby as a silent spectator. Here the ironic jestings of the widow confirm, even for the passionate scholar, the woman's deceit. To his request for a "'buon fuoco, acciò che . . . io mi possa riscaldare, chè io sono tutto divenuto sì freddo, che appena sento di me . . .'" (VIII 7,36), the widow replies: "'Questo non dee potere essere, se quello è vero che tu m'hai più volte scritto, cioè che tu per l'amor di me ardi tutto . . .'" (VIII 7,37). When morning comes, and he is eventually allowed to exit from the courtyard and return home in seriously critical physical conditions, Rinieri's love has died. The realization of having been deceived and ridiculed transforms him from a passionate lover into a relentless vengeance seeker. From now on, he, on his turn, adopts dissimulation as his mode of behavior: "dentro il suo odio servando, vie più che mai si mostrava innamorato della vedova sua'" (VIII 7,45). He is patiently waiting for the right situation to develop: and, once the widow loses her young lover, and wishes him back, the opportunity is provided for the scholar's counter-*beffa*.

In this second *beffa*, words and actions also alternate to heighten the ironic tone. First, a dialogue takes place between the widow and her servant about the scholar's knowledge of magic. The encounter between the servant and Rinieri follows, in which the latter accepts the opportunity to provide the widow with his magic help. Eventually the scholar meets the widow, and his dissimulation matches her credulity. The action then takes place, and another nocturnal scene is enacted, this time in a country background, in summertime:

> . . . in su l'ora del primo sonno, di casa chetamente uscita, vicino alla torricella sopra la riva d'Arno se n'andò, e . . . né veggendo né sentendo alcuno, spogliatasi e i suoi panni sotto un cespuglio nascosi, sette volte con la imagine si bagnò, e appresso, ignuda e con la imagine in mano verso la torricella n'andò.
>
> (VIII 7,65)

The pattern of the action from this point on reveals the difference in the protagonists' characters. There is still an alternation of actions and words, but both agent and victim address each other directly without any third party involved. In addition, instead of several short verbal exchanges, as in the first *beffa*, only two long dialogues between the widow and the scholar are arranged around a detailed description of the woman's sufferings during her exposure to the burning sun of a hot summer day. The first dialogue, of approximately 250 lines, builds up the thematic opposition between female weakness and credulity and masculine ingenuity and shrewdness. These characteristics are suggested in the widow's symbolic rendition of their conflict through the image of a battle between *una aquila* and *una colomba* (VIII 7,79). This imagery is, however, modified by Rinieri, as he sees the woman "'non colomba, ma velenosa serpe'" (VIII 7,87).

> E da che diavol, togliendo via cotesto tuo pochetto di viso, il quale pochi anni guasteranno riempiendolo di crespe, se' tu più che qualunque altra dolorosetta fante? dove per te non rimase di far morire un valente uomo . . . la cui vita ancora potrà più in un dì essere utile al mondo che centomilia tue pari non potranno mentre il mondo durar dee.
>
> (VIII 7,89)

The opposition thus builds toward the theme of the superiority of intelligence and learning in every human endeavor, including love, and reaches its climax in

Rinieri's eulogy of literary power: "'Le forze della penna son troppo maggiori che coloro non estimano che quelle con conoscimento provate non hanno'" (VIII 7,99).[30]

Attention is focused on the woman's skin, that is, on that outward appearance which was the primary source of her vanity and pride; her transformation from beauty to ugliness is described in detail, to the point of grotesqueness:

> Il sole . . . non solamente le *cosse le carni* . . . ma quelle *minuto minuto tutte l'aperse;* e fu la *cottura* tale, che lei che profondamente dormiva costrinse a destarsi.
>   E sentendosi *cuocere* . . . parve nel muoversi che tutta *la cotta pelle le s'aprisse e ischiantasse,* come veggiamo avvenire d'una *carta di pecora abrusciata* . . . E oltre a questo . . . v'erano *mosche e tafani* in grandissima quantità abbondati, li quali, pognendolesi sopra le *carni aperte,* sì *fieramente la stimolavano* . . . *Il sol* di sopra e il *fervor* del battuto di sotto e le *trafitture* delle mosche e de' tafani da lato sì per tutto l'avean concia, che ella, dove la notte passata con *la sua bianchezza vinceva le tenebre,* allora *rossa divenuta come rabbia,* e *tutta di sangue chiazzata,* sarebbe paruta, a chi veduta l'avesse *la più brutta cosa del mondo.*
> (VIII 7, 113-120)

The grotesque mood develops particularly out of the insistent use of heat images. Transformation from beauty to ugliness is intensified by the details of change in skin color, that is, from the *bianchezza* (che) *vinceva le tenebre* to *rossa divenuta come rabbia e tutta di sangue chiazzata.* The two past participles "divenuta" e "chiazzata", stand in contrast to the active verb, *vinceva,* and add to the realization of the change taking place in the woman's situation: from a free, active condition of superior beauty to a passive, restricted state of shame and suffering. Animal imagery also plays a role in Elena's physical deterioration, both to describe her discomfort (*fieramente la stimolavano, trafitture delle mosche e de' tafani*) and her external appearance (*carta di pecora abrusciata*). Furthermore, the repetition of the verb *aprire* in its many forms (*aperse, s'aprisse, aperte*), always in connection with either *carni* or *pelle,* offers a bitter commentary on the woman's sexual excesses. Eventually the whole description conveys the grotesque transformation of a symbol of sex and beauty into a seared piece of meat crawling with insects.[32]

The second dialogue between the two protagonists is much briefer than the first one (only 53 lines) and works out a series of oppositions between the woman's sufferings and the scholar's, as well as differences of time (past vs. present and night vs. day), place (city courtyard vs. country tower); climate, (cold vs. heat), means of relief (fire vs. water and dung vs. rosewater), and consequences (loss of the use of the limbs and deadening of the nerves vs. loss of skin). The woman's request for help in light of the fact that "'se *io feci te nella mia corte di notte agghiacciare, tu hai me di giorno sopra questa torre fatta arrostire, anzi ardere'*" (VIII 7,122) is countered by Rinieri with "'tanta *acqua avrai da me a sollevamento del tuo caldo,* quanto *fuoco io ebbi da te a alleggiamento* del *mio freddo.'*" (VIII 7,125). The scholar contrasts his and the woman's sufferings with chiasmus. ("mio freddo col caldo . . . tuo caldo col freddo . . .") and builds once again to a final comparison of the lady and a *serpe*:

> 'l *mio freddo* col *caldo* del *letame puzzolente* si convenne *curare,* ove quella del *tuo caldo* col *freddo* della *odorifera acqua rosa si curerà;* e dove *io* per *perdere i nervi e la persona* fui, *tu* da questo *caldo scorticata,* non altramenti rimarrai bella che faccia la *serpe,* lasciando il vecchio cuoio'
>
> (VIII 7,126)

We reach the *novella's* climax as both *beffe* come together, their painful consequences for both victims balanced one against the other.

Symbolically, the scholar's suffering in the enclosed city courtyard, in wintertime, at night, represents the dangers of intellectual isolation. At the beginning of the story, his total dedication to the study of philosophical truths is stressed: "avendo *lungamente* studiato a Parigi, *non* per vender poi la sua scienza a minuto, *come molti fanno, ma per sapere la ragione* delle cose e *la cagion* d'esse . . ." (VIII 7,5). By stressing his lengthy curriculum of study, undertaken exclusively for the sake of learning, Pampinea, the story's narrator, seems to suggest the dangers of his exclusive interest in abstract topics of argumentation. He cannot therefore differentiate between abstractions and real life and will eventually invalidate his assessment of actions by basing it on physical rather than intellectual or philosophical motivations. Thus as soon as he sees a creature who attracts him physically, he turns his thoughts from learning to Elena with equally fervent dedication:

> davanti agli occhi si parò questa Elena . . . piena di tanta bellezza al suo giudicio e di tanta piacevolezza quanto alcuna altra ne gli fosse mai paruta vedere; e seco estimò colui potersi beato chiamare, al quale Idio grazia facesse lei potere ignuda nelle braccia tenere . . . seco diliberò del tutto di porre ogni pena e ogni sollecitudine in piacere a costei . . . lasciati i pensier filosofici da una parte, tutto l'animo rivolse a costei.
>
> (VIII 7,6-10)

The most interesting suggestion of the scholar's inability to discern between the superficial and inner beauty is contained in his wish to acquire God's assistance for his sexual pursuit ("colui potersi beato chiamare, al quale Idio grazia facesse lei potere ignuda nelle braccia tenere"). This flaw in a character supposedly trained to be above petty, mundane and superficial relationships, is proof of his momentary loss of wisdom, which is easily recognized and ironically referred to by the widow in her sarcastic remark: "'Hai veduto dove costui è venuto a *perdere il senno* che egli ci ha da Parigi recato?'" (VIII 7,12). The verb *perdere* is used also to describe the effects of the widow's *beffa* on him: "tutto quasi *perduto delle braccia e delle gambe*" (VIII 7,44): "'io per *perder i nervi e la persona fui'*" (VIII 7,126). The use of the same lexical expression, in these passages places the loss of wisdom and the near loss of life in a close relationship of cause and effect. Images of winter cold and snow suggest both potential death and the rigidity of a mind which cannot recognize different areas and/or degrees of intellectual commitment. The closed-in courtyard hints at the solitary condition of the scholar who has not yet developed a relationship with his society because of his exclusive interest in abstract topics of argumentation. The dawn that follows this terrible night of cold and suffering brings the scholar a deeper form of widsom, one that allows him to live in society and to manipulate reality more perceptively and more effectively. "Lo scolare isdegnoso, *sì come savio* . . . senza punto mostrarsi crucciato . . ." (VIII 7,42). We thus see the beginning of a new understanding of the human condition. True wisdom, this *novella* seems to suggest, consists in handling and solving not only intellectual problems, but also problems concerning everyday interactions among human beings. The scholar himself recognizes his own improvement: "'né tanto di me stesso apparai'"—he tells the widow in their first dialogue in the country—"'mentre dimorai a Parigi, quanto tu in una sola notte delle tue mi facesti conoscere'" (VIII 7,85). In the same dialogue with the widow, Rinieri reveals a comfortable familiarity with Florentine habits, especially with gossip: "'Benché tu dichi che mai i tuoi amori non seppe altri che la tua fante e io, tu il sai male . . . la sua contrada quasi di niuna altra cosa ragiona, e la tua . . .'" (VIII 7,105). His long satiric tirade against women reveals a newly-acquired perception of human weaknesses, hardly evident in his first encounter with the widow. This depth of understanding also emerges in the mixed feelings that Rinieri experiences for the woman at the time of her punishment. First, he feels both tenderness and pity for her: "Lo scolare . . . passandogli ella quasi allato così ignuda e egli veggendo lei con la bianchezza del suo corpo vincere le tenebre della notte e appresso riguardandole il petto e l'altre parti del corpo e vedendole belle e seco *pensando quali infra piccol termine dovean divenire, sentì di lei alcuna compassione* . . ." (VIII 7,66). Later, his feelings become even more complex: "Lo scolare . . . veggendo piagnere e pregare, ad un'ora aveva piacere e noia nell'animo: piacere della vendetta la quale più che altra cosa disiderata avea, e noia sentiva *movendolo la umanità sua a compassion della misera* . . ." (VIII 7,80). "Ben conobbe lo scolare alla voce la sua debolezza e ancor vide in parte il corpo suo tutto riarso dal sole, per le quali cose e per gli umili suoi prieghi *un poco di compassione gli venne di lei...*" (VIII 7,124). Through his own experience of physical and mental pain, the scholar has indeed reached a higher level of wisdom, enriched by compassion and awareness of human frailty.

On the other hand, the means of the widow's punishment point symbolically to the dominance of sexual drives in her life, through the images of heat, burning and cooking. Eventually, through a day's suffering, the woman overcomes her passion and, like the scholar, reaches an understanding of her mistake: "dimenticato il suo amante, da indi innanzi e di beffare e d'amare si guardò *saviamente*" (VIII 7,148). The *novella's* two parts are neatly counterbalanced: the former corrects intellectual pride and isolation in the city, and the latter castigates physical sexual excesses in the country. Taken together, the parts seem to restate the theme that has been conveyed alternatively in the city (VIII 1,3,5) and in the country (VIII 2,4,6) in all *novelle* of this day. All urge the improvement of human society through the creation of an inner balance of forces eliminating the excesses both of mind and body which threaten society.

In several *novelle* of the Third Day — the day to which Day Eight corresponds in the general structure of the *Decameron* — we saw the implication of a similar tendency to counterbalance excesses and create a harmonious solution, although there it seemed limited to love situations. And yet, in the Eighth Day, the theme is more precise and is exhibited in all types of situations (not only love) and involves a wider range of individuals. Structurally the first seven *novelle* of the day present an alternating and repeating pattern of characters and themes that clearly conveys the didactic role that this day plays in the overall configuration of the *Decameron*:

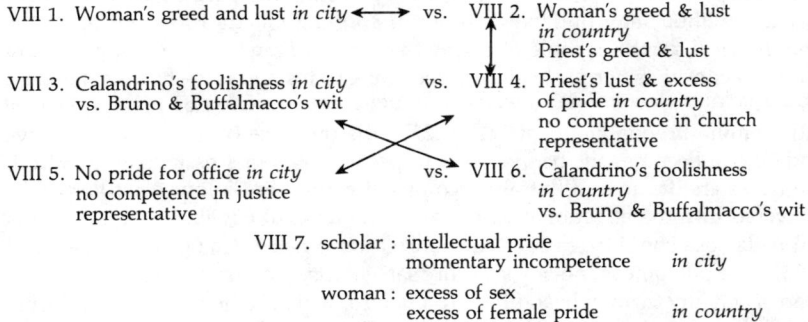

VIII 1 corresponds in theme and character to VIII 2 and partially in theme to VIII 7; VIII 2 corresponds to VIII 4 in character and theme and to VIII 7 partially in theme; it is also analogous to VIII 5 in that throughout professional incompetence the main characters fail to fulfill their social roles. The Calandrino *novelle*, VIII 3 and 6, comically circumscribe *novelle* 4 and 5 which present the most serious social problems of the day: vanity and lechery in the

153

clergy (VIII 4) and incompetency in the judiciary (VIII 5). At the same time, the inner structure of the Calandrino stories presents counterbalancing influences such as Calandrino's excessive foolishness versus Bruno and Buffalmacco's superior wit. Eventually VIII 7, highlights the main concerns of the day through characters, themes, and city versus country motifs.

As for the remaining *novelle* of Day Eight, VIII 8 shows correspondences with III 6, and VIII 9 with III 9. Both VIII 8 and III 6 are narrated by Fiammetta, while the respective queens of the two days, Lauretta and Neifile, recount VIII 9 and III 9. In VIII 8 the make-believe situation of III 6 becomes reality. In III 6, Ricciardo succeeds in making love to Catella by convincing her that her husband is involved with his wife. The supposed *ménage-à-quatre* of III 6 actually materializes in VIII 8, where Zeppa discovers the extra-marital relationship between his wife and his best friend, and redresses the imbalance by making love to his friend's wife: "e da indi innanzi ciascuna di quelle donne ebbe due mariti e ciascun di loro ebbe due mogli, senza alcuna quistione o zuffa mai per quello insieme averne" (VIII 8,35).

The ninth story of the day deals with a medical doctor, maestro Simone, and thus creates a comic contrast to Giletta in III 9, the daughter of the famous "medico chiamato maestro Gerardo di Nerbona" (III 9,4). Maestro Simone is a social misfit, aptly ridiculed by Bruno and Buffalmacco. Superficially, maestro Simone displays all the qualities of an able doctor: he has studied in Bologna, he is correctly attired "di scarlatto e con un gran batolo" (VIII 9,5) and has "sopra l'uscio della via uno orinale, acciò che coloro che avessero del suo consiglio bisogno il sapessero riconoscer dagli altri" (VIII 9,34). And yet, he not only lacks all preparation in the profession, but common sense as well. In III 9, instead, without any outlandish show, the young Giletta turns out to be the only medical doctor capable of curing the King of France. Although her future husband considers her profession unbecoming to his nobility – he asks the king: "'dunque mi volete voi dar *medica per mogliere?* Già a Dio non piaccia che io sì fatta femina prenda giammai'" (III 9,22) – the outcome of the story is positive and Giletta becomes the beloved and respected countess Rossiglione. In VIII 9, the tricksters Bruno and Buffalmacco promise maestro Simone, that he will be delivered into the affectionate arms of "la contessa di Civillari, la quale era la più bella cosa che si trovasse in tutto il culattario dell'umana generazione" (VIII 9,73). The outcome is, however hardly satisfactory for our "medico . . . pecora" who is actually thrown head first into manure, which is the reification of Bruno and Buffalmacco's imaginary "contessa di Civillari." The closing words of the *novella* make clear the combined lesson in professional behavior and in Florentine wit that the tale implies: "Così adunque, come udito avete, senno s'insegna a chi tanto non apparò a Bologna" (VIII 9,112).

On the whole then, Day VIII continues the social criticism of Day VII by hitting particularly social improprieties of behavior or social misfits. Meanwhile its *novelle* direct the readers' attention more specifically at a counterbalancing of excesses and amplify, in relation to Day III, their field of operation.

4. Day IX: An Exercise in Balance

The Ninth Day, like the First, has no specific storytelling topic. The queen of the day, Emilia, declares her intention not to set any topic by using a simile taken from the natural world:

> Dilettose donne, assai manifestamente veggiamo che, poi che i buoi alcuna parte del giorno hanno faticato sotto il giogo ristretti, quegli esser dal giogo alleviati e disciolti, e liberamente, dove lor più piace, per li boschi lasciati sono andare alla pastura: e veggiamo ancora non esser men belli ma molto più i giardini di varie piante fronzuti che i boschi ne' quali solamente querce veggiamo; per le quali cose io estimo, avendo riguardo quanti giorni sotto certa legge ristretti ragionato abbiamo, che sì come a bisognosi, di vagare alquanto e vagando riprender forze a rientrar sotto il giogo non solamente sia utile ma oportuno.
>
> (VIII Concl., 3-4)

A tripartite comparison is made between the *brigata* and the fixed-topic storytelling, the "buoi . . . sotto il giogo" and the "boschi ne' quali solamente querce veggiamo." Free-topic storytelling is compared instead to "giardini di varie piante fronzuti." Nature emerges here in its most typical aspects, the rural as well as the idyllic, so that the scene creates a balanced whole, well keeping with the constant search for balance in actions and situations both in the *brigata*'s life, and in their *novelle*. The first part of this passage conveys a rustic vision of the countryside, with the central image of the oxen and their relationship to the yoke and the action of *"andare alla pastura."* Good balance is underscored in the view of the oxen having "faticato *sotto il giogo ristretti"* and eventually being *"dal giogo alleviati e disciolti, e liberamente dove lor più piace . . . lasciati andare alla pastura."* Here the two verbal forms (1) *faticato* and (2) *ristretti* are set off against (1) *alleviati* and (2) *disciolti*, and the move towards an harmonious outcome is emphasized by the qualifications *liberamente* and *dove lor più piace*. The second part presents a more idyllic view of nature, with "giardini di varie piante fronzuti" and "boschi ne' quali solamente querce *veggiamo."* At this point the human element represented by the storytellers is reintroduced by the verb *veggiamo*, recalling the expression "assai manifestamente veggiamo" with which the passage opens. This in turn prepares for the second term of comparison, rendered by verbal expressions reminiscent of the preceding ones: *"sotto certa legge ristretti ragionato* abbiamo" balances off "hanno *faticato sotto il giogo ristretti,"* *legge* corresponds to *giogo*, and *ragionato* to *faticato*. These comparisons imply a close link between the human concept of law and the yoke, a device belonging to the animal world. Futhermore, the action of the oxen "liberamente . . . lasciati andare in pastura" has its counterpart in the *novellatori's* "vagare alquanto" which implies a figurative form of freedom from the previously mentioned restrictive law. The closing lines of the passage convey the vision of harmonic balance between duty and freedom which coincides with the many-faceted view of life that the *Decameron* proposes to convey: "'io estimo . . . che . . . di vagare alquanto . . . e vagando riprender forze a rientrar sotto il giogo, non solamente sia utile ma oportuno.'" To be "sotto certa legge" or "sotto il giogo ristretti" is thus as important as freedom from either the yoke or the law, inasmuch as both law and freedom are necessary for all creatures to function successfully in their environments.

The balanced view of life conveyed in Emilia's speech is stressed in the Introduction to Day IX by the description of the storytellers freely and joyfully wandering in the countryside "tutti di frondi di quercia inghirlandati, con le man piene o d'erbe odorifere o di fiori; e chi scontrati gli avesse, niuna altra cosa avrebbe potuto dire se non: 'O costor non saranno dalla morte vinti o ella gli ucciderà lieti'" (IX Intr., 4-5).[32] With the introduction of an observer outside their group, "*chi* scontrati gli avesse," the storytellers become the object of a reflexive mood that sees them in terms of death: "O *costor* non saranno *dalla morte vinti o ella gli ucciderà lieti*." This view would seem unrelated in the contextual framework of the storytellers' serene existence in the country villa near Florence, unless the correspondence between Days IX and I, created by Emilia's choice of a free-topic storytelling, is brought to mind. The Introduction to Day I presented the historical situation of the plague and particularly the view that some of the storytellers had of its deadly consequences. The brief interjection in the Ninth Day's Introduction relating the storytellers to death realistically reconsiders dangers faced in Day I, while pointing to the improved physical, psychological, and moral strength which the storytellers have acquired through their self-imposed temporary exile from the plague-infested city. Panfilo will clearly stress these facts in the Conclusion of Day X when he makes the decision for the *brigata* to return to Florence. Thus the presence of the death motif in the Introduction to Day IX creates a strong connection with Day I, hints at the return of the storytellers to Florence at the end of Day X, and prepares for the first *novella* of Day IX, centered on death-related adventures.

Nearly all of the *novelle* of this Day have a structure involving duality, since there is either a double action, an action involving a double response, or two conflicting interests. In IX 1 two lovers desire the same woman, but she refuses them both. The desire of the two lovers is not fulfilled, while the woman does succeed in freeing herself of them both. The same holds true for IX 2, where many nuns do not fulfill their sex drives, while one nun Isabetta, does. In IX 3, instead, everthing turns out the way Calandrino's friends have planned, in a double development of both intention and action. In the end, all desires are fulfilled, both those of Calandrino's friends and those of Calandrino himself, who is the happiest man in the world once he is assured that he has been cured of his "pregnancy." The only dissatisfied character is monna Tessa, Calandrino's wife, who recognizes the trick and "avvedendosene, molto col marito ne brontolasse" (IX 3,33). A different outcome befalls Calandrino in his other *novella* of this Day (IX 5). There his desire for Niccolosa remains unfulfilled while monna Tessa's desire for revenge against her husband for his suspected infidelity is satisfied. The action moves from Bruno and Buffalmacco's intention to play a double *beffa* at Calandrino's expense, that is, (1) to build up his amorous hopes for Niccolosa and (2) to have monna Tessa discover the two together. The entire action of the *novella* follows this double pattern through which all the characters interact to fulfill everyone's but Calandrino's desires.

The *novella* of Angiolieri and Fortarrigo (IX 4) involves two characters, as do most of the *novelle*; its development, which depends on Fortarrigo as the *agent*, takes place in two stages and involves both Angiolieri and another group of characters in each stage. In the first moment Fortarrigo deals with some gamblers and in order to repay them steals money from Angiolieri; in the second moment Fortarrigo pits some field workers against Angiolieri to steal even his horse and clothes. Fortarrigo's intention is fully accomplished while Angiolieri's initial intention to join the Cardinal of the Marca d'Ancona's service with Fortarrigo never materializes. A more satisfactory outcome is seen in IX 6, where the double intention of one character, Pinuccio, (1) to elude the vigilance of Niccolosa's parents and (2) to make love to Niccolosa, involves the sexual interaction of two couples: himself and Niccolosa and his friend and Niccolosa's mother. Only Niccolosa's father is left out of the love game, and in order to have a harmonious ending, he is given a false view of the real situation. The two characters in IX 7 each perform two actions, but reach no positive resolution. The husband, for instance, dreams of his wife's dangerous encounter with a wolf in the forest and warns her not to go there. The jealous wife, suspects an encounter between her husband and a would-be lover, and goes to the forest anyway. The outcome is a real encounter between the wife and a wolf, and her near death. No desires are fulfilled here, while instead in the following *novella* (IX 8), each of the two characters involved fulfills his *beffa* at the other's expense. Furthermore, each character plans his *beffa* by involving the other character with a third party, so as to create an interaction between two characters in each of the two stages of the story. In the first *beffa*, Biondello entices Ciacco to Corso Donati's house with the prospect of eating well, while in a subsequent *beffa* Ciacco repays Biondello by involving him with Filippo Argenti and his wine. Neither of them has a satisfactory experience. In IX, 9, Giosefo and Melisso go to Solomon for advice concerning the relationships of Giosefo and his wife and of Melisso with society at large. Both characters' desires are fulfilled in a second moment when Solomon's advice is put into practice first by Giosefo and then by Melisso. In the last *novella* of this day, no satisfaction is gained either by *comare* Gemmata or *compare* Pietro in their interaction with *donno* Gianni, who was supposed to turn *comare* Gemmata into a mare.

All *novelle* of this Day, according to the introductory remarks of its queen, present unusual views of human frailties. The *novelle* are inspired in part either by other *novelle* in Part II, by their correspondents in Day IV, or by the tales of Day I, with which they have in common the lack of a set topic. Most of the *novelle* of the day seem to consider situations which have not been thoroughly dealt with previously: some present individuals whose love relationships create conflicts with their society (IX 1,2, and 6); others deal with various aspects of friendship (IX 4 and 10); others are concerned with social rights and how to handle them in society (IX 2,5); and others still treat the problem of difficult marital relationships (IX 5,7, and 9).

While a love situation where one woman has more than one lover at the same time has been considered in some of the previous *novelle* (i.e. I 4, II 2, IV 3, VII 6, VIII 7), madonna Francesca's position of being attended by two suitors, both of whom she eschews, is unique in the *Decameron*. In Filomena's opening statements to the tale, she emphasizes the power of the "forze d'amore" that "non solamente a varii dubbii di dover morire gli amanti conduce ma quegli ancora a entrare nelle case de'morti per morti tira . . ." (IX 1,4). She describes the situation of "una valorosa donna" who, "avendo . . . men saviamente più volte gli orecchi porti ad . . . 'mbasciate e . . . prieghi" of her two suitors, "volendosi saviamente ritrarre" used her "senno . . . a torsi da dosso . . . la loro seccaggine . . ." (IX 1,7;4). The first point introduces potential correspondences with Day IV, where indeed love brought death to many lovers, while the theme of the woman's wisdom in knowing how to redress her social position recalls many of Day VII's heroines. Madonna Francesca has a double plan: first, to induce Alessandro to take the place in the tomb "in sul primo sonno" (IX 1,14) of the dead robber Scannadio, and then to convince Rinuccio to carry the body of the would-be Scannadio "in su la mezzanotte" (IX 1,16) from the tomb to her house. Both actions are to be accomplished in the dark and in complete silence; darkness and silence thus provide the ideal situation for the senseless *mise-en-scène* requested by the woman of her lovers. Scannadio, the dead man whose place Alessandro is directed to take in the tomb, is described as "il piggiore uomo che . . . in tutto il mondo fosse." (IX 1,8). This statement echoes "il piggiore uomo forse che mai nascesse" of I 1, thus building up a correspondence between Day IX and Day I through correlations between the first *novelle* of both days. While I 1 was concerned with the *ante-mortem* exploits of Ciappelletto, *novella* IX 1 deals with actions triggered by Scannadio's death and performed around his dead body by characters exclusively interested in their own sexual fulfillment. After Alessandro has taken Scannadio's place in the tomb, Rinuccio then is supposed to move in and perform his deed unaware of the real identity of the man he should be carrying on his shoulders and of the fact that he is still alive. Madonna Francesca thus stages a comedy of errors for her two lovers that consists of actions offering no logical cause or solution. This atmosphere of confusion is underscored by the fact that the action occurs exclusively at night. The nocturnal setting also emphasizes the morbid atmosphere of the tale, centered on the tomb, the corpse, and the superstitions surrounding these elements.

The lovers' passion is dealt with as a very strong and sincere emotion: "di costei presi, sommamente amavano, operando cautamente ciascuno ciò che per lui si poteva a dovere l'amor di costei acquistare." (IX 1,5-6). Yet, when the moment comes to comply with the woman's demands, both men question the advisability of their involvement. For both, however, love triumphs over their fears and they would have succeeded in performing their deeds if the dreaded "famiglia della signoria" had not intervened and offset their intentions.

The nocturnal prank played by madonna Francesca on her two suitors, not devoid of dangerous physical or psychological consequences, brings to mind similar tricks played by women on men in Days VII and VIII, either in order to escape their own downfall (like Ghita of VII 4 and Sismonda of VII 8) or to demonstrate their power over men (like Beatrice in VII 7 and Elena of VIII 7). Madonna Francesca's predicament here is different: she finds herself at a particularly delicate moment in her personal situation, which, however, she can much more easily control by a wise decision than could Ghita or Sismonda. Although madonna Francesca does ask her suitors to perform actions which would prove her power over them, she gives them an option whether or not to perform them. The suitors in VII 7 or VIII 7 never had that chance. Madonna Francesca succeeds in ridding herself of her two lovers with "onesta o colorata ragione" (an expression that recalls another tale where "senno" was essential in eluding a "forza da alcuna ragione colorata." I 3,8), wisely guarding her reputation as an honest widow. In this way, she seems to put into practice what the widow of VIII 7 learned from the *scolare's* lesson: "da indi innanzi e di beffare e d'amare si guardò saviamente" (VIII 7,148). Thus, Madonna Francesca seems instinctively aware of all the lessons on love and its social implications and dangers represented particularly in Days VII an VIII. Her wisdom and wit have gained her peace of mind and social respectability.

Another unusual situation is introduced by Elissa in IX 2 concerning a young nun and the hypocrisy of her abbess. The night-time setting and the theme of love provide links with IX 1. While madonna Francesca demonstrates her intelligence in the planning of her two suitors' nocturnal actions, the nun Isabetta of IX 2, "giovane di sangue nobile e di maravigliosa bellezza dotata" (IX 2,5), shows her wisdom with a ready mind and quick speech. The secret rendez-vous of Isabetta and her "bel giovane," which takes place at night, becomes the cause of suspicion and jealousy on the part of the other nuns, who bring about the intervention of the abbess, herself happily enjoying the embraces of a priest "il quale ella spesse volte in una cassa si faceva venire" (IX 2,9). The nocturnal turmoil of the convent provoked by the over-zealous nuns is comically reflected in the abbess' hurried reaction in the darkness of her cell: "spacciatamente si levò suso e come il meglio seppe si vestì al buio" (IX 2,9). She mistakenly arranges "le brache del prete" on her head in place of her wimple. Darkness and nighttime are therefore once again the setting for a comedy of errors developing this time among three groups of female characters: the nuns "sì focose e sì attente . . . a dover far trovare in fallo l'Isabetta" (IX 2,11); Isabetta, in the role of victim: "vergognosa e timida, sì come colpevole . . . tacendo"(IX 2,14); and finally the abbess, solemnly sitting "in capitolo," unaware of her unusual headdress and intent on excoriating Isabetta, "sì come a colei la quale la santità, l'onestà, la buona fama del monistero con le sue sconce e vituperevoli opere . . . contaminate avea" (IX 2,13). Finally when Isabetta, raising her eyes to face the abbess, recognizes "ciò che la badessa aveva in capo" (IX 2,14), the comic climax explodes in the few words that Isabetta repeats: " 'Madonna, io vi priego che voi v'annodiate la cuffia e poscia mi dite ciò che voi volete.'" (IX 2,14). Every eye then moves from Isabetta to the abbess, and with this change of focus comes a change in the tone of the abbess' speech; reproaches and threats are dropped and the abbess is forced to admit her failure in "potersi dagli stimoli della carne difendere" (IX 2,18). All the nuns are then advised "che ciascuna si desse buon tempo quando potesse" (IX 2,18). This *novella* takes off on I 4 with a change in the sex of the main characters and with a more bustling convent life reminiscent of Masetto's nunnery in III 1. The abbott of I 4 considers opening "in presenza di tutti i monaci . . . la cella di costui e far loro vedere il suo difetto" (13), as a punishment for the young monk; in IX 2 the abbess actually carries out this plan to snare the young nun Isabetta: "la badessa . . . giunse all'uscio della cella, e quello, dall'altre aiutata, pinse in terra: ed entrate dentro nel letto trovarono i due amanti abbracciati . . ." (IX 2,11). The old abbot reproaches the monk in a private session: "fattoselo chiamare, gravissimamente e con mal viso il riprese e comandò che fosse in carcere messo . . . (I 4,20). The abbess reproaches Isabetta more publicly:

> La badessa, postasi a sedere in capitolo in presenza di tutte le monache, le quali solamente alla colpevole riguardavano, incominciò a dirle la maggior villania che mai a femina fosse detta, sì come a colei la quale la santità, l'onestà e la buona fama del monistero con le sue sconce e vituperevoli opere, se di fuor si sapesse, contaminate avea: e dietro alla villania aggiugnea gravissime minacce.
>
> (IX 2,13)

The abbot once proven as guilty as his monk, changes his approach to him: "si vergognò di fare al monaco quello che egli, sì come lui, aveva meritato. E, perdonatogli e impostogli di ciò che veduto aveva silenzio, onestamente misero la giovanetta di fuori e poi più volte si dee credere che la facesser tornare" (I 4,22). The abbess uses the same tactics in the *Decameron's* most blatant *volte-face:*

> Di che la badessa, avvedutasi del suo medesimo fallo e vedendo che da tutte veduto era né aveva ricoperta, mutò sermone e in tutta altra guisa che fatto non aveva cominciò a parlare, e conchiudendo venne impossible essere il potersi dagli stimoli della carne difendere; e per ciò chetamente, come infino a quel dì fatto s'era, disse che ciascuna si desse buon tempo quando potesse . . .
> (IX 2, 18-19)

Aside from these several connections with I 4, this *novella* creates a more animated view of convent life than is visible in any other story on the same topic. Contrary to I 4, the conflict here is not the result of a superior authority learning of an inferior's sexual transgression; but rather it is the zealous detective activity instigated by the other nuns' envy that places Isabetta in conflict with her abbess. A petty and jealous convent atmosphere comes alive in the frenzied nocturnal activities of the nuns: "così taciutesi, tra sé le vigilie e le guardie segretamente partirono per incoglier costei" (IX 2,7).

The outside society, contrary to the other monastery stories, is actively present in this *novella*; the character of Isabetta, "giovane di sangue nobile e di maravigliosa bellezza" (IX 2,5), is carefully linked to her social context. She receives visits from "un suo parente" and eventually falls in love with "un bel giovane che con lui era" (IX 2,5). The love affair between the two is handled in typically courtly terms: "esso, lei veggendo bellissima, già *il suo disidero avendo con gli occhi concetto,* similmente di lei s'accese . . ." (IX 2,5). While both of them "non senza gran pena di ciascuno questo amore un gran tempo senza frutto sostennero," (IX 2,5), it is the young man who eventually sees "una via da potere alla sua monaca occultissimamente andare" (IX 2,6). His presence is also particularly important during Isabetta's trial "in capitolo." The young man, in fact, stays behind in the nun's cell, but in a different frame of mind than did the "giovinetta assai bella," unknowing and passive of I 4: "Il giovane . . . vestitosi . . . aspettava di veder che fine la cosa avesse, con intenzione di fare un mal giuoco a quante giugner ne potesse, se alla sua giovane novità niuna fosse fatta, e di lei menarne con seco" (IX 2,12). The young man stands solidly behind his beloved; in contrast particularly to I 4 he reveals his strong commitment to Isabetta and suggests the reassuring connection between Isabetta and the society outside the convent. Isabetta's wit frees her from a dangerous situation — as wit aided many heroines of Day VII — and yet her victory over envy and hypocrisy seems a natural outcome for a superior individual committed to real love and strongly supported by her own society.

After hearing Fiammetta's tale of Niccolosa and Calandrino, (IX 5), Panfilo presents another interesting new love situation where the female protagonist is also named Niccolosa. The story takes place in "Pian di Mugnone," a river previously mentioned in another Calandrino story, VIII 3, which was narrated by Elissa. Love and nighttime are again essential in this novella, which combines and amplifies the narrative factors of the two stories just discussed. As in IX 2 there are two young lovers whose affair is long maintained without sexual fulfillment: "e più volte per grado di ciascuna delle parti avrebbe tale amore avuto effetto, se Pinuccio (che così avea nome il giovane) non avesse schifato il biasimo della giovane e 'l suo" (IX 6,6). Eventually Pinuccio's desires grew so strong that "caddegli nel pensiero di trovar modo di dovere col padre albergare, avvisando, sì come colui che la disposizion della casa della giovane sapeva, che, se questo facesse, gli potrebbe venir fatto d'esser con lei senza avvedersene persona" (IX 6,7). Pinuccio is accompanied to the inn by a friend, Adriano, while the girl, Niccolosa, is surrounded by her entire family — mother, father, and baby brother. The crucial action takes place at night in a room where there are three beds and a cradle. The comedy of errors in which another pair of lovers is added to the confusion is triggered by some of the characters' intentional and unintentional moves from one bed to another . The complex whole might be represented in the following diagram:

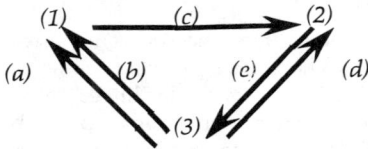

The first move (a) is made by Pinuccio from his bed (3) to Niccolosa's (1); there follows a move by the mother from bed 2 to the kitchen and during her absence another move takes place, which initiates further ones: Adriano gets up for "alcuna opportunità naturale" and moves the cradle from bed 2 to bed 3, so that when the mother comes back she, too, inadvertently moves (b) from bed 2 to bed 3; finally Pinuccio decides to return to his original bed (3), and ends up in Niccolosa's father's bed (2) (move c), triggering the subsequent move of the wise mother and her baby's cradle (d) to Niccolosa's bed (1), thereby allowing Pinuccio to go back for good (e) to his bed (3) with Adriano. Thus two of the characters, Pinuccio and the mother, touch all the beds, with the foreseeable sexual consequences which also involve the characters who do not change beds, i.e. Niccolosa and Adriano. The only one who is left out of the sexual "musical beds" is the father. This does not exclude, however, a reconciliation at the end, with the mother and Adriano successfully covering up for Niccolosa and Pinuccio respectively, as well as for themselves. They convince the father, the "outsider," that all is well. In direct contrast to IX 1 and 2, the younger lovers here do not actively participate in overcoming the difficulties resulting from their love-making, but instead depend on the elder lovers to keep their love secret. In this *novella* we witness a revealing concern on the part of the active characters for the welfare of the others, and for an harmonious view of life. Pinuccio, for instance, tries for a long time to keep from consummating his love for Niccolosa because of his concern for her reputation and for his own; and when he finally decides to act, his main concern is to keep the affair from becoming public. The same concern for a peaceful and honorable outcome is revealed by the mother's actions when she realizes her mistake:

> . . . come savia, senza alcuna parola dire subitamente si levò, e presa la culla del suo figlioletto . . . la portò allato al letto dove dormiva la figliuola e con lei si coricò . . .
>
> (IX 6,24)

She finally convinces her husband of his inability to judge what has transpired: "Voi bevete tanto la sera, che poscia sognate la notte e andate in qua e in là senza sentirvi e parvi far maraviglie . . ." (IX 6,26). Adriano, "veggendo che la donna *saviamente* la sua vergogna e quella della figliuola ricopriva" (IX 6,27) assists her in her attempts to quiet her husband and succeeds in convincing him of Panuccio's habit of walking and talking in his dreams. At the end of the story all the characters interact positively and pleasantly to create a harmonious atmosphere: "venuto il giorno e levatosi, l'oste incominciò a ridere e a farsi beffe di lui e de' suoi sogni. E così . . . i due giovani . . . bevuto con l'oste, rimontati a cavallo se ne vennero a Firenze" (IX 6,31-32).

While friendship between Pinuccio and his "fidato compagno" Adriano is viewed positively in IX 6, a similar relationship comes under attack in IX 4. The two characters, both called Cecco, "l'uno di messer Angiulieri e l'altro di messer Fortarrigo" (IX 4), are introduced by Neifile in ambiguous terms: "Li quali quantunque in molte altre cose male insieme di costumi si convenissero, in uno, cioè che ammenduni li loro padri odiavano, tanto si convenieno, che amici n'erano divenuti e ispesso n'usavano insieme" (IX 4,5). When it turns out that Fortarrigo's *malizia* gets the best of Angiulieri's *senno*, the latter ends up by losing not only all his money but even his clothing, his horse, and all hope of securing a position with the *cardinal nella Marca*: "L'Angiulieri, che ricco si credeva andare al cardinal nella Marca, povero e in camiscia si tornò a Bonconvento . . ." (IX 4,24). This *novella* seems to be the counterpart to I 2, also narrated by Neifile. There two very worthwhile human beings, Abram and Giannotto, although from different religious backgrounds, are both exalted for their honesty, "dirittura e . . . lealtà," wisdom, and friendship. A similar counterpoint with a Day I *novella* occurs in IX 8, where Lauretta continues and amplifies her polemics on the modern "uomo di corte" begun in I 8, in contrast to the "valente . . . costumato . . . e ben parlante" Guiglielmo Borsiere (I 8): Ciacco, "uomo ghiottissimo quanto alcun altro fosse giammai," and Biondello, "piccoletto della persona, leggiadro molto e più pulito che una mosca," who seem to impersonate the modern courtiers that Lauretta described in I 8 as "in rapportar male dall'uno all'altro, in seminare zizzania, in dir cattività e tristizie, e, che è peggio, in farle nella presenza degli uomini . . . s'ingegnano il lor tempo di consumare." (I 8,7-10). The characters' actions are based on cheating, mistrust, and violence, and are enacted in the streets, market place, and *logge* of Florence. At the end, Biondello's realization: "Biondello, che conosceva che contro a Ciacco egli poteva più aver mala voglia che opera . . . *da indi innanzi si guardò di mai più beffarlo*" (IX 8,33), recalls the lesson learned by the widow of VIII 7, which Lauretta herself mentions at the beginning of her story as the main reason for her choice of this *novella*: "me muove la rigida vendetta, ieri raccontata da Pampinea, che fè lo scolare . . ." (IX 8,3).

While IX 8 is clearly not dealing with the topic of friendship, IX 10 is. Here Donno Gianni's close relationship with *compare* Pietro obliges him to perform a supposed magic transformation of *comare* Gemmata into a mare. The story, which is the only "Pugliese" *novella* of the *Decameron,* plays on the conflict between Donno Gianni's awareness and playfulness and the couple's limited intellect and resources. If the outcome is negative, the blame is placed wholly on the dimwitted *compare* Pietro, who "ruins" the magic transformation by crying "O donno Gianni, io non vi voglio coda, io non vi voglio coda" (IX 10,19).

Dimwittedness in the face of scathing intellect is the topic of the Calandrino *novelle* in Days VIII and IX.[33] Calandrino, like *compare* Pietro, stands in comic opposition to those characters of this and previous days whose distinguishing human features are intelligence, wisdom, and control of their lot. Calandrino performs the role of dupe in both Days VIII and IX in a cycle of well-correlated *novelle*. In VIII 3, Calandrino was tricked through words and actions by Maso del Saggio and by Bruno and Buffalmacco. When his beliefs in his own invisibility were shattered, he vented his anger on his wife and gave her a furious beating. In VIII 6, because of his selfishness and obtuseness he was robbed of his hog by Bruno and Buffalmacco, tricked into being accused publicly of the theft, and eventually even obliged to provide his tormentors with "due paia di capponi" in order to keep everything from his wife. Bruno and Buffalmacco based their unwillingness to believe him on his misadventure recounted in VIII 3: "Tu ci menasti una volta giù per lo Mugnone raccogliendo pietre nere: . . . e tu te ne venisti; e poscia ci volevi far credere che tu l'avessi trovata . . ." (VIII 6,54).

Calandrino's avarice and stupidity are preyed upon again in IX 3, where his two usual trickster friends, assisted by the maestro Simone of VIII 9, and by a new character, Nello, make him believe that this time he is pregnant. In IX 5, three of the previous characters, Bruno, Buffalmacco and Nello, return to play an even more devastating *beffa* on Calandrino. This tale centers on the character of Niccolosa, Filippo's whore, whom "un tristo, che era chiamato il Mangione, a sua posta tenendola in una casa da Camaldoli, prestava a vettura" (IX 5,8), with whom Calandrino falls in love. Calandrino's feelings for her befit his irrational uncouth character: "Calandrino cominciò a guatar lei, e parendogli bella . . . subitamente di lei *s'imbardò* . . . tornato a lavorare, altro che *soffiar* non facea . . ." (IX 5,10-12). He expresses his love in this way: "'Gnaffé! tu sì le dirai in prima che io le voglio mille moggia di quel *buon bene da impregnare* . . . se io le pongo *la branca* adosso, per lo verace corpo di Cristo, ché io le farò giuoco che ella mi verrà dietro come va *la pazza al figliuolo*'" (IX 5,27-36). The tricksters make Calandrino believe that Niccolosa too is in love with him and that he can have her through some magic formulas and objects with which they will provide him. Their "amorous encounter" turns out to be a strategic attack by Niccolosa which immobilizes Calandrino: ". . . in su la paglia . . . il gittò, e saligli addosso a cavalcione, e tenendogli le mani in su gli omeri, senza lasciarlosi appressare al viso . . ." (IX 5,57). While holding him down, unable to move, Niccolosa accentuates the comic situation by using expressions such as "'O Calandrin mio dolce, cuor del corpo mio, anima mia, ben mio, riposo mio'" (IX 5,58), which conflict with her actual view of the character to whom the words are addressed. The comedy is intensified by Niccolosa's switch to more vulgar forms of address such as "'tu m'hai con la piacevolezza tua *tratto il filo della camiscia*; tu *m'hai agratigliato il cuor con la tua ribeba* . . .'" (IX 5,58). At this, the view of Calandrino's unsuccessful attempts to realize his sexual urges ("Calandrino, appena potendosi muover, diceva: 'Deh! anima mia dolce, lasciamiti basciare'" (IX 5,59) accentuates the absurdity of his situation. The typical description of a male lover in control of his amorous situation is comically inverted; in both words and actions Caladrino is in a totally passive position, dominated and manipulated by the female character who makes fun of him on behalf of the other characters in the story.

This unusual amorous encounter reaches its climax with the tempestuous arrival of monna Tessa, who finally gets full revenge on her husband, both with physical aggression and verbal abuse:

> "Monna Tessa corse con l'unghie nel viso a Calandrino, che ancora levato non era, e tutto gliele graffiò; e presolo per li capelli e in qua e in là tirandolo cominciò a dire: 'Sozzo can vituperato . . . Vecchio impazzato . . . tristo . . . dolente . . .'"
>
> (IX 5, 63-64)

Our final view of Calandrino is "tristo e cattivo, tutto pelato e tutto graffiato . . . il dì e la notte molestato e afflitto da' rimbrotti della moglie . . ." (IX 5,67).

Calandrino as catalyst for his society's beloved tricks and laughter fulfills a many-faceted role in these four carefully correlated *novelle*. The two stories from the Eighth Day, the former placed in the city and the latter in the Tuscan *contado*, play upon a presence-versus-disappearance motif developed through Calandrino's supposed invisibility in VIII 3 and through his hog's actual disappearance in VIII 6. In VIII 3 Calandrino's supposed invisibility makes it possible for his tricksters friends to shower him with stones, while his own sudden realization that he is not invisible triggers his violent beating of monna Tessa. In VIII 6, the disappearance of the hog not only causes Calandrino a material loss, but the accusation of theft placed on him by his alleged friends and the whole community adds a moral dimension to his distress. While both Calandrino and monna Tessa end up physically debilitated and exhausted in VIII 3, VIII 6 concludes with Calandrino's material loss and moral degradation.

Novelle 3 and 5 of the Ninth Day correlate directly as well as chiasmally with VIII 3 and 6: Caladrino's money triggers his friend's *beffa* in IX 3, which takes place (like VIII 3) in the city. As in VIII 6, Calandrino suffers material loss, since he gives away his money in order to rid himself of a physical impairment (pregnancy) which he is made to believe afflicts him. Calandrino's wife is again blamed and punished for his condition, as in VIII 3, but this time only through verbal abuse. Contrary to the other Calandrino *novelle*, VIII 3 concludes with both tricksters and victim satisfied with their condition (a material gain for the former and a presumed loss of a physical impediment for the latter); monna Tessa is the only exception to the satisfactory outcome.

Novella 5 is the epitome of all the Calandrino stories, as it includes several elements of the previous stories, and presents several new ones. Played largely *in contado*, as was VIII 6, it does, however, move back and forth to the city, as did VIII 3. Calandrino once again, as in VIII 3 and 6, projects a desire, but this time for a human being rather than for a state of being or an object. This wish triggers a *beffa* aimed neither at a material reward for the tricksters (as in VIII 3, 6 and IX 3) nor at an emotional release of their tension through a physical assault against Calandrino (as in VIII 3). The *beffa* in this case moves on two levels: one of pure pleasure out of Calandrino's ridiculous love affair, and one of moral condemnation connected with monna Tessa's punishment of her allegedly unfaithful husband. While the first tale in the Calandrino cycle showed both husband and wife physically exhausted because of Calandrino's violent and irrational beating of his wife, the end of the cycle projects a physically and verbally defeated Calandrino punished, in an act of poetic justice, by his own often-abused wife. This last segment of the Calandrino cycle seems to offer a further connection between this day and the previous ones through its amplification upon the motif of a poor marital situation. While the end of IX 5 provides Calandrino with what he has deserved since his irrational beating of monna Tessa in VIII 3, both *novelle* together clearly provide a rather dismal view of marital relationships. This view is repeated in two other *novelle* of this day, IX 7 and 9, where wives are now the villains of the tales.

In *novella* 7, a woman's stubbornness and ill-intended curiosity cause her downfall in a "bosco assai bello" (IX 7,5). Here the forest once again objectifies violence and uncontrolled passion as a primitive counterpart to the woman's negative character. The "bosco" is introduced at the beginning of the tale in Talano's dream, and it becomes the focus of controversy between him and his wife: "'io per me il dico per bene,'" says Talano, "'e ancora da capo te ne consiglio che tu oggi ti stea in casa o almeno ti guardi d'andare nel nostro bosco'" (IX 7,9). His wife replies: "'Bene, io il farò'" (IX 7,10). But she immediately begins to second guess herself:

> 'Hai veduto come costui maliziosamente si crede avermi messa paura d'andare oggi al *bosco* nostro? là dove egli per certo dee aver data posta a qualche cattiva, e non vuole che io il vi truovi.'
>
> (IX 7,10)

The forest represents two different things to the two characters: to Talano it is a place of danger for his wife; and in Margarita's suspicious view it is a potential place of secreat pleasure for her husband. The *bosco* is thus the projection of each character's frame of mind: a concerned, sincere, and affectionate one on the husband's part, and a suspicious and spiteful one on the wife's. Finally, the forest does become the background of the attack that was foreseen in Talano's dream:

> ... come più nascosamente poté, senza alcuno indugio se n'andò *nel bosco* e *in quello, nella più folta parte* che v'era, si nascose ... E mentre in questa guisa stava senza alcun sospetto di lupo, e ecco vicino a lei uscir *d'una macchia folta* un lupo grande e terribile: né poté ella ... appena dire "Domine, aiutami!" che il lupo le si fu avventato alla gola, e presala forte la cominciò a portar via come se stata fosse un piccolo agnelletto.
>
> (IX 7, 11-12)

The woman's physical mutilation, which entails a destruction of beauty like that undergone by the widow of VIII 7 – a *novella* also narrated by Pampinea – is brought about by her own suspicious and stubborn nature. Margarita undermines her marriage with distrust and deceit, and her ill nature leads to Pampinea's polemic against women which is continued by Emilia in her introduction to IX 9.

Here the wife's ill will and spitefulness inspire her husband Giosefo's search for Solomon's advice. Giosefo, on his way to Jerusalem, meets Melisso from Laiazzo, who is also off to Solomon to seek advice about how to acquire human friendship and understanding. Solomon's replies to their questions at first seem abstruse: Giosefo is commanded to go "al Ponte all'Oca" and Melisso is ordered "Ama!". Only after seeing a mule beaten on the "Ponte all'Oca" does Giosefo understand Solomon's advice and learn an important lesson:

> 'Or ti dico io, compagno, che il consiglio datomi da Salamone potrebbe esser buono e vero, per ciò che assai

> manifestamente conosco che io non sapeva battere la
> donna mia: ma questo mulattiere m'ha mostrato quello
> che io abbia a fare.'
>
> (IX 9,22)

In Giosefo's application of Solomon's teaching, the mule's *battitura* and eventual obedience become the wife's. At this point, Melisso goes back to his own home and is enlightened by a friend concerning Solomon's advice to him: "Tu sai che tu non ami persona, e gli onori e' servigi li quali tu fai, gli fai non per amore che tu a alcun porti ma per pompa. Ama adunque, come Salamon ti disse, e sarai amato" (IX 9,34). The novella's two lessons seem to stand in ironic contrast: on the one hand, Solomon advises a man to achieve harmony through brutality; on the other, he counsels love for love. We might better understand this *novella*, the Ninth Day, and the work as a whole, if we viewed each as an exercise in balance. Pampinea's and Emilia's polemics against women are significant examples of this "balance" when placed in their proper context. In her introduction to IX 9, Emilia says,

> "Amabili donne, se con sana mente sarà riguardato
> l'ordine delle cose, assai leggermente si conoscerà tutta
> la universal moltitudine delle femine dalla natura e da'
> costumi e dalle leggi essere agli uomini sottomessa e
> secondo la discrezione di quegli convenirsi reggere e
> governare . . . e per ciò nel mio giudicio cape tutte
> quelle esser degne . . . di rigido e aspro gastigamento che
> dall' esser piacevoli, benivole, e pieghevoli, come la
> natura, l'usanza e le leggi voglion, si partono."
>
> (IX 9,3-6)

This passage echoes Filomena and Elissa in the general Introduction to the *Decameron*, both of whom imply that women need men's guidance. Filomena says:

> "Ricordivi che noi siamo tutte femine, e non ce n'ha
> niuna sì fanciulla, che non possa ben conoscere come le
> femine sien ragionate insieme e *senza la provedenza
> d'alcuno uomo si sappiano regolare.*"
>
> (I, Introduction,74)

Elissa puts it this way:

> 'Veramente gli uomini sono delle femine capo e senza
> l'ordine loro rade volte riesce alcuna nostra opera a
> laudevole fine . . ."
>
> (I, Introduction,76)

Ironically, these statements are preceded by Pampinea's lucid and well-reasoned review of the sad state of affairs in the city, along with her equally enlightened description of a future restoration of order in the country which they will perform as representatives of the Florentine society. This project is accepted and unanimously endorsed by all seven women in the group. The following events, too, ironically undercut Filomena's and Elissa's statements; in fact, it is the women who choose which men will be their companions in the exit from the city, and Pampinea again is the one who sets down the initial set of laws for the welfare of this group of men and women, during their sojourn in the country (I, Introduction, 53). Pampinea, as queen of the First Day, also enumerates the reasons why storytelling should be the esthetic entertainment for their enlightened life in the countryside. Statements such as Filomena's and Elissa's, then, function as ironic counterparts to the women's actions and decisions, and add to the many-faceted representation of life which the *Decameron* offers. Emilia's statement at the beginning of IX 9, which echoes Filomena and Elissa can be seen in the same light. She plays on the authority of "natura . . . costumi . . . e leggi," and later on "natura . . . l'usanza e le leggi" to suggest that womankind is "agli uomini sottomessa, e secondo la discrezion di quegli convenirsi reggere e governare." Giosefo's wife of IX 9 particularly illustrates the second part of Emilia's assertion: "tutte quelle esser degne . . . di rigido e aspro gastigamento che dall'esser piacevoli, benivole, e pieghevoli . . . si partono." At the same time, in her long introduction to the *novella*, Emilia equates women to citizens in need of assistance and government:

> "E chi ha bisogno d'essere aiutato e governato, ogni ragion vuol lui dovere essere obediente e subgetto e reverente al governator suo: e cui abbiam noi governatori e aiutatori se non gli uomini?"
>
> (IX 9,5)

Women's weaknesses and their need for men's guidance thus reflect a universal human need for government and guidance. The obedience and reverence due to men from women correspond to the loyalty any citizen owes to his governing authority. The typical medieval topos of women's inferiority to and dependence upon men is now endowed with a legalistic implication; both men and women are parts of a system of government in which both parties must work together harmoniously and effectively in order for it to function properly. This concept seems to come into play particularly in IX 2 and 6, where men and women unite to achieve a completely harmonious outcome. In the general structure of the Ninth Day, other storytellers counter Emilia's statements thus providing more than one view of human nature. For example, in the exordium in IX 10, which immediately follows Emilia's tale, Dioneo introduces a simile comparing the women of the *onesta brigata* to "molte bianche colombe" and implies their superiority by envisioning them as the epitome of wisdom and maturity ("discretissime e moderate"); antithetically he describes himself as "uno nero corvo . . . un men savio . . . il quale sento anzi dello scemo che no, faccendo la vostra virtù più lucente col mio difetto . . ." (IX 10,3-4). In the conclusion to the Ninth Day, Panfilo, the king of the Tenth Day, intensifies the complexity of the narrative texture by expressing to the *innamorate donne* his belief in their worth:

> "dicendo e faccendo (the magnificent deeds of the last Day's novelle) senza alcun dubbio gli animi vostri ben disposti a valorosamente adoperare accenderà: ché la vita nostra . . . si perpetuerá nella laudevole fama'"
> (IX Conclusion,5)

Panfilo's words and specifically the gerunds "dicendo e faccendo" which coordinate storytelling and actual performing of actions, are particularly revealing as to the storytellers' future mission towards their society and to the social and moral purpose of their storytelling and actions: "ché la vita nostra . . . si perpetuerá nella laudevole fama." The polemic against women expressed in Emilia's statement and in *novelle* IX 7 and 9 should therefore be considered in the context of the Ninth Day as well as in the total context of the work, which tends to provide a many-faceted view of society as an harmonious balance of opposites.

5. Day X: The Individual in Harmony with his World

The last day of the *Decameron* presents a superior world molded by aware, responsible, and fundamentally good individuals actively involved in the creation of a better society. The storytellers are asked by their king Panfilo to return to a set topic of *novellare* which would deal with "chi liberalmente overo magnificamente alcuna cosa operasse intorno a' fatti d'amore o d'altra cosa" (IX, Conc. 4-5). When this day opens, the ten young people take their usual walk in the countryside and, as if in response to Panfilo's words of the night before suggesting their future mission in their own society, they talk about the future: "molte cose della loro futura vita insieme parlando e dicendo e rispondendo, per lungo spazio s'andaron diportando" (X, Intro.,3).

Liberality and magnanimity are the virtues that the world of Day X aptly displays, on whatever level of the social ladder the characters belong. The *novelle's* protagonists are powerful kings and rulers, such as Alfonso of Spain in X 1, "re Carlo vecchio" in X 6, "re Pietro di Raona" in X 7, Saladin in X 9, and Gualtieri "marchese di Saluzzo" in X 10; popes and bishops, such as Boniface VIII and the "abate di Clignì in X 2; noble people such as Ruggeri of X 1, Ghino of X 2, Natan in X 3, Gentile de' Carisendi and Niccoluccio and Catalina Caccianimico in X 4, messer Ansaldo Gradense of X 5, messer Neri degli Uberti and his family and Guido di Monforte in X 6, Tito Quinzio Fulvio, Gisippo and Sofronia in X 8, or messer Torello da Stra da Pavia and wife in X 9; rich men such as Mitridanes in X 3; professionals, such as the Florentine *speziale* Bernardo Puccini or the "finissimo cantatore e sonatore" Minuccio d'Arezzo or the "dicitore in rima" Mico da Siena in X 7; and eventually even a "guardiana di pecore" such as Griselda and her "poverissimo . . . padre Giannucole" of X 10.

The first three *novelle* deal with liberality as demonstrated by a king to his courtier (X 1), by an abbot and a pope to an excommunicated nobleman (X 2), and by a noble and rich man from China to another equally rich countryman envious of his fame (X 3). The following four deal directly with magnaminity in love: X 4 and 5 by a noble character to the husband of his beloved woman; X 6 and 7 by a king to his subjects — the former involving the girl he loves and her family, the latter the girl who loves him and her family. The Eighth *novella* introduces the topic of friendship connected with self-renunciation in love, while the ninth story projects a contest in magnanimous hospitality between two superior men of different faiths, together with the epitome of a marital relationship. *Novella* 10 pits a ruler against his subjects on the topic of matrimony, and eventually presents the epitome of wife's obedience.

The first three *novelle*, which are not concerned with love, relate more specifically to Day I and seem to correlate, sometimes antithetically, with stories of that day while projecting also some connections with other days, particularly II and IV. In X 1, for instance, the motif of *fortuna* is linked with the topic of a ruler's liberality, and thus offers a possible view of Ruggieri de' Figiovanni as a Day II character. At the same time, his situation reminds us of Bergamino at the court of Can Della Scala or of Primasso at the table of the Abbot of Cluny (I 7). Ruggieri, however, is much more intelligent, aware, and eloquent than any of the male characters of Day II; and his social position as one of the most "valorosi cavalieri" from Florence who "assai onorevolemente in arme e in cavalli e in compagnia . . . se n'andò in Ispagna" to be part of King Alfonso's court, puts him on a much higher and more honorable plane than either Bergamino or Primasso. The King in X I also distinguishes himself beyond Can Grande and the Abbot of Cluny in I 7. Where they display irrational and impulsive bursts of avarice, he responds in a calm and rational way to accusations of illiberality. The Abbot of Cluny appears again in X 2 as an ailing prisoner of the expatriate "rubator di strada," Ghino di Tacco. Here the positive view of the clergy, of the court of Rome, and of the Pope himself, stands in sharp contrast to the polemics against them found in I 2. Another antithetical reference to a Day I story, more specifically I 3, seems to be conveyed in X 3 by the incredible generosity and self-denial of Natan towards the threat of death represented by Mitridanes. The latter, like Saladin in I 3, threatens his opponent in order to get something out of the situation: Saladin needs money and plans a dangerous trap for Melchisedec; Mitridanes wants exclusive recognition for his liberality without competition from Natan, whom he plans to kill. Melchisedec with his *senno* fights back and neutralizes Saladin's plan, but will eventually provide Saladin with all the money he needs without losing either his freedom or life. Natan accepts Mitridane's will and offers himself up in total self-denial. The scene of the aggression in X 3 introduces two elements that recall a similar episode in IV 9: both scenes take place in a natural environment: Rossiglione's "in *un bosco* . . . forse un miglio fuori del suo castello," Mitridanes' in *"un boschetto* . . .forse un mezzo miglio vicin di qui" where Mitridanes finds Natan. The words that Mitridanes uses in the assault are: "Vegliardo, *tu se' mortò*." which closely recall Rossiglione's words when stabbing Guardastagno: "'Traditor, *tu sè morto*. Instead of death and mutilation, however, Mitridanes's action is not fatal: upon recognizing Natan, he renounces his intention and professes his everlasting admiration for the older man's incomparable liberality. While excessive self-gratification in IV 9 had provoked an urge for hate and destruction, self-denial in X 3 creates a need for respect, love, and admiration. Natan's extraordinary behavior conquers his enemy and succeeds in inspiring in Mitridanes a similar sentiment: "'Tolga Iddio che così cara cosa come la vostra vita è, non che io . . . la prenda, ma pur la disideri, come poco avanti faceva; alla quale non che io diminuissi gli anni suoi ma io l'agiugnerei volentier de' miei'" (X 3,39). In all, these first three *novelle* show a much better view of the human world than that observed in the *novelle* of the previous days which treat the same themes. The characters in Day X are much more rational, more understanding, more concerned with their social environment, and more determined to improve their fellow-men, including their antagonists, than were the protagonists in the previous days' *novelle*.

Magnanimity in love is introduced as a subject of discussion by Lauretta in X 4. To that purpose she presents an interpretation of one of the *Filocolo's* "Quistioni d'Amore," the Thirteenth, as a better way to show liberality than any of the previous stories offered, if:[34]

> "è vero che i tesori si donino (implying X 1), le inimicizie
> si dimentichino (X 2) e pongasi la propia vita (X 3),
> l'onore e la fama, ch'è molto più, in mille pericoli per
> potere la cosa amata possedere"
> (X 4,4)

Lauretta describes a happy marriage which foils the desire of the wife's lover, messer Gentile. Like Nastagio of V 8, or Federigo of V 9, messer Gentile is hurt by his unreciprocated love. Madonna Catalina's pregnancy creates a critical situation which culminates when the lady is believed dead. The motif of a person believed dead and then called back to life again with concerns about pregnancy recalls Ferondo's adventure on III 8 — a story also narrated by Lauretta. Ferondo's ordeal, however, was astutely planned by the wife's would-be lover, who was only too eager to get Ferondo out of the way and then back again at the first sign of pregnancy. In X 4, instead, pregnancy is the cause of the lady's sudden catatonia, and her return to life the result of her lover's passionate caresses in the macabre setting of her family tomb. Gentile's final magnanimous gesture of returning madonna Catalina and her newborn baby to her husband elicits Lauretta's restatement of Gentile's unique liberality:

> ("egli . . . non solo temperò onestamente il suo fuoco, ma liberalmente quello che egli soleva con tutto il pensier disiderare e cercare di rubare, avendolo restituì. Per certo niuna delle già dette a questa mi par simigliante."
>
> (X 4,48)

Emilia follows by relating another of the Filocolo's "Questioni," the Fourth. It again concerns liberality in love, and a happy marriage is again the source of pain to a lover whose proposals are continually rebuffed. Like madonna Francesca of IX 1, madonna Dianora, in order to discourage her ardent admirer, demands that he perform what she believes is an impossible task. To her surprise, he accomplishes it. Her husband plays an essential role in the "liberality contest" because he first sacrifices his privileges for another's rights. At the same time, the lover's willingness to help the husband recalls another of Emilia's stories, that of Tedaldo in III 7. The earlier tale, however, differs from X 5 inasmuch as in X 5 no sexual relationship is established between the suitor and the woman; the final rapport between Ansaldo, Dianora, and her husband, contrary to that in III 7, is clearly one of open friendship and esteem.

While in both X 4 and 5, the institution of marriage becomes stronger than ever and absorbs the wife's suitor as a respected friend, in X 6 and 7, interest focuses on pre-marital situations and concerns royal power. Fiammetta recounts, as she has often done before (in II 5, III 6, and IV 1), a story set in the south of Italy, more precisely Naples. It concerns an Angioin King, Carlo I, and some Florentine exiles, Neri degli Uberti and his family. The king's uncontrolled passion for one of Neri's daughters recalls the king of France's infatuation for the Marquise from Monferrato (I 5) — a *novella* also narrated by Fiammetta — who, forces the king to renounce his love through her clever explanation of her hen banquet. In X 6, instead, it is the king himself who, stung by the forthright reprimand of his adviser renounces his disonorable passion, marries off his beloved girl and her sister to noble and powerful lords and "con dolore inestimabile in Puglia se n'andò, e con fatiche continue tanto e sì macerò il suo fiero appetito, che, spezzate e rotte l'amorose catene, per quanto viver dovea libero rimase da tal passione" (X 6,35).

A polemic against the so called "giustizia di re" is expressed in Guido da Monforte's harsh censure of the Guelf king's desire to confiscate messer Neri's beautiful daughters for his own pleasure. Pampinea echoes and balances these condemnatory remarks by addressing the "ghibellino" Pietro d'Aragona in X 7: "Così adunque operando si pigliano gli animi de' subgetti, dassi altrui materia di bene operare e le fame eterne s'acquistano . . ." (X 7,49). In this *novella* the roles are reversed, for it is the young girl who falls in love with the king. Because of her lowly social status as daughter of a Florentine *speziale*, Lisa recognizes the impropriety of her love, and at the same time is incapable of renouncing it. She nears death as she pines for her monarch. But the power of poetry performs a quasi-miracle: through Mico da Siena's verses and Minuccio d'Arezzo's music and singing, the king becomes aware of Lisa's love, deems it highly meritorious, and rewards her with a dowry and marriage to a nobleman of his entourage. Lisa expresses the everlastingness of her love for the king in terms which echo the most famous heroine of the Fourth Day, Ghismonda; in her last speech to the king, Lisa states: "'alla qual legge più volte s'opposero le forze mie, e, più non potendo, *v'amai e amo e amerò sempre'*" (X 7,41-42). Ghismonda's words about Guiscardo were: "'Egli è il vero che *io ho amato e amo Guiscardo* e quanto io viverò, che sarà poco, *l'amerò*, e se appresso la morte *s'ama, non mi rimarrò d'amarlo*" (IV 1,32). The latter part of Ghismonda's speech, which projects her own death and a *post-mortem* continuation of her love, is missing in Lisa's speech. Lisa emphasizes her complete dependence on the king's will as her lord in both feudal and courtly terms; Ghismonda instead strongly emphasizes her right to independence of mind and her personal determination in the choice of a lover. Ghismonda's high social class may contribute to her independence while Lisa's recognition of her own "infima condizione" is stressed throughout the story. A similar plight befell another Florentine character also sketched by Pampinea in the Sixth Day, Cisti . . ., to whose "nobile animo . . la fortuna" had prepared "vil mestiero" (VI 2,3). Cisti's lot, hardly changed by the end of the *novella*, forces Pampinea to consider the relationship between *natura, fortuna*, and man without actually achieving any new solution to the problem: "E certo io *maladicerei e la natura parimenti e la fortuna, se io non conoscessi* la natura esser discretissima e la fortuna aver mille occhi, come che gli sciocchi lei cieca figurino" (VI 2,4-5). The king of X 7 actually does what Pampinea had refused to do in her introductory remarks to VI 2: "più volte seco stesso *maladisse la fortuna* che di tale uomo l'aveva fatta figliola" (X 7,35). He proceeds to *change* Lisa's social position by marrying her to a nobleman and by proclaiming himself "mentre visse *sempre* . . . *suo cavaliere*" (X 7,48).

These last two *novelle*, then, especially when compared with similar *novelle* from previous days, create situations suitable to bring about social change and improved conditions of life.

Friendship tested against love is the general topic of X 8, which Filomena introduces by focusing once more on class differences. She points out the need for replacing royal characters with "nostri pari" whose "opere" must "molto più . . . piacere e esser da voi commendate . . . quando sono a quelle de' re simiglianti o maggiori" (X 8,4). The characters of the story are taken from classical times and the two protagonists, the Roman Tito and the Athenian Gisippo, are both dedicated to the study of philosophy. The theme of friendship is the dominating force that keeps the two together, to the point that Gisippo renounces Sofronia in order to allow Tito to have her. He tells Tito, "forse così liberal non sarei, *se così rade o con quella difficoltà le mogli si trovasser che si truovan gli amici* (X

8,38). Considering examples of more or less satisfactory forms of friendship in previous *novelle* (I 2 and 3; II 9; IV 3,5,7 and 9; VII 3,7, and 10; VIII 3,6,8,9; and IX 3,4, and 5), this story represents the apotheosis of friendship. Gisippo renounces his bethrothed for Tito's sake at the opening of the story in Athens, and Tito, at the end of the tale in Rome, is ready to renounce his own life in order to save Gisippo from being crucified for a murder he never committed. Society in the Tenth Day is always very protective of the individual; thus both friends are eventually spared any punishment. After a happy reunion, a marriage is arranged between Gisippo and Tito's sister in order to strengthen the friendship's ties into a family unit. The several important events of the story are related through the characters' highly sophisticated use of rhetorical eloquence, appropriate to those well trained in philosophy and the humanities as are the two protagonists. (And one should add, in the *ars narrandi*, as Filomena clearly is, given this tale and her madonna Oretta's story at the opening of the second part of the *Decameron*). This rhetorical ability reaches a climax in Tito's speech to all of Athenian society in which he defends his substitution for Gisippo as Sofronia's husband without her or anyone else's knowledge. Tito's eloquent soundness and threatening warnings sway the crowd's sentiment and make them accept Sofronia as really his *"per consentimento degl'iddii e per vigor delle leggi umane e per lo laudevole senno del . . . Gisippo e per la . . . amorosa astuzia"* (X 8,84). These four factors—the gods' consensus, human laws, the individual wisdom and wit—are among the most powerful regulating forces of the *Decameron* world, and by appealing to them for his prerogative to love, Tito becomes an admirable spokesman for men's rights in marriage choice, as Ghismonda was for women in Part I. Ghismonda, however, in spite of her intelligence, eloquence and foresight, and despite her adherence to laws of love based on nobility of heart rather than of blood, was unable to change her lot or to convince her society of her rightful claims. Tito, instead, succeeds where Ghismonda failed; in the favorable environment of Day X, society accepts the superior individual's plea for understanding and cooperation for the sake of more enlightened relationships among men.

Novella 9 fulfills Tito's explicit as well as implicit message. It is narrated by Panfilo, the king of the Day, and as such introduces the last story on the required topic, since by Filomena's decree of Day I, Dioneo is excused from following any prescribed topic in the tenth *novella* of any day. Messer Torello's and Saladin's superiority is measured by the respect they have for each other as human beings and by the means through which they demonstrate their respective admiration. The occasion for their encounter involves the "consentimento degli Dei," as Saladin is in *Lombardia* in order to "personalmente vedere gli parecchiamenti de' signori cristiani a quel passaggio . . . a racquistar la Terra Santa . . ." (X 9,5-6). That is, he is preparing to face the Third Crusade, under the Emperor Frederick I, which will set Christians and Mohamedans against each other. Upon this historical, strife-torn background, the encounter between the two representatives of antagonistic religions assumes a symbolic significance. It pits individual values and laws against the belief in superhuman ideals which causes men to trample on individuals. Man's helplessness in the face of conflicts produced by such beliefs is suggested in the fate of the Christian army overseas:

> montato in galea andò via, e in poco tempo pervenne a Acri e con l'altro essercito di cristian si congiunse. Nel quale quasi a mano a man cominciò una grandissima infermeria e mortalità, la qual durante, qual che si fosse l'arte o la fortuna del Saladino, quasi tutto il rimaso degli scampati cristiani da lui a man salva fur presi, e per molte città divisi e impregionati. Fra' quali presi messer Torello fu uno, e in Alessandria menato in prigione . . .
>
> (X 9, 48-50)

Individual values however, eventually do prevail, at least for messer Torello, who manages to summon the appropriate wisdom and wit at the right time.[35] Messer Torello's art of "conciare uccelli, di che egli era grandissimo maestro," makes him stand out among the throng of prisoners. Eventually Saladin's perception, wit, and esteem restores him to his previous position as a free man of high standing at his own court. Yet the motif of human helplessness in the midst of epidemic and war is played upon again in the disconcerting mix-up over messer Torello's fate among the Moslems:

> Era nel campo o vero essercito de' cristiani, il dì che dal Saladin furon presi, morto e sepellito un cavalier provenzale di piccol valore, il cui nome era messer Torel di Dignes; per la qual cosa, essendo messer Torel di Stra per la sua nobiltà per lo essercito conosciuto, chiunque udì dire 'messer Torello è morto' credette di messer Torel di Stra e non di quel di Dignes; e il caso, che sopravenne, della presura non lasciò sgannar gl'ingannati . . ."
>
> (X 9, 61-62)

The bad news reaches Torello's family and since his attempts to advise his wife of his venture are not successful, she is obliged to remarry as soon as the time has elapsed during which she was bidden to wait. Once Torello realizes that in no earthly way can he reach his home before the term agreed upon has expired, he reacts like most unhappy lovers of the *Decameron:* "in tanto dolor cadde, che, perdutone il mangiare e a giacer postosi, diliberò di morire" (X 9,67-68). Fortunately, in this Day, when human dilemmas and problems of time and space cannot be solved in a normal way, assistance comes from superhuman (and not always divine) intervention. In this case, a luxurious flying bed, devised by magical art, becomes a comfortable means of transportation that deposits messer Torello "in abito barbaresco" in the center of the church "di San Piero in Ciel d'oro di Pavia." He is received in a not too friendly way by the clerics at hand, who are understandably scared out of their wits by the apparition of a man believed "morto . . . dimolti mesi innanzi" (X 9,94). The final banquet scene shows an incognito messer Torello preventing his wife's unwilling marriage to another man. We see the importance of the human customs of marriage and love which both messer Torello and madonna Alatiela respect, as well as the positive impact of Saladin's wise's assistance as a devoted friend. This *novella* therefore becomes the apotheosis of human liberality, friendship and matrimonial love, thus bringing all the topics of the day to a culmination.

In the corresponding day of Part I, Day 5, love is always approached in prematrimonial terms, never reaching the heights of perfect matrimonial devotion presented in Day X. This Day, with the exception of X 6 and 7, which stress moral and political achievements of royal personalities, centers on marriage and its problems in all *novelle* dealing with love. Madonna Catalina of X 4 highlights the helplessness of a married and pregnant woman's condition who, away from her husband, is carelessly disposed of by inconsiderate relatives and eventually saved only through the assistance of her passionate lover. Day IX's polemics on women's vulnerability and defenselessness, echoing Elissa's and Filomena's statement on Day I are pointedly reintroduced in X 4 in narrative action and in verbal utterances as well. Compared to "Quistione XIII" of the *Filocolo*, an important change occurs in this *novella* concerning woman's helplessness away from her husband: while in the *Filocolo* the woman's presumed death occurs in the city and no indications are given as to her husband's absence, in the *Decameron*, a point is made of underlining Niccoluccio's absence by strategically placing it first in the syntactical order, followed by the woman's subsequent retreat in the country, and the eventual doctors' and relatives' carelessness towards her:

> "non essendo Niccoluccio a Bologna e la donna a una sua possessione forse tre miglia alla terra vicina essendosi, per ciò che gravida era, andata a stare, avvenne che . . . un fiero accidente la soprapprese . . . che in lei spense ogni segno di vita e per ciò eziandio da alcun medico morta giudicata fu; e per ciò . . . le sue più congiunte parenti . . . senza altro impaccio darsi, quale ella era, in uno avello d'una chiesa ivi vicina dopo molto pianto la sepellirono"
>
> (X 4,6-7)

This careful arrangement of syntactical order and subsequent change in the narrative action point at a new awareness of the dangers that a woman may endure if she lacks her husband's concern and protection. Messer Gentile's love and liberality provide her momentarily with what she had lost during her husband's absence in preparation for her reinstatement in her family and society. Gentile's story of the servant abandoned by his first master and eventually cured and saved by a a new, more generous and concerned one, further stresses the woman's vulnerability by the obvious—and to modern eyes offensive—comparison of the woman and the servant. These innovations on the *Filocolo* text stress the importance of concern, respect, thoughtfulness, and love in the marital situation. Messer Gentile's lesson to Niccoluccio as a husband is clear, especially considering madonna Catalina's role as a perfectly innocent and honest wife victimized within her family situation.

Such is not the role of madonna Dianora in the following *novella*. Here a happy marriage is clouded by the woman's unwise attempt to rid herself of an importunate lover by asking him to fulfill a seemingly impossible wish of hers. When the lover, with the assistance of a skillful magician, does succeed in fulfilling her wish, madonna Dianora's situation becomes troublesome. Here, the husband's concern for and understanding of his wife is revealed first by his realization of her troubled state of mind and his insistence upon knowing the reason: "volle del tutto da lei di quello saper la cagione. La donna per vergogna il tacque molto; ultimamente, constretta ordinatamente gli aperse ogni cosa". (IX 5,13). Eventually his thoughtfulness and love are also shown in his handling of the whole situation, from his reproach to Dianora for behavior unbecoming to a *savia* and *onesta donna*, to his acceptance of her "purità dell'animo" and the decision to allow her to keep her promise to Ansaldo. The way in which Gilberto frames his decision provides another angle from which to view this unusual matrimonial relationship where the possibility for an extra-conjugal affair is actually controlled by the husband:

> "per solverti da' legame della promessa, quello ti concederò che forse alcuno altro non farebbe . . . Voglio io che tu a lui vada e, se per modo alcun puoi, t'ingegni di far che, servata la tua onestà, tu sii da questa promessa disciolta: dove altramenti non si potesse, per questa volta il corpo ma non l'animo gli concedi"
>
> (X 5, 15-16)

A wife's dependency on her husband's will is here strongly maintained, in contrast to the general theory of Day VII; there, we might recall, intelligent, respectful, and concerned husbands were hard to find. Dianora's unwillingness to accept her husband's will suggests her honesty, while her final acquiescence speaks for her obedience. Such a virtue is lacking in the wives of IX 5,7 and 9. Gilberto's intelligence is evident when he advises Dianora to use her ingenuity with Ansaldo in order to be "da questa promessa disciolta", a suggestion that Dianora very skillfully and successfully follows in her encounter with Ansaldo. The last reason that Gilberto offers for his decision, and which is not present in the *Filocolo,* accentuates the feeling of togetherness that this couple shares: "inducendomi ancora la paura del nigromante, al qual forse messer Ansaldo, se tu il beffassi, far ci farebbe dolenti" (X 5,15). The power of magic, not to be taken too lightly in this story, is real enough to explain Gilberto's fears which clearly project a potential change in their situation together from happiness to sorrow "far ci farebbe *dolenti.*" Matrimonial love, then, in this *novella,* is founded on the husband's concern, thoughtfulness, and respect for his wife, and on his assistance in suggesting intelligent ways to solve a difficult situation. It also relies on the wife's understanding of the vulnerability of her situation (if left by herself without the husband's advice or protection), and on her trust and obedience.

Both *novelle* 4 and 5, then, prepare for Tito's statements in X 8 about the essential factors that brought about his own marriage: in both, the marital laws of love, respect, and obedience, coupled with wisdom and wit, produce a durable marriage. Tito's marital experience turns out well because of his ability to redress society's view of it and of his friend Gisippo's loyalty and liberality. Sofronia's role as a wife in this relationship is rather underplayed. In X 9, then, both husband and wife are first seen acting with intelligence, thoughtfulness, and independence in their liberality to Saladin: while messer Torello does so as a noble man, by offering him "ragionamenti piacevoli," "compagnia d' più nobili cittadini" from Pavia, and eventually more practical masculine gifts such as "tre grossi pallafreni e buoni e . . . nuovi cavalli e forti alli loro famigliari", madonna Alatiela accomplishes her feminine duties as a noble hostess by preparing a "grandissimo convito" on her husband's orders to honor them and eventually by offering them modestly a "piccioletto dono . . . considerando che le donne secondo il lor picciol cuore piccole cose danno . . ." (X 9,30). Eventually messer Torello's identity will be appropriately proven to Saladin through Alatiela's gifts, which Saladin shows in order to reveal himself as "l'uno de' tre mercatanti a' quali la donna vostra donò queste robe . . ." (X 9,57). Marital love in this *novella*—seemingly for the first time in the *Decameron*—is openly expressed both by husband and wife: messer Torello shows her as "sua cara cosa" to Saladin in Pavia, and at the moment of his departure for the crusade he demonstrates his feelings in the respectful, thoughtful way he talks to her. At the beginning of his speech "alla sua donna, la quale egli sommamente amava" he recommends to her "le nostre cose e 'l nostro onore," clearly stating his trust in her managerial ability and marital honesty. He wisely foresees his own potential death and provides accordingly for her future, realizing her great gifts and virtues: "'se' giovane donna e se' bella e se' di gran parentado, e la tua vertù è molta e è conosciuta per tutto . . ." (X 9,44-45). Eventually, when he realizes that for all his planning and provisions, he is going to lose her anyway, his grief makes him wish for death. This is indeed the first time in the *Decameron* when love of this strength and depth occurs in a marital situation. Saladin eventually will provide for his swift return after openly approving of Torello's love:

> "'Messer Torello, se voi affettuosamente amate la donna vostra e che ella d'altrui non divegna dubitate, sallo Idio che io in parte alcuna non ve ne so riprendere, per ciò che di quanti donne mi parve veder mai ella è colei li cui costumi, le cui maniere e il cui abito, lasciamo star la bellezza . . . più mi paion da commendare e da aver care"
> (X 9, 72-73)

Madonna Alatiela is even more demonstrative of her affection for her husband: she tries to dissuade him from going to the crusade with "prieghi . . . e . . . lagrime" and refuses to accept his initial plans for her in case of his death: "'Messer Torello, io non so come io mi comporterò il dolore nel qual, partendovi, voi mi lasciate; ma dove la mia vita sia più forte di lui e altro di voi avvenisse, vivete e morite sicuro che io viverò e morrò moglie di messer Torello e della sua memoria" (X 9,43). When the false news of his death reaches Pavia, "(l)ungo sarebbe a mostrare qual fosse e quanto il dolore e la tristizia e 'l pianto della sua donna" (X 9,64); and when she is eventually forced to consider taking a new husband, she does it "contro suo volere" and only because she is "vinta da' prieghi e dalle minacce de' parenti suoi" (X 9,96). The final scene of the nuptial banquet turns out to be most lively, touching and humorous while at the same time it is a simple testimony of a woman's love for her husband:

> fiso guardato colui il qual forestier credeva e già conoscendolo, quasi furiosa divenuta fosse gittata in terra la tavola che davanti aveva, gridò: 'Questi è il mio signore, questi veramente è messer Torello!' E corsa alla tavola alla quale esso sedeva, senza avere riguardo a' suoi drappi o a cosa che sopra la tavola fosse, gittatasi oltre quanto poté, l'abracciò strettamente, né mai dal suo collo fu potuta, per detto o per fatto d'alcuno che quivi fosse, levare infino a tanto che per messer Torello non le fu detto che alquanto sopra sé stesse, per ciò che tempo da abracciarlo le sarebbe ancora prestato assai.
> (X 9, 107-109)

Once again obedience to her husband's wishes is a proof of the woman's love for him and of the trust that unite the two.

In X 10, obedience is Griselda's most characteristic quality in her relationship with her husband, Gualtieri, the Marquis of Saluzzo. His primary quality, in the context of the story, is *senno*, which Dioneo contradictorily interprets, in his initial and concluding remarks as *matta bestialità*. Gualtieri's wisdom is universally exalted because he chooses Griselda as his wife. She, once elevated to the position of the Marquis's wife in spite of her low birth, "non . . . guardiana di pecore pareva . . . ma (figliuola) d'alcun nobile signore . . . e oltre a questo era tanto obediente al marito e tanto servente, che egli si teneva il più contento e il più appagato uomo del mondo . . ." (X 10, 24-25). The unusual situation created by the marriage between a noble and powerful ruler and a girl of a considerably lower status, recalls the story of Giletta in the Third Day, where, however, the choice is made by the girl and put into effect by the king of France against the young bridegroom's will. In Griselda and Gualtieri's case, it is the latter who makes the choice in order to comply, even if reluctantly, with his subjects' request, and Griselda fully accepts his decision. She answers affirmatively to his questions on the ritual occasion of their first meeting: "domandolla se ella sempre, togliendola egli per moglie, s'ingegnerebbe di compiacergli e di niuna cosa che egli dicesse o facesse non turbarsi, e se ella sarebbe obediente e simili altre cose assai, delle quali ella a tutte rispose di sì" (X 10,18-19). Griselda keeps her promise even in the face of the inhuman treatment that Gualtieri inflicts on her by depriving her of her children and eventually repudiating her for a younger and higher-born wife. At the end, Gualtieri restores her as his legitimate consort, explaining his behavior in moralistic and political terms: "'volendoti insegnar d'esser moglie e a loro (his subjects) di saperla tenere, e a me partorire perpetua quiete mentre teco a vivere avessi'" (X 10,61). He eventually reconsecrates himself as "il tuo marito, il quale sopra ogni altra cosa t'amo, credendomi poter dar vanto che niuno altro sia che, sì com'io, si possi di sua moglier contentare" (X 10,63). Griselda seems the apex of feminine self-denial and generosity in an unusual matrimonial situation, where the husband as feudal lord has all the prerogatives necessary to enforce the total submission of his subjects, especially those from obscure, lowly origins. Yet in Dioneo's interpretation at the end of the story, the roles should be inverted: it is "nelle povere case (che) piovono dal cielo de' divini spiriti, come nelle reali di quegli che sarien più degni di guardar porci che d'avere sopra uomini signoria . . ." (X 10,68). This form of "perspectivism"[36] afforded by the last *novella* of the *Decameron* allows for an open interpretation of what a superior human world can provide to individuals ready to learn from it. Griselda's patience or Gualtieri's socially inspired wisdom may work equally well towards the improvement of a society prepared to accept the laws and qualities implied in their story.

The exceptional individuals of this Day are often exposed to a crucial life experience in nature, just as are the characters in several of the Fourth Day's *novelle*, in almost all of the Fifth Day's, and in the *cornice* itself. In this last day the apotheosis of a whole society is dependent on exceptional individuals and their critical experience in the world of nature. In the first *novella* of the Day, messer Ruggieri's fortune is decided by an event which occurs in a natural environment during his return to Tuscany from the king of Spain's court. Ruggieri compares the mule's unregulated performance in the countryside to the king's behaviors at court:

'Deh! dolente ti faccia Dio, bestia, ché tu se' fatta come il signore che a me ti donò . . . Signor mio, per ciò ve la assomigliai, perché, come voi donate dove non si conviene e dove si converrebbe non date, così ella dove si conveniva non stallò e dove non si convenia sì.'

(X I, 11-14)

His adventure with the mule leads to his return to court, his confrontation with the king, and final resolution of his problem in harmony and contentment: "Messer Ruggieri presolo (il forziere), e quelle grazie rendute al re che a tanto dono si confaceano, con esso lieto se ne ritornò in Toscana" (X 1,20).

While in this *novella* final accord is reached in a feudal environment after the catalyzing event that occurs in the country, the action of X 2 takes place almost entirely in the country environment of the *Maremma senese*. There Ghino di Tacco seizes and keeps the Abbot of Cluny prisoner: "Ghino di Tacco . . . tese le reti, e . . . l'abate con tutta la sua famiglia e le sue cose in uno stretto luogo racchiuse . . . per che l'abate, co' suoi preso veggendosi, disdegnoso forte, con l'ambasciadore prese la via verso il castello . . ." (X 2,7-10). It is finally Ghino, living as an outlaw in the *Maremma senese*, who, with his enlightened perspective, offers the abbot an ideal existence. The abbot's isolation and apparently forced seclusion in the natural world turns out to be a healthy and friendly place of superior existence. The abbot's eventual appreciation of Ghino's efforts brings about a third party's recognition, the Pope's, at whose court the final vision of harmony and liberality is enjoyed: "Venne adunque Ghino, fidato, come allo abate piacque, a corte; né guari appresso del Papa fu che egli il reputò valoroso, e riconciliatoselo gli donò una gran prioria . . . la quale egli, amico e servidore di santa Chiesa e dello abate di *Clignì*, tenne mentre visse." (X 2,31).

In both *novelle* X 1 and 2 the element of *fortuna* plays an important role in the make-up of the central figure, especially in his unhappy situation at the beginning of the story. It is fortune's fault that Ruggieri has not been adequately rewarded by King Alfonso, as the king himself puts it: "'il non avervi donato come fatto ho a molti . . . non è avvenuto perché io non abbia voi valorosissimo cavalier conosciuto e degno d'ogni gran dono: ma la vostra fortuna, che lasciato non m'ha, in ciò ha peccato e non io.'" (X 1,15). The same is true in Ghino's unhappy situation as an outlaw: "'Maladetta sia la fortuna,'" says the abbot, "la quale a sì dannevole mestier ti costrigne!'" (X 2,25-26). It is therefore as a direct counteraction against fortune that the liberality contest takes place: "'certo il vostro valor merita che io m'opponga alle sue (della fortuna) forze,'" states the king to Ruggieri,"' . . . quel forziere che *la fortuna* vi tolse, quello in dispetto di lei voglio che sia vostro . . ." (X 1,18-19); and the abbot's plea to the Pope on behalf of Ghino is similar: "'quel male il quale egli fa, io il reputo molto maggior peccato *della fortuna* che suo: la qual se voi con alcuna cosa dandogli . . . *mutate*, io non dubito punto che in poco di tempo non ne paia a voi quello che a me ne pare.'" (X 2,28-29). *Fortuna*, therefore, is seen as the main cause of the protagonists' unhappy situation. This becomes clear in a natural environment — the mule episode in Ruggieri's case and the outlaw existence in the *Maremma* of Ghino's. Fortune is eventually dominated by man-made actions which change the victims' lot at the end of the stories. We can then speak in these two cases of a close connection between the natural world and the protagonists' unfortunate adventures, as already noticed in many *novelle* of the Second Day and in some of the Third, Fourth, Fifth, and Seventh Days. At the same time, the unfortunate situation in the country, of which the protagonists and their liberal friends are well aware, triggers the positive finale in both *novelle*, as was true in the *novelle* of the Fifth Day. This trend continues with an increasingly intense and vital rhythm in the following *novelle* of Day X.

The story of Natan and Mitridanes (X 3) evolves almost completely in a country background: Natan's place is isolated, "vicino ad una strada per la qual quasi di necessità passava ciascuno che di Ponente verso Levante andar voleva o di Levante in Ponente . . ." (X 3,5); the same is implied about Mitridanes' dwelling "di paese non guari al suo lontano"; and finally the climactic encounter between the two takes place in a *boschetto*. This natural location assumes here an ironic double dimension. As the setting for Natan's planned murder, it connotes selfishness and violence; but later the selfishness and violence are overcome through the scenes of recognition and friendship which take place as well in the *boschetto*.

Decameron X 4, as a reelaboration of Filocolo's "Quistione d'amore" XIII, handles the relationship between city and country in an innovative way. In the Filocolo's "Quistione," the narrative action takes place exclusively in the city. In the *Decameron* story, instead, the country is introduced as the backdrop for the first event in the story: Madonna Catalina retires to her country house to give birth, and there she is believed dead and is buried. The country is then first strictly connected with sickness, death, and sorrow. However, when messer Gentile visits madonna Catalina's tomb for a last passionate farewell, he conquers death by his recognition of life in the appearance of death:

> Il quale . . . trovò costei per certo non esser morta, quantunque poca e debole estimasse la vita: per che soavamente quanto più potè, dal suo famigliare aiutato, del monimento la trasse e, davanti al caval messalasi, segretamente in casa sua *la condusse in Bologna*.
>
> (X 4,12)

The country experience, then, offers in a second moment the opportunity not only to overcome death through love and care, but also to prove, on a later occasion, the magnificent virtue of generosity in the city itself, on a high social level:

> Niccoluccio disiderosamente ricevette la sua donna e
> 'l figliuolo, tanto più lieto quanto più n'era di speranza
> lontano, e come meglio potè e seppe ringraziò il
> cavaliere; e gli altri, che tutti di compassion
> lagrimavano, di questo il commendaron molto, e com-
> mendato fu da chiunque l'udì.
>
> (X 4, 45-46)

The innovative introduction of the element of the country as essential for the development of the narrative action, proves Boccaccio's intention to endow the natural world in general with a positive function in the development of a better social order and human understanding.

A more precise natural image, the garden, also frequently appears in the narrative texture of the *novelle*, and seems to be connected, as in some of the *novelle* of the Fourth, Fifth, and Ninth Days, with a selfish condition of love which must be overcome in order to reconstitute a well-balanced social order.[37]

This particular message is openly conveyed by the fifth and sixth *novelle* of this Day, while in the seventh we find a recapitulation of all the implications of the *locus amoenus* motif throughout the entire *Decameron*. The first *novella* of this Day in which the *giardino* plays a complex role in the narrative texture of the story is the *novella* of madonna Dianora (X 5), another reelaboration of a *Filocolo* "Quistione." Both *quistione* and *novella* present the device of the *giardino*, but the *novella* handles it with significant differences, which highlight the message conveyed. The "giardino pieno di verdi erbe, di fiori e di fronzuti albori, non altrimenti fatto che se di maggio fosse" (X 5,8), embodies the attributes of a traditional *locus amoenus* inasmuch as it stands for love. At the same time, it has initial connotations which suggest a more complex interpretation of its narrative function in the story: first of all, this *locus amoenus*, which should be the natural place *par excellence*, turns out to be not a spontaneous product of nature but rather an abnormal creation magically conjured up in the midst of January:

> ... essendo i freddi grandissimi e ogni cosa piena di neve
> e di ghiaccio ... il calen di gennaio ... apparve ... un
> de' più be' giardini che mai per alcun fosse stato veduto,
> con erbe e con alberi e con frutti d'ogni maniera.
>
> (X 5, 10-11)

The unnatural quality of the garden corresponds to the ambiguity of madonna Dianora's wish, a wish that on the surface seems to stand for a desire for love, but in reality indicates a counter-wish for the elimination of love. Moreover, while a wish is generally expressed in order to be fulfilled, madonna Dianora wishes for the garden in winter only because she believes her wish will never reach fulfillment. A wish, therefore, never expected to be fulfilled, a garden never expected to be realized, finally the actual presence of a contradiction in terms, that is, an unnatural garden, are the elements that create a complex of innuendoes around the motif of the *giardino* in this *novella*. Just as madonna Dianora's wish for a proof of love is in reality the expression of a wish for the elimination of love, the unnatural garden, too, represents not the traditional symbol of natural love, but rather connotes an unnatural love centered on selfishness. In fact, messer Ansaldo's exclusive desire for the woman, without any consideration for her social responsibilities, and madonna Dianora's exclusive interest in escaping messer Ansaldo's solicitations, without any consideration for his feelings, are the main motivations of their actions. Their different reactions to the presence of the garden indicate these exclusively self-centered interests: once the garden exists, messer Ansaldo, though realizing madonna Dianora's counterwish that "per niun'altra cosa ciò esser dalla donna addomandato, se non per torlo dalla sua speranza," does not hesitate to remind the woman of her promise without taking into account her true feelings: "lietissimo . . . fatto cogliere de' più be' frutti e de' più be' fior che v'erano, quegli occultamente fé presentare alla sua donna e lei invitare a vedere il giardino da lei addomandato . . . e ricordarsi della promission fattagli." (X 5,11) Madonna Dianora's reaction to the garden is naturally negative: "s' incominciò a pentere della sua promessa . . . e . . . più che altra femina dolente a casa se ne tornò a quel pensando a che per quello era obligata." (X 5,12-13) She, like messer Ansaldo, lacks concern or understanding for the other's feelings.

The unnatural garden, then, connotes the unnaturally self-centered reactions of the two protagonists of the story. The liberality contest that takes place at the end of the *novella* substantiates this interpretation. Here each of the main characters tries to outdo the others in self-renunciation, indicating, in at least two of them, their recognition that they had previously carried self-indulgence too far. After this display of disinterested generosity that counters the selfishness and conceit exhibited earlier, the garden itself disappears. At this point, to stress even more strongly the equation "unnatural garden = unnatural love" and, consequently, disappearance of garden = disappearance of unnatural love," another element is introduced which specifies the change in the nature of messer Ansaldo's love: "spento del cuore il concupiscibile amore, verso la donna acceso d'onesta carità si rimase"(X 5,25). The *locus amoenus*, therefore, connoted an asocial, self-centered life, as already noticed in the *novelle* of the Fourth Day. Its elimination, then, is imperative for the re-creation of a socially harmonious existence. In fact, the vision of harmony and social balance at the end of X 5 is strictly connected with the disappearance of the magic garden, which is the narrative correspondent to selfish love and individualistic, instinctual desires. And, the husband's compassion for messer Ansaldo's devotion to his wife wins him in return Ansaldo's respect and courtesy, plus an everlasting sentiment of esteem and friendship:

". . . voi al vostro marito di tanta cortesia, quanta la sua

> è stata, quelle grazie renderete che convenevoli
> crederete, me sempre per lo tempo avvenire avendo per
> fratello e per servidore."
>
> (X 5,22)

Madonna Dianora also participates in the "strettissima e leale amistà" that binds her husband and messer Ansaldo. In a new role as Ansaldo's sister rather than as his beloved ("'non altramente che se *mia sorella* foste,'" as Ansaldo himself says), her gratitude, too, is everlasting: "'di che io vi sarò *sempre* obligata'" (X 5,23) The opposition "presence vs. disappearance of the garden", highlights the process of the individual's transformation and provides a social implication to the story, inasmuch as it presents as highly desirable a change from a purely egotistical condition of existence to a magnanimous view of social behavior that saves the individual from self indulgence and isolation and makes him an integrated part of the social context.

This message is repeated in X 6, the *novella* of king Carlo d'Angiò and messer Neri, in which the *locus amoenus* is the narrative correspondent of the king's selfishness and lust for one of messer Neri's daughters. The king's unreasonable passion, fomented by the garden environment, grows to such a point that, unable to control himself any longer, he plans to possess not only one, but both twins: "dover non solamente l'una ma amendune le giovinette al padre torre." (X 6,25) Finally this plan is abandoned and at this point in the story the beautiful garden where the king's lust had been kindled and fostered disappears from the narrative scene. Here the garden's disappearance coincides not only with the elimination of the king's selfish passion, but also with the reappearance of his interest for social justice and harmony. The story in fact ends on this note:

> Così adunque il magnifico re operò, il nobile cavaliere
> altamente premiando, l'amate giovinette laudevolmente
> onorando e se medesimo fortemente vincendo."
>
> (X 6,36)

Finally in X 7, (the last story of the *Decameron* in which the *locus amoenus* appears with a negative narrative function underlying love and selfishness) we find that this device provides a stage for another king, Pietro of Aragon, to show his qualities of leadership and honor and for the girl who loves him to reveal the unselfishness and nobility of her love. The garden is the backdrop for two important scenes involving the king: the first corresponds to the king's visit to Lisa, bedridden by lovesickness:

> . . . e in su l'ora del vespro montato a cavallo, sembiante
> faccendo d'andar a suo diporto, pervenne là dov' era la
> casa dello speziale: e quivi, fatto domandare che aperto
> gli fosse *un bellissimo giardino* il quale lo speziale avea,
> in quello smontò e dopo alquanto domandò Bernardo

> che fosse della figliuola . . .
> (X 7,30)

The garden here permits an encounter between people of different social levels, a king and a *speziale*. It is finally in this same garden that Lisa's emotional and intellectual superiority is rewarded in the presence of the whole society, aristocratic and bourgeois:

> . . . il re . . . montato un dì a cavallo con molti de' suoi baroni a casa dello spezial se n'andò, e *nel giardino entratosene* fece lo spezial chiamare e la sua figliuola; e in questo venuta la reina con molte donne e la giovane tra lor ricevuta, cominciarono maravigliosa festa.
> (X 7, 37-38)

The final vision is here, too, of social harmony, openly stressing the positive interaction of rulers and subjects, as opposed to exclusively self-centered actions: "Così adunque operando, si pigliano gli animi de' subgetti, dassi altrui materia di bene operare e le fame eterne s'acquistano . . . (X 7,49) In this way, the garden is still present here reproposing the same message of the Day IV *novelle*, where it was synonomous with self-centered and anti-social love. In this *novella*, however, the presence of superior human beings, endowed with noble and magnanimous feelings provides the possibility of a symbolic transformation in the meaning of the garden. It can still be a symbol of love, but only of an unselfish form of love, based on human concern and understanding in view of a better social existence. The next step will be to find the garden motif devoid of all amorous connotation, and in the story of messer Torello (X 9), the next to the last story of the *Decameron*, the garden has this meaning.

Here, the garden functions exclusively as a setting for social interaction among highly refined and magnanimous people with no sign of its usual meaning as a setting for love. We must conclude that it is this new meaning of the garden which will prevail at the end of the *Decameron*. The garden in the country villa where messer Torello entertains the unknown visitors ("fece ordinare una bella cena e metter le tavole *in un suo giardino* . . . " (X 9,11), corresponds to the dining hall in the city where all "i gentili uomini di Pavia" are invited by him to honor and dine with his foreign guests: "nella sala, dove splendidamente era apparecchiato, vennero; e . . . a tavola messi con grandissimo ordine e bello, di molte vivande magnificamente furon serviti . . ." (X 9,25) This interesting correlation between the *giardino* (in the country) and the *sala* (in the city) summarizes the outcome of the *giardino* symbolism in the *Decameron*. From the correspondent of a self-centered love between two people isolated from society, it has changed into the correspondent of the highest form of social interaction. It is now a place of encounter for unselfish and magnanimous human beings, representative of the aristocratic as well as the bourgeois classes, who are deeply concerned with a close and fulfilling relationships which will result in their mutual benefit and the furtherance of world harmony. Indeed, here we have two worlds, with messer Torello representing the best of western civic society, and Saladin, the highest standards of eastern society. This goes beyond the *novella* of King Pietro and Lisa, which dealt with the different classes of one society whose interrelation brought about the final internal social harmony represented by the *giardino*. In X 9, we have two totally different societies, and yet a similar outcome is foreshadowed when messer Torello and Saladin join in the initial *giardino* festivity. Their perfect understanding and mutual admiration, fostered by the garden site, convey the ultimate vision of the harmony where East and West meet and are totally integrated in splendid conviviality.

In the *Decameron*, then, the *locus amoenus*, in addition to its traditional role as a place of love fulfillment plays an innovative role linked with the themes of solitude and alienation. The presence of the *giardino* seems to warn against the dangers of an all-absorbing passion which alienates the individual from society, either by enclosing him in a private world with his lover (as especially in the *novelle* of the Fourth Day), or be isolating him through his own self-centered desires (as in the fifth and sixth *novelle* of the Tenth Day). The *giardino* motif, then, conveys a message well in harmony with the overall message of the *Decameron:* the individual has to overcome his selfishness and interact with society so that, through communication and understanding a better world can be re-created.[38]

After the vision of social harmony in country and city presented in the *novella* of messer Torello, in the *novella* of Griselda, which concludes the *Decameron,* the natural world predominates: it not only triggers the action of the story, as in the preceding *novella,* through the strong connection between Griselda and nature ("una povera giovinetta . . . d'una villa vicina . . . figliuola di Giannucole . . . e . . . guardiana di pecore . . . X 10, 9,24), but it also provides all the elements which place Griselda in opposition to the courtly society to which she does not belong. Nature is in fact the generator of all Griselda's traits: innocence, moral strength, wisdom, humility, patience. And it is because of the gifts provided her by the natural background that she overcomes her trials and tribulations, and ultimately re-creates a balanced human society around herself.[39]

All the important details of the "creation" of the heroine as Gualtieri's chosen companion take place in the world of nature represented by the *villetta* near his court. There Gualtieri and "tutta la compagnia" go to the "povera casa" of Griselda's father, inside which Gualtieri proposes to the girl, imposing upon her the ritual of acceptance and obedience typical of her character. The ritual of her undressing and dressing takes place in front of Giannucole's country hut:

> Allora Gualtieri, presala per mano, la menò fuori e in presenza di tutta la sua compagnia e d'ogn' altra persona la fece spogliare ignuda e fattisi quegli vestimenti che fatti aveva fare, prestamente la fece vestire e calzare e sopra i suoi capelli così scarmigliati come erano, le fece mettere una corona . . .
>
> (X 10, 19-20)

What occurs later has its foundation in these initiatory ceremonies performed in the natural background of the country. It is as if this creature grown and developed in the world of nature were endowed with all the powers needed to create a perfected human social situation of which no other creature could conceive. Indeed this is the message of Griselda's words to Gualtieri towards the end of her ordeal, when she suggests that her strength derives from her rustic background, since "in continue fatiche da piccolina era stata." (X 10,59). A creature born and raised in the country thus becomes in this last novella of the *Decameron* the symbol of perfection: "nelle povere case piovono dal cielo de' divini spiriti." (X 10,68). The essentiality of the world of nature is thus elevated to the maximum in this final vision of a socially inferior country creature who becomes the symbol of marital bliss, thus intensifying the message of the importance of family harmony in society. In this case a woman totally connected with the world of nature is the centripetal force that holds together the smallest social nucleus of civic life. At the same time, Griselda's exemplary function influences each family nucleus around her, thus creating the possibility of a better private life for all the people who come into contact with her. Furthermore, by the social position acquired through her marriage to Gualtieri, a wider social implication is involved in her influence on other people's lives. While the whole society improves under the impact of her perfection, the interrelation between ruler and subjects too becomes one of total reliance and contentedness: "essendo ogni uomo lietissimo . . . savissimo reputaron Gualtieri . . . e sopra tutti savissima tenner Griselda . . ." (X 10,66). The urban world of the court thus reaches perfection through the exemplary influence of a creature of nature who performs the harmonious social renovation it needed through individual self-sacrifice and total understanding.

Human experience in Day X has therefore reached a very high level of accomplishment in all areas of social and personal endeavor. Wisdom, intelligence, verbal dexterity, emotional awareness, and magnanimity are virtues shared by all the protagonists of this day's *novelle*. These are the qualities used in solving the human situations dealing with either power confrontations (X 1,2,3,6,8,10), and/or emotional issues (X 4,5,6,7,8,9,10). The society emerging at the end of each story is a harmonious one where all parties, whatever social class they belong to, are integrated into a serene, pleasant, and balanced condition of life. As the ideal background for the display of socially concerned attitudes and virtues, the natural world plays an important role in helping to pull the narrative levels of the *novelle* and of the *cornice* together in total harmony. Storytellers and *novelle* characters are now equally capable of controlling their respective worlds with the same intelligent, successful, and harmonious use of leadership. At this point, Panfilo, the Day's king, proposes the return to the city left "domane saranno quindici dî, per dovere alcun diporto pigliare a sostentamento *della nostra santà e della vita*" (X Concl., 3). Panfilo, indeed, states precisely the superior achievement of the *brigata's* way of life: "niuno atto, niuna parola, niuna cosa né dalla vostra parte né dalla nostra ci ho conosciuta da biasimare: continua onestà, continua concordia, continua fraternal dimestichezza mi ci è paruta vedere e sentire . . ." (X Conc., 4-5). Once the fictional worlds of the *novelle* and of the *cornice* have reached such a superior plateau of human perfection, the *brigata* can return to the city.

CONCLUDING REMARKS

In his *Conclusion,* the general Narrator takes leave of his audience of "Nobilissime giovani", stressing the honesty and true-to-life qualities of his *novelle* as well as the variety of styles and messages which they have presented.

The *novelle* have ranged from short and uncomplicated in narrative structure, as in Day I or VI, to lengthy and complex, as in Day IV or X. There are variations in compositional form (from the elegance and complexity of IV 1 or X 8, to the concise staccato style of I 6, IV 4, or VIII 5), in narrative mood (from comic relief in I 4, II 1, or VIII 3, to tragic suspense in most *novelle* of Day IV), and in characterization (with the vast gamut of human types of both sexes and all social classes). As to message, each day of storytelling has led to the creation of an ideological framework in harmony with the *cornice* world of the storytellers.

In Part I, the Day I stories create a conflicting atmosphere by presenting characters whose moral weaknesses are a threat to their society. This atmosphere is in tune with the chaotic Florence that the storytellers have escaped. At the same time, the Day I characters skilfully use wit and verbal dexterity to resist the dangers of their social environments. Individuals unable to control their lot become the main topic of Day II, while the Day III *novelle* reveal a confined world in which resourcefulness and ingenuity may prevail. However, in Day IV, even individuals's endowed with intelligence and affected by the deepest emotions, are powerless in the face of an antagonistic society which forces them to choose between their rights to personal justice and their duties to that society's laws and traditions. In Day V, similar individuals succeed in achieving the blessed state of matrimony by recognizing their society's rights and laws and by making intelligent compromises regarding their own rights to love. At the end of Part I, love and marriage provide a harmonious solution to the conflict between the individual and society. Society has made clear the laws and traditions an individual should conform to and respect in order to be accepted within its boundaries. And the individual has learned that a human being can only survive by coming to terms with his or her society.

Part II examines all possible solutions where resourceful and capable individuals try to conform to, maintain, and even improve upon their society's laws and traditions without damaging their personal status. Day VI openly restates Day I's message about the importance of wit and verbal agility in all human encounters. The moral weaknesses of Day I's characters here give way to the sensible foresight and social awareness of superior individuals such as

Cisti, Giotto and Forese, Madonna Filippa, Guido Cavalcanti, and Frate Cipolla. Women's verbal and intellectual facility is the topic of Day VII, where the institution of marriage becomes the *novelle's* main concern. In Day VIII, malpractice in such institutions as the religious and judicial systems is criticized and education and competency in philosophy, medicine, or business are questioned. The social censure present in both Days VII and VIII urges a reconsideration of all such issues with the purpose of banning excesses and counterbalancing them by a constructive attitude fostering social and personal improvement. The Day IX *novelle* with their handling of unusual love affairs, difficult friendships and marital relationships, contain a similar message, constantly stressing the need for balance in all facets of human life. Finally Day X presents the human world at its best, where superior individuals are integrated into effectively administered social systems.

By the end of Day X, the ideological message is clear. It is through superior individuals that a society attains social and moral improvement. It is significant that the superior individuals of the "onesta brigata" decide to return to their city, conceivably still devoid of moral, political, or natural law or order, at this particular time. During their two-week sojourn in the country, they have aptly recreated a world of their own, a world of order, harmony, beauty, and joy, that has effectively contrasted and overshadowed the chaos, sickness, and sadness oppressing the city of Florence. As superior individuals, they have conquered even though momentarily and through fiction, chaos and death, with personal intelligence and social concern. The model they have created, of a society where order and harmony reign, may work for themselves and for their contemporaries as an alternative to social disruption, or simply as in inspiration for a better form of personal life.

At the same time, the *Decameron's* message reaches out to the larger audience of readers for whom the general Narrator has recounted the *brigata's* experience in the country, and collected in writing the *novelle* which they had told each other. For these readers, and for all those of future generations, the Narrator's message is the same: The fictional world of the *Decameron* works as a model for a better human world based on an effective integration of responsibile individuals and their society.

NOTES

1. See especially Pamela Stewart's article "La novella di Madonna Oretta e le due parti del *Decameron*",, in *Yearbook of Italian Studies* (1973-75), 27-40; A. D'Andrea's "Appendice: Per la struttura del *Decameron*" in his "Le rubriche del *Decameron*", ibid., 41-67; 63-67; A. Freedman, "Il cavallo del Boccaccio: fonte, struttura e funzione della meta-novella di madonna Oretta", in *Studi sul Boccaccio* (1975-76), 225-41.

2. This is a thesis thoroughly discussed by Vittore Branca in his *Boccaccio Medievale* (Firenze: Sansoni, 1975), especially in his chapter "Tradizione medievale", 3-30; 16.

3. As noted by Stewart, in "La novella di Madonna Oretta", p. 33.

4. See particularly the above-quoted article by Stewart and G. Almansi's "Lettura della novella di madonna Oretta", in *Paragone* (1972), 139-142.

5. I have discussed this topic in "The Hiccuping Rhythm of Chichibio's Adventure: A Comic Farce", in *An Anatomy of Boccaccio's Style* (Napoli: Cymba, 1968), 83-96.

6. According to Branca, Montughi is a "collina fuori della porta S. Gallo, sulla valle del torrente Terzolle, fin da quei secoli popolata di ville delle più cospicue famiglie fiorentine. Derivò il nome da Mons Ugonis, che alludeva probabilmente ai beni posseduti dai Marchesi di Toscana." *Decameron*, ed. Vittore Branca (Firenze: Le Monnier, 1965); VI 6, note 1, p. 728.

7. See F. Fido's essay on "Boccaccio's *Ars Narrandi* in the Sixth Day of the *Decameron*", in *Italian Literature: Roots and Branches. Essays in Honor of Thomas G. Bergin*, eds. Giose Rimanelli and Kenneth J. Atchity (New Haven: Yale university Press, 1976), 225-42; 235. On Day VI, see also G. Bosetti, "Analyse 'structurale' de la VIe journée du *Décaméron*", in *Studi sul Boccaccio* (1973), 141-58.

8. On this particular *novella*, see K. Pennington's "A Note to *Decameron* 6,7: The Wit of Madonna Filippa", in *Speculum* (1977), 902-5.

9. ibid., p. 903.

10. ibid.

11. My colleague, Dr. Fredi Chiappelli, has suggested this possibility.

12. Pennington, "A Note to *Decameron* 6,7 . . .", 904-5.

13. On the general topic of medieval superstitions, see Maurilio Adriani, *Italia magica* (Roma: Biblioteca di Storia Patria, 1970); Francesco Albergamo, *Mito e magia* (Napoli: Guida Editori, 1970), and Arturo Graf, *Miti, leggende e superstizioni del medioevo* (Torino: Ermanno Loescher Editore, 1925).

14. On incantations connected with spitting, see P. Pajello, "Lo sputo e la saliva nelle tradizioni popolari antiche e moderne", in *Archivio delle tradizioni popolari* (1887), 250-54.

15. On Apuleio as source of this *novella*, see the exhaustive study of

Laura Sanguineti White, *Apuleio e Boccaccio: Caratteri differenziali nella struttura narrativa del Decameron* (Bologna: ED.I.M., 1977), especially Ch. III, 60-68, and Ch. IV, 157-98.

16. On "vermini" incantations, see Giuseppe Bonomo's chapter dedicated to "Scongiuri contro i vermi intestinali" in *Scongiuri del popolo siciliano* (Palermo: Palumbo, 1953), 91-141. See also T. Casini's "Scongiuro e poesia", in *Archivio delle tradizioni popolari* (1886), 560-68.

17. The particular structure of this novella is discussed by C. Segre in his "Funzioni, opposizioni e simmetrie nella Giornata VII del *Decameron*", in *Studi sul Boccaccio* (1971), 81-108; 92-93.

18. The theme of "beffa" is discussed by A. Fontes-Baratto in "Le thème de la beffa dans le *Decameron*", in *Formes et significations de la "beffa" dans la littérature italienne de la Renaissance*, ed. André Rochon (Paris: Université de la Sorbonne, 1972), 11-44.

19. See Gene Brucker, *Florentine Politics and Society, 1343-1378* (Princeton: Princeton University Press, 1962), p. 11.

20. This *novella* has been the source of later *novelle* where certain narrative details have been changed so as to reflect more appropriately social customs of Renaissance England: for more specifics, see my essay on "*Tarlton's Newes out of Purgatorie:* The Beginning of the 'Beffa' *Novella* Tradition in XVI Century England" *The Blue Guitar* (1975), 317-23.

21. Vittore Branca notices a shift in this *novella*, especially in the "spezzatura del ritmo narrativo e stilistico" of the *novella*, in "Registri strutturali e stilistici" of his *Boccaccio Medievale*, 130-32. See also Guido Almansi, *L'estetica dell'osceno* (Torino: Einaudi, 1974).

22. For the role of women in medieval society and marriage, see AA.VV. *The Roles and Images of Women in the Middle Ages and Renaissance,* ed. Douglas Radcliff Umstead (Pittsburg: University of Pittsburg Press, 1975).

23. I have discussed the function of the use of magic and superstition in the *Decameron* as applied to the character of Calandrino in my essay on "Magic and Superstition in Boccaccio's *Decameron*", in *Italian Quaterly* (1975), 5-32; 18-21.

24. ibid., 29-30

25. Among other forms of *ridiculum* Ernst Robert Curtius discusses "involuntary nudity" as one very popular in Medieval times: see "Kitchen

Humor and other *Ridicula*", in *European Literature and the Latin Middle Ages* (New York: Harper Torchbooks 1963); 431-35; 433-35.

26. Branca points out the comic rhythm of Maestro Simone's description in "Strutture della prosa", in *Boccaccio medievale*, 63-64.

27. I have discussed the "comic" of this *novella* in "Comic Modalities in the *Decameron*", in *Versions of Medieval Comedy*, ed. Paul G. Ruggiers (Norman: University of Oklahoma Press, 1977), 430-49; 444-48.

28. For an explanation of these terms, see *Decameron*, ed. V. Branca, VIII 9, 76-77, notes 5 and 6, p. 987.

29. I have discussed this episode in "Magic and Superstition . . .", 21-26.

30. On this novella see G. Almansi, "Alcune osservazioni sulla novella dello scolaro e della vedova", *Studi sul Boccaccio* (1974), 137-46; M. Leone, "Fra autobiografiea reale e ideale nel *Decameron*, VIII 7", *Italica* (1972), 242-65; G.I. Lopriore, "La novella dello scolare", *Nuova Italia* (1941), 128-39.

31. See Claude Lévi-Strauss, *Le Cru et le cuit* (Paris: Plon, 1964).

32. This statement already introduces in this earlier context, the eventual return of the storytellers to the plague-infested city, together with their potential for overcoming death or at least fear through happiness and awareness.

33. On Calandrino as the "beffato" *par excellence*, see A. Fontes-Baratto "La 'beffa' dans le *Decameron*", 29-30.

34. On the problem of the relationship between *Decameron* X 4 and 5 and the *Filocolo* 's "Questioni", one can find still useful information in P. Rayna, "L'episodio delle 'Questioni d'amore' nel *Filocolo* del Boccaccio", *Romania* (1902), 28-81. See also S. Battaglia, "Dall'esempio alla novella", *Filologia Romanza* (1960), 21-84; D. Dutschke, "Boccaccio: A Question of Love (a Comparative Study of *Filocolo* IV 13 and *Decameron* X 4)", *Humanities Association Review* (1975), 300-12.; V. Kirkham, "Reckoning with Boccaccio's 'Questioni d'amore'", *Modern Language Notes* (1973), 45-59.

35. See F. Fido, "Il sorriso di Messer Torello", *Romance Philology* (1969), 154-71; M. Landau, "La novella di messer Torello e le sue attinenze mitiche e leggendarie", GSLI (1883), 59-78.

36. See L. Spitzer, "Linguistic Perspectivism in the *Don Quijote*", in *Linguistics and Literary History: Essays in Stylistics* (Princeton: Princeton University Press, 1967), 41-85; especially 50-52.

37. I have discussed this topos of the *locus amoenus* in "La funzione nar-

rative del giardino o 'locus amoenus' nel *Decameron*", in *Teoria e critica* (1973), 1-22; see also M. Bevilacqua, "Il giardino come struttura ideologico-formale del *Decameron*", *Rassegna della letteratura italiana* (1976), 70-79.

38. M. Cottino-Jones, "La funzione narrativa del giardino . . .", 21-22.
39. See my discussion of Griselda in "Fabula-vrs-Figura: Another Interpretation of the Griselda Story", in *Italica* (1973), 38-52.

INDEX

Adriani, Maurilio 193
Albergamo, Francesco 193
Alighieri, Dante 86-87
Almansi, Guido 98,99,100,193,194,195
Alonso, Pedro 38
Alphabetum Narrationum, 88
Apuleio 96,103,193
Atchity, Kenneth J 193

Baratto, Maio 97,98,100
Barthes, Roland 65,100,102
Battaglia Salvatore 38,195
Becker, Marvin B. 3,33
Bevilacqua, M. 196
Biographies des Troubadours, 101
Biscaro, G. 98
Bonomo, Giuseppe 194
Book of Sinbad, 20,38
Bosco, Umberto 97
Bosetti, G. 193
Bramanti, V. 97
Branca, Vittore 36,37,41,97,99,193,194,
    195,196
Brucker, Gene 2,3,32,33,34,44,49,98,129,
    195

Cappelletti, Licurgo 102
Casini, T. 194
Cazale-Bernard, C. 98
Cerreta, F. 99
Chiappelli, Fredi 193
Cole, H. 100
Comedia delle ninfe, 19
Conti di antichi cavalieri, 20
Cottino-Jones, Marga 34,38,97,99,100,101,
    193,194,195,196
Croce, Benedetto 99
Curtius, Ernst Robert 194-195

D'Andrea, Antonio 38,192
Deligiorgis, S. 99
Des Tresces, 129
Devoto, D. 101
Di Francia, Letterio 39
Directorium vitae humanae, 38
Disciplina clericalis, 38
Dutschke, Dennis 195

Elegia di madonna Fiammetta, 19
Exempla, 20

Factorum ac dictorum memorabilium, 20
Fassò, Luigi 98
Ferrante, Joan 97
Fido, Franco 193,195
Filocolo, 19,91-92,172,173,177-179,185,
    187,195
Filostrato, 19
Fiore dei filosafi, 20
Fiori di virtù, 20
Firenzuola, Agnolo 34
Fontes-Baratto, A. 194,195
Freedman, A. 192

Gaiffer, B. 99
Galila and Dimna, 20
Genealogia deorum gentilium, 7-8,9,35
Getto, Giovanni 97,100,107
Giacon, M. 102
Giamatti, A. Bartlett 36
Grabher, Carlo 97
Graf, Arturo 99,193
Green, Louis 3,32,34,44,98

Hauvette, Henri 101

Ihoannes da Capua 38
Iser, W. 34

Jacopo da Varazze 38
Jacques de Vitry 20

Kamber, G. 102
Kirkham, Victoria 100,195
Kleinhenz, Christofer 98

Landau, M. 195
Langlois, A. 101
Legenda aurea, 38
Leone, M. 195
Levi-Strauss, Claude 195
Libro dei sette savi, 38
*Libro de los enganos y asayamentos de las
    mujeres,* 38
Lopriore, G.I. 195
Lucente, G. 99

Mannucci, F.L. 98
Marchionne 1,33
Marcus, Millicent 98,100
Marino, Lucia 36
Martines, Lauro 33
Meiss, Meillards 33
Molho, Anthony 33
Muscetta, Carlo 97

Nelson, Lawry Jr. 34
Neri, Francesco 97
Novellino, 20,21-24,30-31,38

Oberziner, M. 99
Osgood, Charles S. 35-36

Pace, A. 101
Padoan, Giorgio 97-100Pajello, P. 198
Panchatranta, 38
Passavanti, Iacopo 88
Pastore Stocchi, M. 101
Penna, Mario 97
Pennington, K. 111,193
Perrus, C.L. 100,102
Petronio, Giuseppe 97,99
Pitré, G. 99
Potter, Joy H. 34

Radcliff Umstead, Douglas 194
Rayna, P. 195

Repetti, E. 34
Ricci, Pier Giorgio 35
Rimanelli, Giose 193
Rochon, André 194
Rolfs, D. 101
Ruggiers, Paul 34, 192

Sanguineti White, Laura 102, 194
Sapori, Armando 33
Scaglione, Aldo 33
Segre, Cesare 99,102,194
Specchio de vera penitenza, 88
Speculum historiale, 38,89
Spitzer, Leo 195
Stewart, Pamela 38,39-40,97,192,193
Story of Barlam and Josafat, 20

Tayler, William E. 36
Teseida, 19
Todorov, Tzvetan 61,100
Toldo, P. 100
Tuttle, Edward F. 100

Valerius Maximus 20
Valori, E. 101
Villani, Giovanni 3,33,36
Villani, Matteo 1,2,3,33,34,36
Vinay, G. 98
Vincent de Beauvais 38,88

Wheelock, J. 100

SUBJECT INDEX TO THE
DECAMERON

Proemio 4,5,6,8-9,18

Day I 41-49,94,103-104
    Introduction 1,9,11,18,20,33,37,168
    I 1, 5,46-49,116
    I 2, 5,163
    I 3, 5,21,24-32,43,171
    I 4, 5,9,43-44,160-161
    I 5, 5,44-45,173
    I 6, 5,45
    I 7, 5,43,171
    I 8, 5,42,163-164
    I 9, 5,18,42
    I 10, 5,9,45-46,104
    Conclusion 9,11-12,37

Day II 49-60
    II 1, 54
    II 2, 34,51,54
    II 3, 34,51
    II 4, 34,52,54
    II 5, 34,55-57
    II 6, 34,52-54
    II 7, 52,54
    II 8, 34,51,54
    II 9, 54,57-59,134-135
    II 10, 54,59,134-135
    Conclusion 12-13,37,61

Day III 60-66
    Introduction 60
    III 1, 34,60,62,63,65
    III 2, 34,65
    III 3, 34,61,64-65
    III 4, 34,143
    III 5, 34,65
    III 6, 65-66,154
    III 7, 34,61,66
    III 8, 34,62-63
    III 9, 34,63-64,154
    III 10, 63
    Conclusion 13,37

Day IV 66-79
    Introduction 6-7,66-67
    IV 1, 13,34,67-68,70,75,78,79
    IV 2, 13,67,69,70,78,79
    IV 3, 67
    IV 4, 68,69,76-77,78
    IV 5, 34,67,69,75-76,78
    IV 6, 69,70-72,79
    IV 7, 69,73-75,79
    IV 8, 34,69,70
    IV 9, 67,68,69,77-78,79
    IV 10, 13,69
    Conclusion 13-14

Day V 86-96
    V 1, 81-83,101
    V 2, 14,90-91,101
    V 3, 34,81,83-86,101
    IV 4, 14,34,93,101-102
    IV 5, 14,34,94,102
    IV 6, 81,91-93,102
    IV 7, 34,93-94,102
    IV 8, 81,86-88,102
    IV 9, 34,81,88-90,102
    IV 10, 94-95
    Conclusion 14,15,37,95

Day VI 103-117
    Introduction 15
    VI 1, 104,105,106-107,173
    VI 2, 107,114,173
    VI 3, 107-108
    VI 4, 108-109
    VI 5, 109-110
    VI 6, 105,110
    VI 7, 34,105,110-112,114
    VI 8, 98,112-113
    VI 9, 113-114
    VI 10, 106,115-116
    Conclusion 14,15-16,117

Day VII 118-135
    VII 1,   34,119-120,131
    VII 2,   120-121,131
    VII 3,   121-122
    VII 4,   34,122-124,127,131
    VII 5,   34,124-127
    VII 6,   34,130
    VII 7,   131-133,159
    VII 8,   34,127-130,133
    VII 9,   133-134
    VII 10, 134
    Conclusion 13,16,37,135

Day VIII 135-155
    VIII 1,   136,153
    VIII 2,   136-138,153
    VIII 3,   138-139,153,164,165-166
    VIII 4,   98,141-143,154
    VIII 5,   143-144,153
    VIII 6,   138-141,153,164,165-166
    VIII 7,   28,98,141,147-153,154,158
    VIII 8,   147,154
    VIII 9,   144-147,154
    VIII 10, 147
    Conclusion 16,37,155-156

Day IX 155-170
    Introduction 156
    IX 1,156,158-160
    IX 2,   156,159-161
    IX 3,   156-157,164,166
    IX 4,   34,157,163
    IX 5,   157,164-165,166
    IX 6,   157,162
    IX 7,   98,157,166-167
    IX 8,   157,163-164
    IX 9,   98,157-158,167-169
    XI 10, 164,167,169-170
    Conclusion 17,37,170

Day X 170-190
    X 1,171,181-182
    X 2,   171,182-183
    X 3,   171-172,183
    X 4,   171,172-173,177-178,183-184
    X 5,   171,173,178-179,184-185
    X 6,   171,173,186
    X 7,   171,173-174,186-187
    X 8,   171,197,187
    X 9,   9,171,175-177,179-180,187
    X 10, 171,180-181,188-189
    Conclusion 17,37,190

    Author's conclusion 17,191